T. S. ELIOT
PATTERN OF IMAGES

कर्मण्येवाधिकारस्ते मा फलेषु कदाचन।
मा कर्मफलहेतुर्भूर्मा ते सङ्गोऽस्त्वकर्मणि॥ 2.47

Karmanye vadhikaraste Ma Phaleshu Kadachana,
Ma Karmaphalaheturbhurma Te Sangostvakarmani

To action alone has thou a right and never at all to its fruits. Let not the fruits of action be thy motive neither let there be in thee any attachment to inaction.

T. S. ELIOT
PATTERN OF IMAGES

Manjula Batra

STERLING PAPERBACKS
An imprint of
Sterling Publishers (P) Ltd.
Regd. Office: A1/256 Safdarjung Enclave,
New Delhi-110029. CIN: U22110DL1964PTC211907
Tel: 26387070, 26386209; Fax: 91-11-26383788
E-mail: mail@sterlingpublishers.com
www.sterlingpublishers.com

T.S. ELIOT
Pattern of Images
© 2017, Manjula Batra
ISBN 978 93 86245 08 3

All rights are reserved.
No part of this publication may be reproduced, stored in a retrieval system or transmitted, in any form or by any means, mechanical, photocopying, recording or otherwise, without prior written permission of the author.

Printed in India

Printed and Published by Sterling Publishers Pvt. Ltd., Plot No. 13, Ecotech-III, Greater Noida - 201306, Uttar Pradesh, India

Foreword

I do not pretend to remember what I wrote on T. S. Eliot in 1966, but I do know that Manjula Batra's *T. S. Eliot: Pattern of Images* has outdated and outclassed my work.

I am no expert on technical aspects of English verse. Manjula appears to have inherited her interest in poetic images from her father, Professor C. D. Verma, an illustrious scholar and multifaceted personality.

Eliot is a 'Time' poet. Time and Consciousness are major themes of his poetry and plays. Eliot also uses Time-Consciousness as a technique. Manjula has discussed this aspect of his technical excellence in detail. She has gleaned 'Temporal Images' and 'Spatial Images' scattered all over his poetry and plays.

Interplay of Time and Consciousness in Eliot occurs on several planes at once. Through images, Eliot transforms abstract time of clocks and calendars into concrete experiences of conscious existence and human condition. Time is perceived on psychological, historical, spiritual planes and Manjula has successfully established thematic connections with the correlative patterns of images and arranged them in various categories.

Eliot's Time-Consciousness images achieve the same effect of tension and intensity which the Soviet film-makers of the 20th century achieved through montages for cinematic impact. In Eliot's poetry, 'words move, music moves' into patterns of 'first intensities' or timeless moments forging the Kantian *noumena* and *phenomena*, abstract and concrete categories, into living insights and startling epiphanies.

Likewise, Manjula Batra carefully examines 'Spatial Images' and shows how Eliot achieves transformation of place into space and how individual experience merges into spiritual experience, achieving transparency of time while transiting from one plane to another.

Besides being a poets' poet, Eliot was also a culture-hero of his age and times. Accordingly, Manjula dwells deeply on Eliot's 'Classical Images' and highlights his use of 'the classical myths, symbols, images and motifs' that impart extra amplitude and dimension to his observations on contemporary life. Eliot freely plunders the resources of all major cultures, eastern or western, modern or ancient, to achieve 'unity in diversity' for his poetic expression.

I was especially impressed by Manjula Batra's analysis of 'Manichaean Images' that, according to her, 'reveal the traces of Manichaean mythology'. Duality is a persistent theme in Eliot's plays and poems. In his *Choruses From The Rock*, on the duality of Good and Evil, he emphatically states:

'The world turns and the world changes/But one thing does not change. /In all of my years, one thing does not change./ However you disguise it, this thing does not change:/The perpetual struggle of Good and Evil.'

His essay on Baudelaire, I believe, is an authentic statement of Eliot's position on Good and Evil. Eliot goes beyond Christianity, resolves the dilemma of damnation and salvation and affirms that doing evil is better than doing nothing. He, however, seeks the final answer to the question of duality in Krishna's teaching to Arjuna on the field of battle where the ultimate duality of Life and Death dissolves into fearless, detached action:

'I sometime wonder if that is what Krishna meant …when he admonished Arjuna /On the field of battle… And do not think of the fruit of action.' (*Four Quartets*)

Professor Manjula Batra's *T. S. Eliot: Pattern of Images* opens yet another academic window for re-viewing Eliot's poetic world. Both teachers and students will find the book of immense help in understanding Eliot's technique and re-interpreting the meaning of his plays and poetry afresh.

Professor Jitendra Kumar Sharma
M.A. (U of T); Ph.D. (University of Toronto, Canada); formerly of Toronto, Guelph, McGill, Jawaharlal Nehru Universities

Rohini, Delhi 110085   February 24, 2016

Acknowledgements

I'm deeply indebted to

- My father Dr. C. D. Verma, a great scholar and the first discerning teacher I've ever had who honed my intellect and unlocked my creative faculties, and my late mother Mrs. Chander Mohini Verma, the most loyal and understanding friend to me whose constant motivation and inspiration made this book possible.
- My Guide and guru Dr. U. S. Bhardwaj, for his valuable suggestions at the formative stage of this venture.
- Dr. Jitendra Kumar Sharma, for his intellectual inputs as well as critical analysis of the study, which equipped me with a new insight into the subject.
- My husband CA Harish Batra and darling sons Rishabh and Rakshit, for ensuring time, constructive criticism and moral support all through this venture.
- My publisher, who worked tirelessly to finish the book against tight deadlines.

June 2017 **Manjula Batra**

Preface

T. S. Eliot's poetry, at first glance, evokes a sense of incomprehensible ambiguity and complexity, leading the reader to dither from approaching it. As a research scholar, however, I experienced the thrill of a challenge as I set out to decipher the mesmerising economy of Eliot's imagery and the layers of meanings his words are charged with. Gradually, I came to realise that Eliot is known as the most influential figure in English literature today only because he achieved distinction in the precision of language and imagery. I felt like a scientist, 'inventing a thing of beauty' in a work of art with a dull exterior, as I went on to explore a recurrent, cyclical pattern of images in his poetry and plays. Within this circular pattern, the images compose a simultaneous rather than a developing order, like segments in a revolving circle or panels in a medieval altar painting, each individual, with a separate flavour, and yet existing as part of a greater whole.

During the last fifty years or so, the word 'image' has taken on a fresh mystical potency. Yeats heralded the trend, but Eliot elevated the image to 'the first intensity', presenting it as it is, and yet making it represent something much more than itself. So Eliot has created a new mode of release and expression for others. This magic of Eliot's art is easier to comprehend in the light of the formative influence of Dante, his all-pervasive and profound influence, indeed.

Eliot read Dante around the year 1911 with the help of a prose translation. He, at once, fell in love with the

Italian poet's language and committed long passages to his memory. However, in the beginning, Dante evoked in Eliot the same dislike as Eliot did in me when I set out to study his work. Eliot didn't like his pre-Raphaelite imagery. But in the course of time, the fascination of Dante's imagery was too much for him. It was from Dante, the great reformer of his own language , that he learned how to polish and refine his language, how to enlarge his emotional range and how to bring his poetry in line with the European tradition. Trying to model Dante's style and bringing into practice his precision of diction, his clear visual images, Eliot himself became, by the sheer alchemy of his genius, 'the most universal poet in a modern language' ,the term Eliot used to eulogise Dante.

The study of Eliot's images provides a new method of approach to his poetry and plays, because the images used by him throw light upon his thoughts and temperament, as also on the themes and personae of his work. The images, thus collected and analysed, not only constitute an innovative world in themselves, for they mirror the richest experience and the most profound and roaring imagination known to the reader, but also unlock his ambiguity to the reader.

Observations

T.S. Eliot (1888–1965) is a pioneer of the 20th century formalistic criticism and an innovator of formalistic poetry in which the poet lays stress more on the 'form' than on the 'content'.Those who are brought up on the Romanticpoets will not find themselves comfortable with the form of Eliot's poems and plays as they are not built upon the functional images which are essential to be understood.The best approach tointerpretand understand Eliot's poems is through the interpretation of images used by him in each of his poems and plays.

Dr. Manjula Batra keenly and intelligently studies the pattern of Eliot's images and makes observation that his images mostly work on three levels of cognition: temporal, spatial and psychological corresponding to time, space and psychology. The author, interestingly, illustrates the use of images by Eliot through his major poems and plays, which makes it easy for the reader to comprehend this ambiguous artist.

In addition to this tripartite pattern of images, she has also revealed the traces of classical and Manichaean mythology of the ancient in Eliot's images of dualism.

I am sure the reader will find the book interesting and useful.

Prof (Dr.) U. S. Bhardwaj
Former Associate Professor in English,
Jawahar Lal Nehru (P.G.) College, Faridabad

Contents

Foreword		v
Acknowledgements		viii
Preface		ix
Observations		xi
1.	Introduction	1
2.	The Pattern of Images	16
3.	Temporal Images	37
4.	Spatial Images	71
5.	Psychological Images	101
6.	Classical Images	143
7.	Manichaean Images	200
8.	Conclusion	234
	Bibliography	245

1

Introduction

The present study aims at critically examining the pattern of images in the poetry and plays of T. S. Eliot. The poems and plays selected for this purpose are *The Love Song of J. Alfred Prufrock* (1915), *Portrait of a Lady* (1917), *Rhapsody on a Windy Night* (1917), *The Waste Land* (1922), *Murder in the Cathedral* (1935) and *The Family Reunion* (1939).

    T. S. Eliot is a modern artist. And in modern poetry, image is the only manifestation of an almost mystical theory of perception, a phenomenon which brings to an end the romantic theory of direct expression of perception. In the present century, from Henry James's *represent* through Joyce's *epiphanies* to Eliot's *objective correlative*, the modern writers have a dominant belief that every pattern of feelings has its correlated system of objects and events. So, if a writer sets down the pattern of objects in exactly the right relations, without irrelevancies or distortions, he evokes in the reader the same pattern of feelings. And the pattern of objects, or, in other words, images, suited Eliot's talent, which had a great power of visual and aural perception. Eliot, therefore, must be approached through a pattern of images, running through his work, as woof and warp.

    The available studies on Eliot's poetry and plays, by and large, deal with his modernity, allusiveness and psychological and archetypal exploration of his themes, but few of them exclusively concentrate on the imagery which forms the largest part of his poetry and plays as an 'aesthetic whole'. This usual approach to Eliot's work overshadows the intrinsic and textual aspects. Being a new critic, Eliot's linguistic assets require the greatest attention. Though critics like Leonard Unger have made attempts to classify the images of Eliot, yet an exclusive and independent study of the pattern of recurrent images in Eliot's poetry and plays has not been attempted till now. Eliot's works, usually considered to be difficult and obscure, need to be endowed with an explicit and logical pattern of images to make them easily comprehensible. The present study is a modest attempt in this direction.

Eliot's images work at three levels: Temporal, Spatial and Psychological, that is, images relating to time, space and psychology. This pattern can be exemplified through the following lines of *Prufrock*:

> Let us go then, you and I,
> When the evening is spread out against the sky
> Like a patient etherized upon a table;

Since the poem is an internal debate in the mind of the protagonist, 'you' is a psychological image revealing a split personality. In the second line 'evening' is a temporal image conveying the time of the day and the 'sky' is a spatial image carrying a sense of space and void existing between the earth and the sky. The third line—'like a patient etherized upon a table'—emanates from and becomes a corollary to the second line. The etherisation conveys the void in the patient's mind. He is conscious and yet conscious of nothing. His consciousness has been arrested in a moment like that of the patient etherized on the table. So 'etherized patient' is a psychological image, conceptually referring to the twilight zone of Prufrock's mind.

These three categories of images primarily dominate Eliot's works. However, in addition to these broad categories of images, which G. Wilson Knight would call 'atmospheric' images, Eliot's poetry and plays have classical and Manichaean images at well.

It is pertinent to recall briefly Eliot's theories of language (he being an imagist poet and a new critic) to understand the need for images which hold a key to his work. His sustained preoccupation throughout has been with the 'verbal equivalent for states of mind and feeling.'[1] Highlighting the importance of imagery in a work of art, T. S. Eliot states in his essay on *Hamlet*:

> The only way of expressing emotion in the form of art is by finding an 'objective correlative'; in other words, a set of objects, a situation, a chain of events which shall be the formula of that particular emotion; such that when the external facts, which must terminate in sensory experience, are given, the emotion is immediately evoked.[2]

The 'objective correlative', which Eliot elsewhere calls 'words, images and phrases', is the medium which 'depersonalises' or 'objectifies' the poet's emotion and transmutes it into an art emotion. It is a picture made out of words, phrases and images which gives quality, creates atmosphere and conveys emotion. Imagery—that is, images taken collectively—signifies all the objects and qualities of sense-perception referred to in a work of art, whether by literal description, or by allusion, or in the analogues used in its similes and metaphors. Images may become wholly psychological, linking one emotional or intellectual experience to another with the help of metaphors and similes, the range extending from the 'mental pictures' experienced by the reader to the totality of the work.

'New criticism' which originated with the publication of T. S. Eliot's *The Sacred Wood* (1920), has gone far beyond the older criticism in stressing imagery as a major clue to

---
1. Eliot, T. S., *Selected Prose* (Harmondsworth: Penguin Books, 1953), p. 112.
2. Ibid., p. 102.

poetic meaning, structure and effect. New critics concentrate exclusively on the language of poetry and account for its structure in terms of the layers of meaning the words are charged with. I. A. Richards makes a two-fold semantic division of the language of poetry into denotation and connotation, the former being the literal or dictionary meaning and the latter being the suggestive meaning or associations brought forth by the poetic context. This is extended to embrace imagery:

> The imagery of prose is, in the main, single and explicit; the imagery of poetry, complex and suggestive.[3]

In romantic poetry, as Cleanth Brooks points out in his essay 'Metaphor and the Tradition',[4] imagery was decorative, used to exalt the subject, for the image used possessed 'an independent power to please'. But in modern poetry, according to I. A. Richards, images are expansive and are used for the expression of subtler states of emotion. Richards notices the lack of poetic effect of mere sound divorced from meaning in romantic poetry, what T. S. Eliot calls 'Dissociation of sensibility'. In modern poetry, content of image rather than the form is the primary concern of the poet. In Wordsworth's following lines:

> The holy time is quiet as nun
> Breathless with adoration

The sound is divorced from meaning. The image is used to exalt the subject. But when Eliot compares 'evening' to 'a patient etherised upon a table', it becomes a concrete example of 'unified sensibility' — a synthesis of thought and feeling, of fancy and imagination, as Cleanth Brooks opines: 'Fancy can be used to attain heights of imagination.'[5] Thus, intellect merges with the depth of emotion to produce a modern and complex image.

---

3. Foakes, R., *The Romantic Assertion* (London, 1918), p. 18.
4. Brooks, Cleanth, *Modern Poetry and the Tradition* (London: University of North Carolina Press, 1967), p. 6.
5. Ibid., p. 8.

Eliot himself emphasizes the need of unified sensibility in his essay, 'Tradition and the Individual Talent', when he highlights the importance of imagery for the poetic effect:

> This balance of contrasting emotion is, so to speak, the structural emotion provided by the drama. But the whole effect is due to the fact that a number of floating feelings having an affinity to this emotion, by no means, superficially evident, have combined with it to give us a new art emotion.[6]

'The structural emotion' is the logical design of the poet's experience; 'the floating feeling' is the texture or the imagery and the 'art emotion', the overall effect is composed of these two ingredients. Thus, Eliot's poetry is, as Hulme puts it, 'all dry and hard', precise and finite. It fits the three criteria by which modern poetry is judged, as Brooks suggests. The first criterion reflects that poetry should be treated as if it were contemporary poetry; it can be detached from its context in time and studied with reference to its historical meanings. The second criterion is a demand for complexity. The third criterion is the demand that every line must be able to withstand the most severe scrutiny. Thus, what the new critics look for in a poem is 'a structure of meanings contained largely in its metaphor. . . . It represents an outlook that is generally hostile or indifferent to romantic poetry.'[7] And Eliot does use images of thought, the complexity of which consists in the balance and tension between conflicting elements held in suspension in the unity of the poem or drama and emerging in irony and paradox. What Richards calls 'denotation' and 'connotation' are termed as 'perceptual' and 'conceptual' metaphors by Ezra Pound. In Eliot, intensity of language is achieved through these two types of metaphors. Pound draws distinction between these two metaphors:

---

6. Eliot, T. S., *Three Essays* (New Delhi: Oxford University Press, 1974), p. 24.
7. Foakes, R., *The Romantic Assertion*, p. 21.

The essence of the conceptual metaphor is in the unrealizable, apt, half ironic suggestion; the perceptual metaphor is a precise realizable picture.[8]

When Eliot writes:

The readers of the Boston Evening Transcript
Sway in the wind like a ripe corn

The apparently harmless visual image of the readers swinging in the winds of doctrine like a field of ripe corn hides a powerful judgment on those readers who lack inner conviction and are, therefore, swayed by the changing opinions, views and news of the *Boston Evening Transcript*. Similarly, in the title *Prufrock and Other Observations*, the last word 'observations' is a clever blend of conceptual and perceptual metaphors since Eliot is ' trying to qualify the perceiver's vision as well as the object of the vision'.[9] In this sense, there is a clever deceptiveness in the word 'observations'. It implies detachment and the scientific objectivity of a disinterested analyst and observer. Through these metaphors, Eliot gave new possibilities of poetry in a new stock of imagery of contemporary life. His imagery, thus, becomes instrumental in highlighting the theme by artfully making it objective.

The categories of temporal, spatial and psychological images become all the more explicit and logical when studied in terms of Richards' 'denotation' and 'connotation', and Pound's 'perceptual' and 'conceptual', metaphors, for they are at the heart of Eliot's poetry. Temporal and spatial images, in fact, are what the poet perceives and intends to denote in the thematic context. It is the psyche (the psychological image) that transforms those harmless images or perceptual metaphors into connotative and conceptual

---

8. Eliot, T. S., ed., *Literary Essays of Ezra Pound* (London: Faber and Faber, 1954), p. 419.
9. George, A. G., 'The Dimensions of Contemporaneity in T. S. Eliot' In *Asian Response to American Literature*, ed., C. D. Narasmhaiah (Delhi: Vikas Publications, 1972), p. 71.

metaphors. Thus Eliot, Richards, Brooks and Pound worked out the same linguistic principles. Northrop Frye added a new dimension to these principles in his *The Anatomy of Criticism* through his statement:

> Whenever we read anything, we find our attention moving in two directions at once. One direction is outward or centrifugal (perceptual), in which we keep going outside our reading, from the individual words to the things they mean, or in practice, to our memory of the conventional association between them. The other direction is inward or centripetal, in which we try to develop from the words a good sense of the larger verbal pattern they make. In both cases we deal with symbols, but when we attach an external meaning to a word, we have, in addition to the verbal symbol, the thing represented (the image) by it.[10]

Symbols (as devices of imagistic patterns) so understood may be called verbal units. A poem's meaning is literally its pattern or integrity as a verbal structure. Its words cannot be separated and attached to sign–values: all possible sign-values of a word are absorbed into the complexity of verbal relationships. That is why the image is a key to the meaning of any modern poem, more particularly of Eliot's poems and plays. Hence, the representation of natural objects and ideas, showing the relation of the 'spatial' to the 'conceptual world'[11] are simply two different branches of centrifugal meaning.

The association of Eliot with Hulme and Irving Babbit led to the development of Eliot into a new critic from the old fashioned man of letters. New criticism, in fact, may be described as the extreme form of the imagist movement led by Hulme and Pound. Hulme strengthened *imagism* and *Vorticism* by insisting on a concrete style, free from abstractions. What impressed Eliot and confirmed some aspects of his own philosophical attitude was Hulme's

---
10. Frye, Northrop, *The Anatomy of Criticism* (Princeton: New Jersey Press, 1957), p. 73.
11. Ibid., p. 79.

doctrine of discontinuity. The value of the concrete to poetry had never been in question when imagery functioned within a narrative or discursive framework. In the 20th century, both symbolist and imagist poets liberated the poetic image from narrative, descriptive, or logical continuity. That is to say, images are not bound together by an explicit theme, and obviously not related to each other. *Prufrock* is the best example of Eliot's use of Hulme's concept of discontinuity.

The device is again used in *Portrait of a Lady* to express abrupt revulsion of feelings: 'Let us take the air, in a tobacco trance'. Here the discontinuity is accentuated by the separate concreteness of both the juxtaposed elements and by the ostensibly non-committal equality of the two images, which leaves conceptual interpretation of the equation entirely to the reader.

The second major imagist poet, Ezra Pound, emphasises the perfect control the poet should exercise on his materials and medium. Hence he attaches great importance to the language. He refers to the three distinct properties of language which, when developed harmoniously, energise language and make it fit for creative use. They are, in Pound's specialised language, 'melopoeia', 'phanopoeia' and 'logopoeia', meaning (to simplify Pound's elaborate explanation), music, image and sense, respectively. To him, the idea of an image is three-dimensional, like a piece of sculpture, vivid, static and four square (that is, equally balanced on all four sides, firm, unyielding, unhesitating , hence solid), as pictures on Keats' 'Grecian Urn'. It is by developing these three properties cumulatively that the poet constitutes the complex meaning of poetry. Pound defines literature as 'language charged with meaning'. So it is the harmonious development of the latter two elements out of the three suggested by Pound—visual and ideational elements—which, according to Eliot, contribute to the vividness and stability of the work. These are, in other words, the perceptual and conceptual metaphors which Pound approved and Eliot employed.

Introduction

The other basic tenets upon which imagist movement rested are the following:

a) Direct statement of a thing, whether subjective or objective, which implies absolute economy of expression, and as close a resemblance of the word to the real object as art can achieve. Hulme insisted upon an accurate and concrete description. And the poet, he says, cannot be precise about the things he sees unless he is precise about the feelings which attach him to them. It is this need for expressing the relationship between things and feelings which compels the poet to employ images. This is the same need which demands that, within the poem, the images should be linked by some internal necessity stronger than the mere tendency of words to congregate in patterns. Eliot's images are precise, in the sense that they are linked with one another through the conceptual context and central motif of the poem or the play, though the apparent logical and narrative connection may be lacking.

b) To use absolutely no word that is not essential and ceaselessly endeavour to discover and employ fresh metaphors and forceful phrases.

This emphasis on economy, directness and concentration on the essential, concrete and vivid word means that an imagist poem will be brief and static. In an imagist poem, what is important is a moment of revealed truth, rather than a structure of constructive events or thoughts. Plot or argument of older poetry is replaced by a single dominant image, or a quick succession of related images; its effect, as Pound says, is meant to be instantaneous rather than cumulative.

Northrop Frye observes pertinently in his *The Anatomy of Criticism* that the imagist movement, headed by Eliot and Pound in England, is directly related to what Mallarme, Rimbaud and Valery did in France or Rilke in Germany, for all of them started the movement generally called 'symbolism'. In the theory of symbolism, Frye says, we have the complement to extreme naturalism, an emphasis on the literal aspect of meaning and a treatment of literature as centripetal verbal pattern, in which elements of direct or verifiable statement are subordinated to the integrity of that pattern. The conception of 'pure' poetry, or evocative verbal structure injured by assertive meaning, was a minor by-product of the same movement. Symbolism, as expressed in Mallarme, maintains that the representational answer to the question 'What does this mean?' should not be pressed in reading poetry, for the poetic symbol means primarily itself in relation to the poem. The imagists also best apprehended the unity of a poem as a unity of mood, a mood being a phase of emotion and emotion being the ordinary word for the state of mind directed towards the experiencing of pleasure or the contemplating of beauty. And as moods are not long sustained, literature, both for symbolists and imagists, is essentially discontinuous, longer poems being held together only by the use of imagistic structures. Poetic images do not state or point to anything, but by pointing to each other (as do 'evening' and 'etherized patient') they suggest or evoke the mood which informs the poem or the play. That is, they express or articulate the mood.

Eliot's images are constructed in such a way that they intensify the mood or the basic idea emotionally. He rarely uses a simple image. Many more words are needed to paraphrase one of Eliot's images than what it contains, that is, the image is highly compressed and intense. Most of his images are complex and loaded with meaningful and multiple connotations. He acquired this art from master artists including the French Symbolists. His mind responded to various influences. Irving Babbit taught him the doctrine of classical balance and impersonality, which shows itself in his intellectual imagery. Montgomery Belgion, in an article, 'Irving Babbit and the Contingent', mentions a man and a book as having exercised the strongest influence on Eliot.

The man was Babbit and the book was Arthur Symons' *Symbolist Movement in Literature* (1899) which Eliot read in 1908. Belgion points out:

> The man and the book I referred to proved beneficial to Eliot precisely because he was content to obtain from each what each could give: the sense of tradition from the professor, the fostering of individual talent from the Symons volume.[12]

Symons' book helped Eliot 'discover' the symbolist poetry of France as a part of self-discovery, and also helped him reinforce the theory of impersonality that Babbit had taught him. However, the prime discovery Eliot made through Symons' book was Laforgue, in whom he encountered the discovery of 'one's own form and of the poetic possibilities of [his] own idiom of speech'.[13] Laforgue had a disposition to jibe clownishly at sentiment. This habit, though it shaded his poems with a subtle pathos, brightened them with a tinsel novelty all the more bizarre because of their slang. Splitting or 'doubling' himself into a languid sufferer and satiric commentator, he wrote poems deriding in one passage the tenderness of another. Eliot accommodated this idiosyncrasy to his own needs of language; it helped him veil personal agonies with impersonal, ironical images.

However, it was Baudelaire who first proclaimed the value of symbols; Verlaine used them instinctively, and it was left to Mallarme to erect a sort of metaphysics to explain and justify them. They are called symbolists because they attempt to convey a supernatural experience in the language of visible things and, therefore, almost every word is a symbol and is used not for its common purpose but for the associations which it evokes of a reality beyond the senses. <u>So the basis of</u> symbolism is the theory of correspondence

---

12. March, Richard and Tambimuttu, eds., *T.S. Eliot, A Symposium* (Chicago: Henry Regnery, 1949), p. 42.
13. Eliot, T. S., *To Criticize the Critic* (London: Faber and Faber, 1965), p. 136.

which means that every material and natural object may be used as a symbol for spiritual, moral and intellectual ideas. The affinity between the ideas and the objects rests upon the various known attributes of the object. This theory corresponds to the imagistic principle of 'close resemblance of the word to the real object'. The value of a symbol or an image depends upon its expansiveness, which may be defined in terms of I. A. Richards' 'connotative' expansion of meaning.

The influence of Baudelaire is clearly visible in the 'Unreal City' of *The Waste Land* as Eliot himself acknowledges in his notes to the poem. Here Eliot creates in his own language the Baudelarian ideal of blending the familiar and the strange. And the exclamation in *Prufrock*, 'But how his arms and legs are Thin', is French, not English. Eliot's symbols and images, then, become psychological images (as in Baudelaire) used to convey the modern psychic complexes. Images from the external world correspond to the inner life and thus the world (for Eliot as well as Baudelaire) becomes a storehouse of images to be evoked and loaded with deep spiritual meanings by the magic of poetic imagination. Therefore, all the images present a fusion between sordidly realistic and phantasmagoric, the juxtaposition of the matter-of-fact and the fantastic. In his essay on Baudelaire (1930), he elaborates this point:

> It is not merely in the use of imagery of common life, not merely in the use of imagery of the sordid life of a great metropolis but in the elevation of such imagery to the first intensity — presenting it as it is, and yet making it represent something much more than itself that Baudelaire has created a mode of release and expression for other men.[14]

In Eliot, this intensity is achieved by the conceptual and perceptual metaphors or connotative and denotative images. Middleton Murry underscores the significance of such imagery:

---

14. Eliot, T. S., *Selected Essays* (London: Faber and Faber, 1951), p. 426.

> The highest function of imagery is to define indefinable spiritual qualities. All metaphors and similes can be described as the analogy by which the human mind explores the universe of quality and charts the non-measurable world. Of these indefinable qualities some are capable of direct sensuous apprehension. . . . Sensuous perception is of the qualities of the visible, audible, tangible world; of the spiritual qualities, of the more recondite world of the human personality there is intuition.[15]

Thus, Murry echoes Baudelaire's words: 'In certain almost supernatural states of the soul'. To Eliot, his constant accumulation of vivid 'sense perceptions' (spatial and temporal images) supplies the most potent means by which he articulates his spiritual intuitions or concepts (psychological images).

What the modern reader looks for in imagery is freshness, intensity and evocative power. Intensity is achieved through closeness of the pattern within which a poem's images are related, even when the emotional tone of the image does not perfectly correspond with the idea presented. And the evocative power aims at the participation of the reader's consciousness.

It is evident, then, that the working principle behind the image-pattern in Eliot's works (poetry and plays) is the 'congruity of image'. What he aims at is the consistency of impression, for without this poetic truth cannot be communicated. Consistency of impression leading to a whole poem means that images are the natural language of their theme. So the principle that organises the images is a concord between image and theme. For example, consider the images, in the first three lines of *Prufrock*. Here between 'evening' and 'patient etherized', there is a rational void. But a spark leaps to fill the gap so that the etherized and unconscious pale evening and unconscious consciousness of the protagonist illuminate each other reciprocally, a light

---
15. Martin, Graham and Furbank, eds., *Twentieth Century Poetry: Selected Essays and Documents* (London: Open University Press, 1979), p. 9.

which extends beyond them and reaches out in some way over the modern human situation all around. These images are tied together by 'Intellectual logic'. Their component parts, the ideas for example of 'patient' and 'evening', have been brought into an association from which each part profits, and each part contributes to the complete image, and ultimately to the poem as a whole. This is called the perception of the similar in the dissimilar.

So images are not things apart or complete, except in the sense that a whole poem or play may be a composite image. If the work is to be whole, and not a series of meaningless images, a pattern of images must be created, a relationship equivalent to that which underlies all reality — living or inanimate — must be established. In Eliot, this pattern is created by recurrent images working on three levels: temporal, spatial and psychological, that is, images relating to time, space and psychology. These images play an important part in conveying emotion or tension and sustaining it.

They provide the 'atmosphere'. But Eliot uses classical and Manichaean images as background and undertone. This second category of images emphasise the leading motif or the theme and reveals the temperament and character of the person using them. So at the mental plane, he uses temporal, spatial and psychological images, and at the thematic plane he uses the classical and Manichaean images.

The mastery of Eliot's imagery does not lie in the use, however beautiful and revealing, of isolated images, but in the total harmonious impression produced by a succession of subtly related images. So all the temporal, spatial, psychological, classical and Manichaean images are inter-related. His images appear to grow out of one another, and at the same time fulfil an independent existence of their own.

The complex inter-relation and inter-play of the recurrent images assumes a particular pattern in his poetry and plays, which holds a key to the proper understanding of the thematic layers in his works. In any intellectual study, we expect a principle of unity, and it is exactly this that we have been lacking to have a fuller understanding of Eliot. The purpose of the present study is to draw attention to the poetic unity in Eliot's recurrent images. The pattern of images traced in the following pages has not been taken up for a serious academic discussion so far.

/ 2

The Pattern of Images

T. S. Eliot is a highly conscious artist. Every word, every phrase—nay every image—that he uses has a definite purpose to serve. The more one explores the images used by him, the greater the explication of his thematic layers and the deeper the enjoyment. Eliot believes that the entire output of a 'major' poet constitutes a single work, that there is a meaningful inter-relationship between compositions and that individual pieces are endowed with meaning by other pieces and by the whole concept of a writer's work. Elsewhere, he speaks of the 'world' that a poet creates, and remarks that all Shakespeare's work is one poem. Like so many of Eliot's generalisations, this is particularly true of his own poetry. He cannot be sampled in anthologies. One understands each of his poems after having read the others. But his total work is an imaginative world and must be approached through his imagery. If there is a fragmentary aspect in much of his work, there is also a continuity and wholeness, which he achieves through a pattern of recurrent images.

A frequent practice of Eliot was 'doing things separately' and then 'making a kind of whole of them' so that the fragmentary quality of the work is finally operative in the unity of the whole. This practice of 'congruity' in incongruous elements is common among the entire school of New Criticism, French symbolists and imagists. Like Baudelaire, Eliot's 'sense-perceptions' — scattered in the form of metaphors and similes as 'things separately' — supply the most potent means by which he articulates his 'spiritual intuitions' or concepts. These concepts, which govern or dominate the pervading 'atmosphere' of the poem, are the organising principle, 'fusing' those sense-perceptions together.

According to Leonard Unger, 'The characteristic poem [of Eliot] . . . is analogous to the series of slides, highly selective and suggestive.'[16] The fragmentariness of Eliot's poetry is, thus, a structural device, for it is related to subject and meaning. In *Preludes*, Eliot makes explicatory comments about fragmentary images:

> I am moved by fancies that are curled
> Around these images, and cling:
> The notion of some infinitely gentle
> Infinitely suffering thing.

'These images' constitute the main body of Eliot's poems. The poet has tried to guide the reader towards the 'meaning' of the poem by mentioning the 'fancies' (the 'sense-perceptions') which attend the images. The title of *Four Quartets* announces most succinctly 'the quasi-wholeness and the quasi-fragmentariness' which are characteristic of Eliot's work. The title *Four Quartets* 'allows for the separate unity of each of the *Quartets*, and at the same time makes each a part of the larger whole.'[17]

The technique is particularly applicable with reference to Eliot's use of imagery. Just as the recurrent themes of time, alienation, and isolation contribute to the continuity, 'so does a steadily developing pattern of interrelated images and symbols.'[18]

---

16. Unger, Leonard, *T. S. Eliot: Moments & Patterns: A Study in Sources and Meaning* (Minneapolis: University of Minnesota Press, 1959), p. 20.
17. Ibid., pp. 26–27
18. Ibid., p. 31

There is, for example, the underwater imagery of the poems of the *Prufrock* group:

> I should have been a pair of ragged claws
> Scuttling across the floors of silent seas

*   *   *

> We have lingered in the chambers of the sea
> By sea-girls wreathed with seaweed red and brown
> Till human voices wake us, and we drown.

*   *   *   *   *   *

> The memory throws up high and dry
> A crowd of twisted things;
> A twisted branch upon the beach

Commenting on these lines, Leonard Unger says: Comparable images, of water and underwater, of rain and river and sea, continue to appear throughout the poetry, reflecting and echoing each other with cumulative effect.[19]

There is a similar development of flower and garden imagery, from beginning to end, and even extending into the plays. The 'hyacinth girl' of *The Waste Land* is related to the 'Smell of hyacinths' in *Portrait of a Lady* and to the girl 'her arms full of flowers' in *La Figlia Che Piange*. The rose-garden dialogue of Harry and Agatha in *The Family Reunion* remains enigmatic, unless related to this garden imagery in Eliot's poetry, and especially to the symbolic rose-gardens of *Ash-Wednesday* and *Burnt Norton*. Each garden passage, whether early or late, gains in clarity and scope of meaning when read in relation to the others.

We see that these recurrent images in Eliot change their associations under the impact of the character and atmosphere. For example, 'sea' (pp. 23-26) in *Prufrock* becomes an image of escape from reality into imagination

---

19. Unger, Leonard, *T. S. Eliot: Moments and Patterns: A Study in Sources and Meaning*, p. 32.

while the same 'sea' in 'Death by Water' in *The Waste Land* (pp. 316–17) becomes an image of harsh realities—the sea of temptations through which the human beings are voyaging and getting caught in the whirlpool of death. It also becomes a symbol of spiritual regeneration, which death by water leads to.

Such changing associations make it difficult to categorise Eliot's images in water-tight compartments, for images are not merely objects but ideas which the perception evokes in the poet's mind, and these concepts and ideas link Eliot's images. On the basis of these concepts, Eliot's imagery functions on three levels: temporal, spatial and psychological. It is amazing that the recurrent pattern holds a key to Eliot's poetry which, following the symbolist tradition, abounds in private images.

Within this broad framework, most of Eliot's images function, some independently as woof and some as warp, but in the ultimate analysis they become part of the same texture. That is to say, a temporal image may have psychological and spatial overtones and connotations and a spatial image may thematically relate to psychological and temporal context and so on.

In Eliot's poetry and plays, images appear to grow out of one another. There is an overlapping of these three types of images. Nevertheless, the recurrent imagery forms a definite structure which includes 'the structural emotion', and which, in turn, coalesces into 'the floating feeling' to create the overall poetic effect, or the 'art emotion'. By using these three types of images, Eliot creates one texture of imagery in spite of the woof and warp of the images being independently visible. By following the inter-related and inter-linked pattern of images, one can arrive at and grasp the inner meaning of the poem.

Let us examine lines from another poem to prove the efficacy and successful application of the aforementioned pattern. In the following two lines of *Portrait of a Lady*:

> Among the smoke and fog of a December afternoon
> You have the scene arrange itself.

'Smoke and fog' are spatial images, while 'December afternoon' is a temporal image. The artificially arranged scene reveals the mind of the lady; hence it becomes a psychological image. The same pattern is followed in *The Waste Land*:

> April is the cruelest month, breeding
> Lilacs out of the dead land, mixing
> Memory and desire, stirring
> Dull roots with spring rain.

Temporal, spatial, psychological, then again temporal—this is the recurrent structure of the images of these lines. This pattern of imagery—the implicit interaction and interplay of the images, rather than the explicit statements, or overt speeches/actions of the characters—constitutes the working out of the primary subject, or 'theme'.

By taking into account the imagery of *Murder in the Cathedral* and *The Family Reunion*, it may be indicated as to how the progressive pattern breaks surface in his plays. The opening speech of the Chorus in *Murder in the Cathedral* abounds in all the three categories of images:

> Here let us stand, close by the cathedral.
> Here let us wait,
> Is it the knowledge of safety, that draws our feet
> Towards the cathedral? What danger can be
> For us, the poor, poor women of Canterbury?

The sense of danger and waiting reveals the intuitive foreknowledge of the mind of the Women—hence it becomes a psychological image. 'Cathedral' and 'Canterbury'—the spatial images, are then followed by the concrete temporal imagery:

Since golden October declined into somber November,
And the apples were gathered and stored

Similarly, the opening speech of Amy in *The Family Reunion* is built around the three kinds of images:

Not yet! I will ring for you.
   It is still quite light.
   I have nothing to do but watch the days draw out.
   Now that I sit in the house from October to June,
   And the Swallow comes too soon and the spring will be over
   And the cuckoo will be gone before
   I am out again.
   O Sun, that was once warm,
O Light that was taken for granted . . .
   . . . Will the spring never come?
   I'm cold.

In the first line, 'light' is a spatial image, establishing the atmospheric background. The second line converts the entire speech into a lament of Amy's advancing age and indicates her delicate health, which keeps her housebound. So 'I have nothing to do' becomes a psychological image exposing the death-in-life state in which she lives. The 'days' becomes a temporal image and the 'house' and 'sun' are spatial images. The temporal images bring out the central idea of the play—the attempt to prevent 'the clock to stop in the dark', to arrest time in eternity. It is autumn, summer seems a long way off. The expression 'I'm cold' becomes a psychological image, for it conveys a chill, a sense of fear that underlies this speech.

Leonard Unger[20] analyses a large number of images recurring as a pattern in Eliot's poems. He categorises these images under the following heads :

1.   Flowers and gardens: eventually the rose and the rose gardens.

---
20. Unger, Leonard, *T. S. Eliot: Moments and Patterns*, pp. 161–62.

2. Water images of various kinds, especially underwater.
3. Months and seasons, days of the week, periods of the day or night and the time of day.
4. Smoke and fog.
5. City streets.
6. Parts of the human body — especially arms, hands and fingers, legs and feet.
7. Human hair.
8. Stairs.
9. Images of music.
10. Images of smell.

Unger comes out with a thesis that mind or 'awareness' is the coordinating image for which all the other images exist. That is to say, all images, by implication, serve the purpose of externalising the inner working of the mind or the psychology of the protagonist. However, the images picked up by Unger occur and recur in association with one another and, as such, can be easily classified under the three broad categories of images as mentioned here, that is temporal, spatial and psychological. The temporal and spatial images, taken as conceptual metaphors, ultimately turn out to be psychological, since all the images are interrelated.

Even spatial images are of two types: infinite spatial images and intervening spatial images. The former group deals with cosmic elements, such as the moon, the sun, the sky and the related elements like rain, thunder, and so on. The latter group deals with earth, sea, river and distant places. An in-depth study of some poems of Eliot will substantiate the fact that a pattern of imagery exists in them. That this pattern has a wider context and range becomes clear when we examine in detail the works under study. Some instances justifying the relevance of such a pattern are enumerated here.

Eliot's poem *Rhapsody on a Windy Night* provides an accurate synthesis of the three types of images:

> Twelve o'clock.
> Along the reaches of the street
> Held in a lunar synthesis,
> Whispering lunar incantations

'Twelve o'clock', a temporal image, is followed by the spatial images, 'the reaches of the street' and 'lunar synthesis'. Moon hypnotises the deserted street. The moonlight seems to be whispering stories of the night— 'lunar incantations'—into his ears. What are the stories of the night? They are sordid experiences and actions of the man, witnessed by the street. These 'lunar incantations' dissolve the floors of his memory (signifying madness); he becomes moony, lunatic:

> Every street lamp that I pass
> Beats like a fatalistic drum,
> And through the spaces of the dark
> Midnight shakes the memory
> As a madman shakes a dead geranium.

The spatial image of darkness turns into a conceptual comment on the disorderly inner mental state of a person in a drunken state. His consciousness is in twilight zone, with the street lamp dismally lighting the darkness. The consciousness of the protagonist has been reduced to the level of a mad man shaking a dead geranium. Therefore, this stanza fuses the spatial setting with the psychological state of the protagonist.

The entire poem provides a synthesis of the spatial and temporal settings. The protagonist, experiencing a 'vision of the street', soliloquises in response to visual and temporal images. It is relevant to recall the words of Sunil Kumar Sarkar in his book *T. S. Eliot: Poetry, Plays and Prose*:

The poem has a clock-time structure (that is, temporal structure), divided by the hours announced at the beginning of the strokes: 'twelve o'clock', 'Half-past one', 'Half-past two', 'Half-past three', 'Four o'clock', which Bergson would call a 'spatial' structure. This structure is spatial because the times are synchronised with the speaker's pauses at street lamps. But as each lamp mutters an 'incantation' to direct his gaze towards new spatial images, these pass into his consciousness and unite with memories already there to make up subjective time where space is non-existent.

Therefore, throughout the poem, images function on three levels: temporal, spatial and psychological.

As the above discussion shows, *Rhapsody on a Windy Night* includes not only the third and fifth group of images listed by Unger, but also those images which Unger excludes, such as 'moon', 'memory', 'madman', and so on. So the three categories of images are multi-dimensional, and include other images on the perceptual as well as conceptual level. The following lines from *Prufrock* will further elucidate the point:

> I have seen them riding seaward on the waves
> Combing the white hair of the waves blown black
> When the wind blows the water white and black.

The 'underwater' and 'hair' images, included in the second and seventh groups by Unger, have spatial and psychological overtones. There is also the psychological image 'mermaids' and the spatial image 'wind' which 'blows the water white and black'. The mermaids represent imagination and beauty, uncontaminated by the touch of the 'earth', whereas 'the women . . . talking of Michelangelo' symbolise beauty contaminated by the touch of the earth. Prufrock is afraid of reality. His timidity is so piteous that he asks himself nervously: 'Shall I part my hair behind?' He is growing old and wants to conceal his age. He knows the enchanting song of the mermaids, and the magnificence of the sea, but he will only walk by the borders of the waves. The white streaming hair of the sea-horses, the waves on which the mermaids ride (in his imagination), overwhelms him. In order to forget the sordid reality of the world, Prufrock enters into a dream world, a reverie, a psychological necessity for him. It is the sound of the human voices in the drawing room that brings him back to ordinary life.

The image of 'stairs' frequently occurs in the poems of Eliot, including *Prufrock*, *Portrait of a Lady*, *The Boston Evening Transcript*, *Rhapsody on a Windy Night*, *La Figlia Che Piange*, etc. In every case, the stairs are a literal reference, an image related to space. In all the passages where the image of 'stairs' has been used, stairs serve as the settings for arrivals and departures. Prufrock is contemplating a possible crisis of decision, having mounted the stairs, whether to enter and join his friends or whether to turn back and descend the stairs. In *Portrait of a Lady*, the gentleman mounts 'the stairs and turn the handle of the door/And feel as if I had mounted on my hands and knees.' Here too, he is confronted with the problem of whether to meet the lady or not. In *La Figlia Che Piange*, the man has departed, leaving the girl to 'stand and grieve' at the top of the stairs. In the passage concluding *Rhapsody*, the man is returning to the solitude of his own quarters, and his sexual anxiety is emphasised here as it is done in the whole poem. The figurative mounting on hands and knees in *Portrait of a Lady* suggests a kind of dehumanisation, as if through his abashment the crestfallen young man has become a bungling animal. In *The Boston Evening Transcript*, the relation between the speaker and his 'cousin Harriet' is troubled by ironic implication. Between the man and the woman there are no 'appetites of life' but only the Boston Evening Transcript. In every case, the relation of the speaker to stairs includes what may be called a posture of awareness. Hence 'stairs' becomes a psychological image.

Music, too, is a psychological image. In *Portrait of a Lady*, the man and woman have just arrived in the woman's room after attending a concert of Chopin's *Preludes*. As the 'conversation slips', the sounds of violins and concerts echo in the mind of the man, thus indicating a diffusion of awareness and a quality of strain and distress in the man's relations with both music and the woman.

In the second section of the poem, there are two images of music, and both present music as unwelcome invasions of awareness. Similarly, the smell of the hyacinths in the *Portrait* contributes intimations of poignancy to the occasion on which the street-piano is heard. As an invasion of awareness, the 'smell of hyacinths' is also comparable to the distracting 'perfume from a dress' in *Prufrock*. Thus, all the images listed by Unger fall within the pattern evolved in this study:

1. Water, Fog, Street: spatial images.
2. Parts of human body like arms, eyes, etc. become temporal images, being symbols of individual or social time. Months, seasons and days are also temporal images.
3. Stairs, music, smell: psychological images.

In order to fully understand the above categorisation of images in Eliot's poetry, one must, for purposes of comparison and elucidation, look at G. Wilson Knight's classification of Shakespearean imagery in *The Wheel of Fire* (1930). It is interesting to note that the 'Introduction' to *The Wheel of Fire* was written by Eliot, in which he appreciates Knight's classification: 'I think, Mr. Wilson Knight has shown insight in pursuing his search for the pattern below the level of "plot" and character.'[21] So Knight's study and classification of images of Shakespeare seems to be complementary and supplementary to Eliot's imagery, and relevant to the present study.

---

21. Knight, G. Wilson, *The Wheel of Fire* (London: Methuen and Co. Ltd., 1930), rpt. 1965, p. XVIII.

According to Knight:

> One must be prepared to see the whole play in space as well as in time . . . there are . . . a set of correspondence which relate to each other independently of the time-sequence which is the story. . . . This I have . . . called the play's atmosphere.[22]

For Knight, 'spatial' and 'atmosphere' are synonymous, by which he means the 'omnipresent and mysterious reality brooding motionless over and within the play's movement.'[23] With the poet as with the reader, the time-sequence is uppermost in consciousness, the pervading atmosphere or static background tending to be unconsciously apprehended or created. Knight opines that the character is ultimately confused with this atmospheric quality; he obeys a spatial as well as temporal necessity. He further emphasises that symbols or images illuminate the consciousness, the pervading atmosphere and working of the human psyche, for 'the character is intimately fused with this atmospheric quality'.

Applied to Eliot's use of imagery, Knight's classification helps to understand the concepts incorporated in temporal, spatial and psychological images. What Knight terms as 'spatial' or 'atmospheric' images in Shakespeare's context may be understood in terms of psychological imagery in Eliot's poetry. For the pervading atmosphere, the 'spatial quality' as Knight calls it, is a projection of the protagonist's consciousness.

Death pervades *Hamlet* and dominates the consciousness, just as in Eliot's *Prufrock* the consciousness is governed by the divided self and lack of communication (as both in *Murder in the Cathedral* and *The Family Reunion*, the sense of evil and guilt creates the pervading atmosphere). The entire scenery of the poem, indoor and outdoor, is finally the psychological landscape of Prufrock himself. The streets, rooms, people and fancies, all register on

---
22. Knight, G. Wilson, *The Wheel of Fire*, p. 3.
23. Ibid., pp. 4–5.

Prufrock's consciousness; they, in fact, become a part of his consciousness. That happens in his consciousness and takes place in time and space. What is, in short, 'spatial' in Shakespeare, is psychological in Eliot.

Consciously used metaphors of time and space in Eliot's poetry tend to illuminate the psychic atmosphere. The common element, thus, in the present study and that of Knight, is the pervading atmosphere—psychology or mental state. This reminds us of Unger's remarks that mind or 'awareness' is the coordinating image, synthesising all other images.

Knight's temporal elements can be divided into two parts in the context of Eliot: spatial and temporal, that is, images relating to cosmos and elementary nature (Like the earth, water, sea, river, etc.). These spatial and temporal images, thus, are the visual perceptions (perceptual metaphors) linked through the psychological conception of them (conceptual metaphors).

A similar exercise of tracing a pattern of imagery in Shakespeare has also been done by Caroline E. Spurgeon in her book *Shakespeare's Imagery and What it Tells Us* (first printed in 1930). She begins by recounting various sources of Shakespeare's imagery and then proceeds to concentrate on the range and subject matter of images with simultaneous commentary on their dramatic and artistic function in the plays of Shakespeare. Using the 'eclectic' method, to quote Knight, like Unger, Spurgeon classifies Shakespeare's images into eight categories:

1. Natural imagery
2. Animal imagery
3. Body imagery
4. Daily life imagery
5. Learning (law, science, religion, etc.) imagery
6. Arts imagery
7. Domestic imagery

8. Imaginative states (emotions, abstractions, etc.) imagery.

Knight, however, regards Spurgeon's analysis of Shakespeare's imagery a very limited one. His classification appears to be a catalogue of all possible images used by Shakespeare on the perceptual level, but excludes the dominating atmospheric impressions shaping into psychological and intellectual concepts. Her rigid codification based on fields of Shakespeare's interest, often leads to 'negative inferences' which are likely to be misleading. For instance, she writes that since *Julius Caesar* is poor in imagery, it lacks excitement in composition. But actually, no single work of Shakespeare tingles with vivid, fiery and, to use Masefield's words, 'startling life' as does Julius Caesar. The truth is that the pervading atmosphere of 'fire' is here generated by events and descriptions more important than any imagery, visual metaphors and similes. However, for Spurgeon, imagery includes only images, symbols, metaphors and similes, and her classification is not applicable to the complex modern poetry of Eliot, for in Eliot's poetry, 'ideas' unlock the mystery of imagery and vice-versa. In this sense, Knight's classification is more relevant to modern poetry, including that of Eliot.

Knight's thesis offers a clue to the interpretation of images of a great poet. He himself admits in the 'Prefatory Note' to his book, *The Imperial Theme* (1931), that his 'criticism has been associated with the "Cambridge" school of literary criticism, headed by such names as T. S. Eliot, I. A. Richards and, later, F. R. Leavis' (p. vi). Since Eliot is a new critic, his poetry demands poetic 'interpretation' (like that of Knight in the case of Shakespeare) rather than 'criticism' (like that of Spurgeon). As regards the tempest-music opposition which is the recurrent imagery in Shakespeare's plays, Knight says:

> Tempests are all important. Taken in opposition with music they form the only principle of unity in Shakespeare.

'Characterisation', plots, meter, even typical 'values' change, plays are tragical, historical, comical, or personal . . . but all may be shown to revolve on this one axis.[24]

A similar kind of unity is found in Eliot's poetry and plays associating and connecting all the fragmentary aspects of his work.

The ten categories of images discovered by Unger in Eliot's poetry are covered by the pattern of images evolved under three heads—temporal, spatial and psychological—in the present study. Similarly, Knight's classification also includes images and symbols picked up by Spurgeon. As Knight's pattern is different from Spurgeon's classification, similarly the pattern traced in the present thesis is different from that of Unger. There is no rigid codification. Perceptions are concentrated in conceptions. Knight observes:

> Moreover, tempest-imagery is only one very obvious and recurrent thread in wider pattern of 'disorder', though often bodied into imagery of universal disorder : comets and meteors, earth-quakes, and such like which may blend with 'disease' imagery. Conversely, music is enmeshed in other pleasant suggestions, especially delicate airs (to be contrasted with the Tempests), flowers, gold, jewels and all rich stones. On the purely human plane, these groups are associated with disorder, conflict and all fierce passions on one side; and love, concord, peace, on the other. Tempests, also, are to be related to all Shakespeare's 'weather' thought, blending with rain, clouds, fog, all dark or wintry effects; whereas music harmonizes with spring and summer, light and warmth. Moreover . . . tempests are often associated with trees, especially the cedar, oak and pine, and rough beasts; also we find gentile beasts— especially birds suggesting the opposite, though birds may in turn be evil, as in *Macbeth*, so that our tempest-symbolism cannot be finally abstracted from all Shakespeare's imagery, suggestions, symbolism.[25]

---

24. Knight, G. Wilson, *The Shakespearean Tempest* (London: Methuen and Co., 1953), p. 6.
25. Ibid., p. 17.

We may propound the thesis, then, that the recurrent images of Eliot--- temporal, spatial and psychological – cannot be finally abstracted from all his imagery, suggestions, symbolism, dramatic effects, reflecting impressions of man's physique and psyche, flowers and beasts, earth and water, air and fire; sun, moon and stars; light and dark. The three kinds of images are inter-related and they cannot be discussed in isolation. The temporal and spatial images taken as conceptual metaphors turn out to be psychological. In addition to such meaningful recurrence of symbolic imagery, there is, at times, a merging of one kind of imagery with another, as in the following lines from *Marina*:

> Whispers and small laughter between leaves and hurrying feet
> Under sleep, where all the waters meet.

Here the garden (temporal) imagery and the water (spatial) imagery are related to each other, and related also to that deeper realm of consciousness in which such associations occur. Three categories of imagery, each already intricate and extensive, have been joined to produce a pattern that is still larger, more intricate and multi-dimensional.

In the continuity of Eliot's imagery, there is not only an accumulation of meaning, but an alteration of meaning, a retroactive effect of later elements upon earlier ones. For example, the lines from *Marina* have a relevance to the final lines of *Prufrock*. Marina is a girl, the daughter of Shakespeare's Pericles, and as her name indicates, a 'sea-girl'. There are, thus, in both passages, the details of under-water, of sleep, and of the sea-girls. Considered alone, the sexual fantasy of the passage from *Marina* is expressive of Prufrock's isolation and alienation: 'Till human voices wake us, and we drown'. But when considered in relation to *Marina* and to the entire pattern of the rose-garden imagery, Prufrock's erotic daydream becomes an intimation of what is represented in later poems as a spiritual vision. The image of 'mermaids' in Prufrock's self-indulgent reverie (psychological image) becomes just an antecedent type of the female figure that is later to represent spiritual guidance such as the lady in *Ash-Wednesday* (psychological image extended to religious archetype or the race-mind) who is:

> Blessed sister, holy mother, spirit of the fountain
> Spirit of the garden.
> *   *   *   *
> And spirit of the river, spirit of the sea.

This is not to say that the earlier apparent meaning of the spatial (water) image in *Prufrock* is cancelled out by that in *Marina*. But while each image remains itself, it takes on an additional connotation and qualification of meaning in the larger context. Eliot's observation in *Tradition and the Individual Talent* about literature in general that 'the past (is) altered by the present as the present is directed by the past', is precisely applicable to his imagery in particular and poetry and plays in general.

Most of the images used by Eliot in his poetry and plays belong to one of the three categories and since their major function is to create atmosphere, in the context of Knight's interpretation, they may be termed as 'atmospheric images'. In addition to these broad categories of images, a second pattern of classical and Manichaean images emerges if Eliot's works are studied in correlation to the classical plays and myths. These images provide structural outline to his poems and plays. This second pattern of classical and Manichaean images gains intensity in the light of Eliot's doctrines presented in his essay *Tradition and the Individual Talent*. In this essay, Eliot considers the relationship of any poem by any poet to other poems by other poets which forms the poetic tradition. Eliot defines 'tradition' as the aggregate of poetic modes created by the long line of poets from Homer to the poets of yesterday. No living poet can stand outside this tradition. This is not a plea for a slavish imitation of the past, but for a hard-won involvement in a real sense of history. He looks for an almost mystical blending of the temporal and the timeless in the poet's perception, a sense that past and present confront each other endlessly; each new work adds to—and at the same time redefines—a tradition which is so much greater than the individuals who contribute to it.

Applied to Eliot's imagery, his 'atmospheric images' reflect his individual talent which draws strength from the present—the modern age. But his classical images as well as Manichaean (mythological) images redefine the classical tradition and, at the same time, relate present to the past. The temporal (atmospheric images) and the timeless (classical and Manichaean images) are blended in the poet's perception. By this blending, Eliot, as he opines in his essay, aims at 'a principle of aesthetics'. Because from this give-and-take of conformity between the poet and the tradition, the present and the past, emerges 'the individual talent'.

Eliot brings in all the Greek images in his poems and plays to highlight the themes and subject matter which, in turn, seem to be derived from classical plays with artistic deviations. Hence, if at the mental plane, Eliot uses 'atmospheric'—spatial, temporal and psychological—images, at the thematic plane he uses classical and mythological (Manichaean) images. However, the unifying factor, again, is the fact that all the images ultimately become a device to throw light upon the working of the protagonist's mind.

To comprehend the depth of these classical images, it is significant to delve deep beneath the ready framework of thematic layers of his works. Since *The Waste Land* is about the spiritual renunciation of the modern barren minds, Eliot brings in the Sophoclean character of Tiresias, with a prophet's grandeur and grace. Historically, Tiresias is connected with the story of King Oedipus of Thebes, which is clearly and demonstrably the classical legend of the wasteland brought about by the sin of Oedipus, the sin arising from the violation of sanctity. His bisexuality suggests sterility, the condition of the wasteland. Each characteristic of Tiresias becomes an image, a symbol of the barren condition of the modern wasteland. Since all the thematic myths are united in Tiresias's consciousness, he becomes the major classical and mythological image.

All the poems and plays of Eliot are based on the quest motif and, therefore, like Greek tragedies, this quest covers three stages: guilt, suffering and purgation or insight. It is a journey from the prison of isolation towards self-realisation and beatitude. Since the subject matter is classical, the poems and plays are replete with classical images. The protagonist of *The Family Reunion*, Harry, also moves from guilt through suffering to purgation and insight.

The central experience in this play is an experience of conversion, so the imagery is designed to support Harry's guilt. The Furies transforming into 'bright angels' becomes the classical image that presents the journey towards realisation.

Guilt in *Murder in the Cathedral* is presented in the same manner as in *Oedipus Tyrranus*—through the ever-increasing sharp and fearful reaction of the Chorus starting only with a sense of reverence towards their respective heroes. Oedipus is regarded as 'God' by his companions while Becket is thought of as 'Son of Man' (p. 25). Later, the rotten smell in the air in *Murder in the Cathedral* corresponds to the 'night's agony grows into tortured day' in *Oedipus Tyrranus*; 'Now a new terror has soiled us' in the former is reflecting the latter's 'Fear is upon us'. However, since there is an overlapping of the above two categories of images—modern and classical—the cumulative effect is only psychological. The classical image of ritual ('spring is an issue of blood, a season of sacrifice'—*The Family Reunion*) also becomes a temporal image of season, which serves to highlight the guilt in Harry's mind and so, eventually, becomes a psychological image as well. Thus, Eliot brings in the 'great tradition of the past' and mingles it with the present.

The mythical method of Eliot is also derived from the classical writers, but the style of juxtaposing mythical elements is definitely modern. Hence, his myths can be categorised under the title of 'Manichaean images'. The mythology of Manichaeism is present in all his poems and plays. The religion of Mani, which originated in Mesopotamia in third century, AD., posited a state of war between spirit and matter, light and darkness, good and evil. Its mythology explains the present mixed state of things as a result of partially successful assault by the darkness on the light and the whole duty of Man is to restore the separation, largely by ascetic practices. Hence, Eliot's poetry and plays reflect this psychic need of modern man through Manichaean images which, in turn, present an opposition between positive and negative elements. In *The Waste Land*, the mythological images of death and rebirth, of Philomel's spiritual transformation and the last significant images of 'DA' — *Datta, Damyata* and *Dayadhavam* (Give, Control and Mercy) — are the Manichaean images, juxtapositioning the barren state of modern wastelanders and their constant effort to restore fertility and order. These images are working only in correlation to the psychic need of the protagonist.

Similarly, Eliot's temporal images of season make up not only a cycle but an opposition. 'Youth and age, spring and winter, dawn and darkness, rain and sea, form two contrasting states.'[26] Blake calls these states innocence and experience, and his terms are useful even for Eliot.

For poets with a religious imagination, there are also heaven and hell, the paradisal and demonic realities lying under the 'Manichaean' amalgam of good and evil in human

---

26. Frye, Northrop, *T. S. Eliot: Writers and Critics* (Edinburgh and London: Oliver and Boyd, 1963), p. 50.

life. Heaven and hell can be represented in poetry only by images of existence, hence images of innocence, the garden, perpetual spring, eternal youth, are closely associated with heaven or paradise, and images of repugnant experience, the desert, the sea, the prison, the tomb, are associated with hell. But for any poet who follows this structure of imagery, including Eliot, there are four worlds, and heaven and innocence, hell and experience, are distinguished as well as associated. So they become Manichaean images of opposed worlds and elements.

Thus, we see that Eliot makes a frequent use of images and all the images used by Eliot belong to one of the five categories: temporal, spatial, psychological, classical and Manichaean images. And when his poems and plays are interpreted according to the pattern of images traced above, they emerge thematically cogent and structurally well-knit.

3

Temporal Images

In the preceding chapter, it was observed that images in Eliot's poetry and plays assume a specific pattern that centres around five categories of images: temporal, spatial, psychological, classical and Manichaean. Often the 'atmospheric' images merge with classical and Manichaean images. In Eliot's works, no ideas are so consistently used, considered and later overtly discussed as ideas about time and the need to transcend it. His *Four Quartets*, particularly, makes a long meditation, interspersed with lyrics, on the conquest of time and the meaning of history. According to Unger, 'The central subject of the work of Eliot is the relation of the individual consciousness and identity to the passage of time'.[27] Both the concept of time and the presentation of it change and develop through Eliot's works, paralleling the movements from boredom, frustration and despair to significant action, acceptance and security. While the emphasis moves from individual experience of time as in *Prufrock* to the possibility of experiencing timelessness as in *Four Quartets*, the technique and imagery develop towards greater use of overtly stated doctrine combined with symbolist passages.

Although Eliot's scholarship has recognised the importance of time as a theme, there has been surprisingly

---

27. Unger, Leonard, *T. S. Eliot: Moments and Patterns*, p. 27.

little attempt to examine its effect on the poetry and plays as a whole. Most discussions focus on defining a single *time* concept—Heraclitean, Neoplatonic, Bergsonian—presumed to be present throughout his plays. In Eliot's works, the concept of time is largely determined and developed by temporal images. The emphasis of Prufrock's life, at least partially, stems from his failure to apprehend a timeless reality beyond the aimless cycle of daily routine ('I have measured out my life with coffee spoons').

Gerontion's terror reflects the paradox of history filled with meaning, but empty to him. In the later poems, the question of time is increasingly religious, 'How and to what extent can humanity achieve apprehension of and union with a timeless God?' The anguished seeking of *Ash Wednesday* and the almost weary resignation of *Journey of the Magi* or *A Song for Simeon* depend on the apparent opposition of time and eternity, and opposition reconciled only in 'Little Gidding' of Eliot's *Four Quartets*. The temporal images, thus, not only suggest a development in theme and technique, but also an association, inter-linked and correlated, in his poetry and plays.

The problem of antimony of time and consciousness finds expression in Eliot's poetry and plays at three levels:
i. Psychological
ii. Historical
iii. Spiritual

i. In his early poetry, *Prufrock And Other Observations* (1917), consciousness apprehends time in psychic terms. The psychological experience of time, the memory of the past of the individual, the fulfilled and unfulfilled urges of man in time, determine his 'facticity' or 'what he has been'. Every moment of his conscious existence is determined by his projection of this 'facticity'. In the entire volume *Prufrock and Other Observations*, the time is generally late afternoon, evening or night; for instance, the beginning and middle of *Prufrock*, the beginning and end of *Portrait of a Lady, Preludes I, III* and *IV, Rhapsody on a Windy Night* and *The Boston Evening Transcript*. Evening or night in Eliot's poetry is often a time when the pulses of life quicken, as in the rhythms at the beginning of *Prufrock*, or in 'The Fire Sermon' of *The Waste Land*, 'the violet hour, when the eyes and back turn upward from the desk, when the human engine waits,/Like a taxi throbbing waiting'. Evening is a time when the pressures of the social and workaday world are eased, and the individual may be prompted to search for a deeper and more intense life within himself. But imprisoned in the cell of past memories, which determine his present, the protagonist is not capable of transcendence. 'No transcending vision ever appears in these poems which is defined and bound by time'.[28]

ii. In the 1920 poems (of which *The Waste Land* may be described as the most representative), individual consciousness is lifted to the plane of history. Man's 'facticity' is not a 'past' of his individual consciousness alone, but includes the 'past' of the tradition of his culture. Just as the individual 'facticity' has been projected in the concrete act of 'conscious choice', so also with man's corporate 'historicity'. Every new stage or turn in the historical process offers possibilities for the reaffirmation of man's individual and historical being. In *Murder* in the *Cathedral* also, Eliot presents Becket as achieving historical timelessness through the conscious act of martyrdom.

iii. The concept of time as a spiritual phenomenon is propounded in *Four Quartets* and *The Family Reunion*, which commits man to every phase of cosmological process, imparting to him, as it were, a new insight into the cyclic movements of history. Even on the plane of history with its powerful undertones of flux, growth

---

28. Gish, Nancy K., *Time in the Poetry of T. S. Eliot: A Study in Structure and Theme* (London: The Macmillan Press Ltd., 1981), p. 2.

and decay, 'time the destroyer is time the preserver'. Thus, the treatment of time in Eliot's poetry and plays is three-dimensional.

a) Time Psychological

It is Bergson's persistent preoccupation with time that stimulated Eliot's thoughts on the psychic character of time. Eliot himself acknowledged that at a certain period of his life he was very influenced by Bergson's *Matter and Memory*. This must have happened about 1911, when Eliot was hearing Bergson's lectures in Paris and working on *Prufrock, Portrait of a Lady, Preludes* and *Rhapsody on a Windy Night*. 'The world of these poems, like that of Bergson, is one of constant flux, constant becoming without permanence or transcendence'.[29] Bergson describes time as a 'succession of states, each one of which announces what follows and contains what precedes'. Moreover, two major aspects of Bergson's philosophy illuminate many of Eliot's Poems:

(a) The split between inner and outer world corresponding to inner duration and external clock time.
(b) The emphasis on memory as the only source of unity in a discrete world.

According to Bergsonian psychology, the mind is constantly engaged in a double duty; it perceives and it remembers what it perceives.

In Bergson's *Matter and Memory*, an image is definable as a perception or as the perceived thing itself, so the subject and object merge, resulting into *dedoublement*. So we may regard, 'Let us go, then you and I' and 'Time for you and time for me' and '. . . the afternoon, the evening, sleeps so peacefully' as expressions of a consciousness aware of itself. The perceiver absorbs images into his consciousness, where they persist as memories. In the aggregate, memories, thus, form a *duree*. As seen in *Prufrock*, they affect the perception of things in the perceiver's future.

---
29. Ibid., pp. 2–3.

As a result of this 'time-space-continuum', or the psychic concept of time in Eliot—as also in Proust and Joyce—the straight-line structure has yielded place to a circular motion; the mind is always in a flux; past as a social time and individual time impinges on the present and future.

In addition to using time as a theme, Eliot also uses it as a technique. Through historical and contemporary juxtaposition of allusions, he achieves what may be called a 'transparency' of time.

The split between consciousness and the external world and the contrast between inner duration and scientific clock time are apparent throughout 1917 poems of Eliot. So time here appears as a psychological phenomenon. *The Love Song of J. Alfred Prufrock*, the landmark of early poetry, inaugurated a duel between time and consciousness.

The following comments by Camus can be pertinent to *The Love Song of J. Alfred Prufrock*:

> Likewise and during every day of an unillustrious life, time carries us. But a moment always comes when we have to carry it. We live in future: 'tomorrow'; 'later on'; 'when you have made your way'; 'you will understand when you are old enough'. Such irrelevancies are wonderful, for after all, it's a matter of dying. Yet a day comes when a man notices or says that he is thirty. Thus he asserts his youth. But simultaneously he situates himself in relation to time. He takes his place in it. He admits that he stands at a certain point on a curve that he acknowledges having to travel to its end. He belongs to time and, by 'the horror that seizes him, he recognizes his worst enemy: 'Tomorrow'. He was longing for tomorrow, whereas everything in him ought to reject it.[30]

There is an identical situation in Camus' *The Myth of Sisyphus* and *Prufrock*. Prufrock is confronted with the problem of growing older, achieving nothing, spending his time in tea-parties and chatter to 'assert youth', but leading only to age and death. More consciously aware of time,

---
30. Camus, Albert, *The Myth of Sisyphus* (Harmondsworth: Penguin Books, 1975), pp. 19–20.

he obsessively talks of it: 'There will be time, there will be time'. So, fundamentally, there are only two 'characters' in the Prufrock drama: time and consciousness. Their metaphysical aspect finds ironic correlation in the 'psycho-social' personality of the protagonist and his 'environment' which he calls his 'universe' and whose laws he 'dare' not disturb or challenge. Temporal images, thus, get related to psychological images.

The form of the poem is largely determined by temporal images. The nature of time is revealed not only in Prufrock's direct assertions about it and his almost obsessive concern with it, but in Eliot' specific use of symbolist techniques. The juxtaposition of images focuses on and intensifies the repetition of daily events and the passing of time without direction or purpose. Time appears as the etherized evening, restless nights, October night, days, hours, minutes, evenings, mornings, afternoons, dusk and sunset. These repeated temporal images assume the 'masquerades' of decisions and revisions, coffee spoons, tea and cakes and ices, door-yards, sprinkled streets, teacups and skirts that trail along the floor, and are joined with images of passing time: 'I have seen the moment of my greatness flicker'; 'I grow old . . . I grow old'; 'Shall I part my hair behind?'; 'No: I am not Prince Hamlet, nor was meant to be'.

And these images are interspersed with Prufrock's explicit talk of time: 'There will be time, there will be time' and such expressions are ironically reiterated. These images emphasise the outer life of clock time, of external events and situations in which Prufrock wishes to act but cannot. They also present the continual flow of his thoughts, revealing not only his fear but his desire for something else, something profound and inexplicable: 'It is impossible to say just what I mean.' The poems' sad tone develops with the movement of his thoughts from 'there will be time' to 'And would it have been worth it, after all . . .?' Time in the poem, then, is both : that which Prufrock

Temporal Images 43

thinks about,(clock time), and his own inner duration of which he is only inarticulately aware. By making the poem a dramatic monologue, Eliot was able to focus on individual experience of the world of flux, especially the flow of Prufrock's feelings. David Ned Tobin states:

> In (Eliot) one finds a characteristic Tennysonian theme: the desire to somehow transcend the whole process of time and lose oneself in death-like oblivion. Eliot took up this theme as early as *Prufrock* where the word 'time' tolls like the fatal angelus of 'The Dry Salvages', announcing not the time for prayer, but only the heavy presence of time itself. Time stretches before the speaker in 'Deserts of vast eternity' littered with cups and coffee spoons.[31]

The poem opens with a situation which symbolises 'no placid, peaceful city sunset'.[32] The spectator's sunset on the one hand, and the probing surgeon on the other, capture the split between the inner and the outer world; the romantic world of evening and nature on the one hand, and the enclosed space of the antiseptic, operating room on the other. Prufrock's inner hopes, aspirations and fears, divorced from the public life and hence as futile as the social events, make the evening 'like a patient etherized upon a table'. Thus, Eliot's psychic concept of time may be understood from what G. J. Whitrow observes:

> The psychological origin of the concept of time is, therefore, to be found in the conscious realization of distinction between desire and satisfaction. The sense and purpose of associated effort is the ultimate source of the ideas of cause and effect.[33]

Cyclic time comes and goes, while human time — psychic, social, historical — lingers and keeps vibrating in

---

31. Tobin, David Ned, *The Presence of the Past: T.S. Eliot's Victorian Inheritance* (Michigan: University Research Press, 1983), p. 130.
32. *Drew, Elizabeth, T. S. Eliot: The Design of His Poetry, p. 58.*
33. Whitrow, G. S., *The Natural Philosophy of Time* (London: Thomas Nelson and Sons, 1961), p. 52.

the consciousness of man. Prufrock, with his excessively intellectualised awareness of 'cyclic time' is delighted to observe the objective world of 'a soft October night', but he is too weak to translate this softness of October night in terms of emotions. So in psychological terms, this cyclic time of 'nights' and 'evening' would be accounted the cruellest and the hardest of nights. Hence this conflict between 'you' and 'I' — 'you' is the symbol of social awareness, and 'I' is the romantic self. Nancy K. Gish tells us that:

> Bergson's theory of the self and the external world contains not only a split between the inner and outer world, but within the self between the outer social life, which is like a crust of solidified states, useful for social life but no longer vital, and the inner true self which is rich and indefinable but seldom known.[34]

This psychic failure is caused by the 'social time'. 'Cyclic time' sharpens his desire, 'social time' declares its instantaneous death:

> In the room the women come and go
> Talking of Michelangelo.

These women do not invoke 'cultural past' as the name of Michelangelo might suggest, but are ghosts of Prufrock's past. He has 'known them all'. They had been his companions in the futile process of measuring life with coffee spoons.

This familiarity becomes a taboo for him, for the memory of his past interferes with his present desire and future actions, and his life becomes an interplay between memory and desire. The women are symbols of 'social time' which would crush the awakening self of Prufrock. This experience of 'social time' is too threatening and frightful compared with the sickly, nauseating features of the 'phenomenal time' seen in the aspect of the 'evening spread out against the sky / Like a patient etherized

---

34. Gish, Nancy K., *Time in the Poetry of T. S. Eliot*, pp. 11–12.

upon a table'. His fractured psyche and social awareness clash with the experience of 'cyclic time'. The impact of his social environment on his 'self' is crushing. So in his preparation to meet 'you' (his self) he meets another aspect of time—'individual time', his own past which is burdened with unfulfilled potentialities, vague urgings, undetermined fancies. Thus 'you', as a psychological image, also becomes a temporal image.

Afraid of the 'social time', Prufrock turns his consciousness away from 'the women' talking of Michelangelo, perhaps only to gather courage to face the social vultures ready to pounce upon his precarious being. And once again he throws a lingering glance at the 'corners of evening' chasing the lengthened and winding movements of 'the yellow smoke that rubs its muzzle on the window panes'. However, his awakened consciousness must cause an encounter of his self with the temporal tyrant. So, once again, he returns to the nightmare scene where women come and go, talking of Michelangelo. But it is not without a presentiment that he notes:

> There will be time, there will be time
> To prepare a face to meet the faces that you meet;

To conquer the past amounts to meeting and not caring for 'the faces that you meet'. On the one hand, he imagines the possibility of life in heroic terms: 'There will be time to murder and create', 'To have squeezed the universe into a ball'; on the other hand, he cannot reject his classification by others—'a formulated phrase'—any more than he can reject his 'social past' and continue to be himself. He quivers:

> And time yet for a hundred indecisions,
> And for a hundred visions and revisions,
> Before the taking of a toast and tea.

This incessant repetition of 'there will be time' not only implies doubt, but is itself a way of losing time, of thinking so constantly about it that it passed without use. Prufrock can neither forget it nor escape it.

By now Prufrock has realised that the time for questioning, contemplation and abstraction will soon be over and the 'moment' of crisis with demands of living and action is approaching. As Albert Camus puts it:

> What distinguishes modern sensibility from classical sensibility is that the latter thrives on moral problems and the former on metaphysical problems.[35]

Prufrock is Camus' 'modern man'. The 'metaphysical' universe occupies more than the immediate experience of this world and life. Prufrock cannot presume so much as to disturb the universe. By fulfilling himself in the moment of 'now' he could have rearranged things in order according to his own choice. But he is convinced of his impotency before the massive barrier of time; to compromise with time is far easier than to confront it.

The social environment and the resulting self-consciousness destroys the 'strength to force the moment to its crisis'. So Prufrock returns to the world of time, the world of non-being, the world of misused possibilities where 'the afternoon, the evening, sleeps so peacefully/smoothed by long fingers', 'Time', 'The eternal Footman'[36], was there to 'hold his coat' and open the door to the place of self-fulfilment. Prufrock's impotence only made it 'snicker'.

---

35. Camus, Albert, *The Myth of Sisyphus*, p. 95.
36. It may be of incidental interest to remark that in Hindu mythology, Yama, the god of Death, employs four Footmen called Yama Doots (the agents of Yama or Death). Whenever a mortal dies, these Footmen are sent down to earth to carry his spirit to Heaven or Hell according to the earthly merits and demerits of the deceased appearing against the balance sheet of his life-account. Again, in Hindu mythology, 'Kaal' or Time is synonymous with Death or Yama.

His consciousness invokes his 'historicity'. If he could hold on to his consciousness up to and beyond the moment of crisis, he could have been as great as 'prophet'. But 'Here is no great matter'. He acknowledges his lack of courage. His life has been reduced to a mock-heroic counterfeit of the miracle of history. The mocking voice of his rejected self can be heard in the lines:

> I am Lazarus, come from the dead,
> Come back to tell you all, I shall tell you all.

But soon he decides not to take arms against a sea of troubles. Albert Camus, talking about the 'modern consciousness', says:

> Weariness comes at the end of the acts of a mechanical life, but at the same time it inaugurates the impulse of consciousness. It awakens consciousness and provokes what follows. What follows is the gradual return into the chain or is the definitive awakening.... In itself, weariness has something sickening about it.[37]

Prufrock returns to the chain of his eventless life and resumes the time-ridden existence, a life of indecisions and revisions and hesitations and questionings, a life of 'living and partly living':

Shall I part my hair behind? Do I dare to eat a peach? Weariness overtakes him:

> I grow old . . . I grow old . . .
> I shall wear the bottoms of my trousers rolled.

And he is drowned in the sea of time.

The Love Song of J. Alfred Prufrock, thus, is the most representative example of psychological time, depicting the failure of modern man in his confrontation with time. 'Time', as a temporal image, gives expression to modern man's awareness of time as that which crushes man's being at every turn.

---

37. Camus, Albert, *The Myth of Sisyphus*, p. 18.

Similarly in *Portrait of a Lady*, the 'cyclic time' of the seasons transforms itself into the psychological time of the characters. The lady has saved a 'December afternoon' for a private talk with her 'gentleman'. The dark room is faintly lighted by 'four wax candles', and the room resembles 'Juliet's tomb'. It suggests that the man-woman relationship is fraught with failure and frustration. 'December afternoon', a temporal image, indicates lack of warmth to the extent of the protagonists being cold and artificial in their dealings. In spite of much conversation and talk about music, the heart-to-heart communication is missing.

In the second movement of the *Portrait*, temporal imagery merges into flower imagery; phenomenal time makes a greater thrust into the individual consciousness. The 'cyclic', 'seasonal', and 'biological' operations have reference to the workings of the lady's consciousness:

> Now that lilacs are in bloom
> She has a bowl of lilacs in her room
> And twists one in her fingers while she talks.

The bloom of lilacs duly symbolises the cruel 'youth' which has no 'remorse' and reminds the lady of her own past. 'April Sunsets' impel the lady to recall her 'buried life, and 'Paris in the spring'. This is another example of interplay between memory and desire. There is a sense of a lost past, a vanished joy. Lilacs in Eliot's poems are always associated with the headiest onset of sexual desire. So lilacs serve to intensify the feelings of the lady. Grover Smith traces the inter-relation between temporal and psychological imagery by relating it to the theme of the poem:

> The poem has three parts, or quasi-dramatic scenes, timed by the seasons. Each, constructing a different stage in the young man's attitude, takes its dominant tone from a particular pattern of imagery. There is first a foggy December afternoon of after-the-concert tedium; then April twilight of pathos and unease; and lastly, an October night of crisis when he can no longer dissemble but must act

upon the disclosure that he and the lady have nothing in common. [38]

Precisely through his confrontation with the hidden personal values in the 'cycle', as he becomes troubled by her attention to these tokens of awakening life, the young man is forced to experience the psychological climax of the affair. As the lady has no power of attracting him, he plunges helplessly into an emotion compounded of embarrassment and arrogance. Plucked and artificially arranged, the April lilacs will quickly and quietly die, the sooner as her tense fingers crush them. The flower image, thus, becomes the end:

> Well, and what if she should die some afternoon,
> Afternoon grey and smoky, evening yellow and rose

These temporal images — smoky and grey afternoon, evening yellow and rose — are quite in keeping with thoughts of death which keep coming to the mind of the gentleman.

Similarly, in *Rhapsody on a Windy Night*, the temporal imagery has significant connotations. It is an important example of Eliot's perception of time in relation to memory and consciousness; it is perhaps the only poem which makes a direct use of memory as a technique. In the struggle between time and consciousness, as the 1917 poems show, the last twist usually belongs to time. All the images spring from the speaker's consciousness of time as a succession of moments. It is midnight when the young man is walking alone along 'the reaches of the street'. The dark night shakes his memory as insistently as a madman shakes a dead geranium and out flow his perceptions of the disgusting reality, marked by time-bound pauses: half-past two, half-past three, four in the morning. Time, here, serves to sharpen his awareness. The last line of *Rhapsody*, 'the last twist of the knife' could as well be re-written as:

---

38. Smith, Grover, *T. S. Eliot's Poetry and Plays: A Study in Sources and Meaning* (Chicago: The University of Chicago Press, 1974), p. 11.

The last twist of time.

Thus, the temporal images in these poems articulate feelings of resignation, generated by 'observation' of a world of flux, a world where there is nothing but time. So the 1917 poems have been aptly captioned as *Observations* by their author, for they are scientific observations of the phenomena of time without any mystical wonder. They are the reflection of a world caught in the 'aspect of time', and they represent certain 'modes' of perception. Eliot's poetic vision is focused here on life. But his vision is to deepen and 'acuminate' into and beyond 'horror' of historical time.

b) Time Historical

History for Eliot is not determined by political forces and economic factors alone. For him the history of man is history of the culture he has evolved for himself. In 'Little Gidding' Eliot writes:

> A people without history
> Is not redeemed from time, for history is a pattern
> Of timeless moments.
> So, while the light fails
> On a winter's afternoon, in a secluded chapel
> History is now and England.
> With the drawing of the Love and the voice of this calling.

Temporal images move from transience and flux to timelessness—a transcendence of time which can be achieved through history alone. Eliot says: 'A new unity can only grow on the old roots.'[39] Eliot, in emphasising the importance of 'the past' as a mode of realisation of the being of man on the historical plane, is not very far from the position taken by some of his contemporary thinkers and philosophers on this issue.

What Eliot postulates for the poet as a literary perpetuator of tradition is, by extension, true for man as

---

[39] Eliot, T. S., 'The Classics and the Man of Letters' in *To Criticize the Critic* (London: Faber and Faber, 1965), p. 160.

a being placed in the historical situation and amid the flux of historical time:

> . . . the historical sense, which we may call nearly indispensable to anyone who would continue to be a poet beyond his twenty-fifth year; and the historical sense involves a perception, not only of the pastness of the past, but of its presence: the historical sense compels a man to write not merely with his own generation in his bones, but with a feeling that the whole of the literature of his own country has a simultaneous existence and composes a simultaneous order.[40]

* * *

That the past experience revived in the meaning
Is not the experience of one life only
But of many generations.[41]

In their historical role, then, temporal images correlate the past and the future through the agent of Bergson's 'Memory', for past endures through memory into the present. Bergson says in *Creative Evolution*: 'Duree is the continuous progress of the past which gnaws into the future and which swells as it advances, leaving on all things its bite . . .'[42]

Like Bergson, Eliot looks upon history as the struggle and fulfilment of man's being in time. History, in other words, is 'temporal becoming'.

> Thus, what is now happening ceases to happen and becomes past as future events become present, so that past events become more past and future events less future. This process of temporal becoming . . . [43]

---

40. Eliot, T. S., 'Tradition and the Individual Talent' in *Selected Essays* (London: Faber and Faber, 1951), p. 15.
41. Eliot, T. S., 'The Dry Salvages' in *The Complete Poems and Plays* (London: Faber and Faber, 1969), p. 187.
42. Bergson, Henri, *Creative Evolution*, tr. Arthur Mitchell (New York: Henry Holt & Co.,1937), p.4.
43. Gale, Richard M., ed., *The Philosophy of Time: A Collection of Essays* (New Jersey: Humanities Press, 1968), p. 66.

This is the dynamic concept of time, which is the concept of historical time and which, however, merges into the static concept of time. For the 'memory' of the dynamic time or 'temporal becoming' (the act of changing by which in transforming himself man incessantly re-invents his own being: 'To exist is to change, to change is to mature, to mature is to create oneself endlessly.')[44] results in the static concept of history—that is a 'pattern of timeless moments'. It is Prufrock's refusal to change in relation to time that leads to his failure. So he represents a large segment of mankind existing at an unconscious level.

To Eliot, then, an individual consciousness takes up the challenge of time on behalf of the conscious mass of humanity. The key moments in the history of mankind are those which have presented the drama of human suffering through selfless sacrifice, when consciousness has refused to yield to the forces of time. Such moments become timeless because, while all else is forgotten in time, they still are sacredly preserved in the conscience of the race perpetually. Purified historical action divests the human experience of its temporality.

The awakening of the epochal or historical consciousness and its merging in the individual consciousness is the basic theme of Eliot's 1920 poems, *The Waste Land* and *Murder in the Cathedral*. Therefore, the temporal images in these works depict the relation between time and timelessness, humanity and God.

With *Gerontion*, Eliot begins a technique which he uses again in *The Waste Land*, the landmark of 1920 poems, where he combines symbolist technique with passages of prose-like commentary. The temporal images are employed to depict the decayed 'past' and historical 'vacuity'. Not only here, but also in the later poems, this commentary is primarily about time inseparable from the images which surround the consciousness. Nancy K. Gish remarks: 'In *The Waste Land*, there are no discursive sections though

---

44. Poulet, George, *Studies in Human Time*, (New York: Harper and Brothers, 1959), p. 35.

concept of time, based on sources which discuss it overtly, underlay the pattern of imagery.'[45] The theme of *The Waste Land* is a natural development from that of *Prufrock* and *Gerontion*. *Prufrock* is as much concerned with the experience of an endless hell as *Gerontion* and *The Waste land*. Yet, Prufrock's life is unstable, inexplicable; it is covered with layers of external action, as the images of 'days', 'hours', and 'minutes' suggest. He can find no words, no voice to express precisely what he desires. Although Gerontion is also uncertain, but his uncertainty is a nervous tension created by the contrast of his life with the meaning inherent in history. He is uneasily aware of this meaning, but cannot apprehend it. In this connection Nancy K. Gish states;

> Both (Prufrock and Gerontion) experience their failure through an inability to control or transcend time, whether the daily routine or the sequence of history which contained a timeless moment. The voice Prufrock desired and the vision of history Gerontion could not attain are both, to some extent, present in *The Waste Land*.[46]

So by changing from monologue to a fluid, shifting perspective, Eliot was able to retain the sense of individual futility and despair, while placing individuals in a context of all time, and to present both the misery of daily routine and the terror of emptiness as part of a larger horror. In *The Waste Land*, time — social, psychological and historical — lingers behind every major metaphor.

A significant aspect of the historical time highlighted in Eliot's poetry and plays is the cyclical time, manifested into the constant movement of seasons, months and nature. The psychic perception of cyclical time is made apparent by the temporal images employed in the section, 'The Burial of the Dead':

> April is the cruelest month, breeding
> Lilacs out of the dead land,

---

45. Gish, Nancy L., *Time in the Poetry of T. S. Eliot*, p. 46.
46, Ibid., p. 50.

As in *Prufrock*, 'April' of the 'cyclic time' — the month of spiritual regeneration, pilgrimage and revival, hope and peace in *Canterbury Tales* — appears to the fractured psyche of the Waste landers as the 'cruelest'. The paradox becomes clear with the next image of 'rain', which reminds them of their spiritual starvation:

> . . . mixing
> Memory and desire, stirring
> Dull roots with spring rain.

Here, there is an implied contrast between an 'April' that breeds lilacs out of the dead land and one that brings no new life into the dead hearts of the denizens of the Waste Land. The revival and rejuvenescence brought about in nature by the spring rain awakens the 'desire' of a life in their dead hearts, and this 'desire' brings back the 'memory' of the past 'April' which brought about fertility and regeneration. The present 'April' reminds them of past history when warm days of the spring time, of the resurrection season, brought rain, the water of life, with sunlight:

> Summer surprised us, coming over the Starnbergersee
> With a shower of rain; we stopped in the colonnade,
> And went on in sunlight, into the Hofgarten

Once again past and present are juxtaposed; the present 'April' when compared with 'April in the past becomes the 'cruelest', mixing memory and desire. 'Memory' is past-directed, 'desire' is future-directed. What hangs in-between is the vacuum brought about by 'fear' to live in reality. While the life in cyclic time sharpens the desire of the waste landers and intensifies the awareness of their inability to rouse themselves from death-in-life, social and psychic time declares its instantaneous death. They prefer death:

> Winter kept us warm, covering
> Earth in forgetful snow

Cleanth Brooks remarks:

> The first section of 'The Burial of the Dead' develops the theme of the attractiveness of death, or of the difficulty in rousing oneself from death in life in which the people of the waste land live. . . . Men dislike to be roused from their death-in-life.[47]

The death of 'winter' and the life of 'spring' usurp each other: 'I read, much of the night, and go south in the winter'. This image reminds us of social time in *Prufrock*, 'measuring life with coffee spoons'.

The adjective 'cruelest' for the temporal image 'April' in the first part finds a concrete expression in the image of 'parching sun' in the second part:

> . . . you know only
> A heap of broken images, where the sun beats

This leads once again to memory mixed with desires:

> And I will show you something different from either
> Your shadow at morning striding behind you
> Or your shadow at evening rising to meet you;

'Evening' here becomes a temporal image of past memory, or backward-looking gaze; it is also an image of desire, 'rising to meet you', a forward-looking gaze. The images of 'shadow' and 'sun' also refer back to Bildad's words to Job:

> We are but of yesterday, and know nothing, because our days upon earth are a shadow. . . . So are the paths of all that forget God. . . . He is green before the sun.[48]

---

47. Brooks, Cleanth, 'The Waste Land: Critique of the Myth' in C. B. Cox and Arnold P. Hinchliffe, eds., *T.S. Eliot: The Waste Land* (London: Macmillan, 1968), p. 130.
48. Job, 8: 9, 13, 16.

Through the interaction of the historical and cyclical images, Eliot emphasises the fact that the same thing is seen in all the time. This juxtaposition of all time, of past and present, denying real change or development and thus precluding renewal, predominates and intensifies the sense of Hell:

> Unreal City,
> Under the brown fog of a winter dawn,
> A crowd flowed over London Bridge,
>
> * * * *
>
> With a dead sound on the final stroke of nine.

The ninth hour of the present winter-dawn brings back the memory of the historical event—Christ's crucifixion. As a temporal image then, 'the fog of winter Dawn', qualifies the suffocating hellish atmosphere of 'unreal City'—London—where the spiritual values suggested by the ninth hour are lost. This temporal image is also related to the theme of sterility: there is perpetual winter in Eliot's wasteland. The attempt to bury the memory of 'spring' is suggested—to quote F. R. Leavis and F. O. Matthiessen—by the last temporal images in 'The Burial of the Dead':

> That corpse you planted last year in your garden,
> Has it begun to sprout? Will it bloom this year?

The passage of one year that the crops will take to sprout suggests, as a temporal image, the periodical hopes and expectations of the waste landers. But the next image refers back to the 'winter' image of the opening lines: 'Or has the sudden frost disturbed its bed?' The death of any hope of regeneration and the 'fear' are suggested by this image of 'winter'.

The impotent and empty figures in *The Waste Land* are as oppressed by time as Prufrock or Gerontion, yet the poem as a whole portrays no temporal moment. Both the daily cycle that oppressed *Prufrock* and structured *Preludes* and *Rhapsody on a Windy Night* and the seasonal cycle which structured *Portrait of a Lady*, appear but as incidental pieces rather than overall form. The poem, as shown earlier, opens not with April's cruelty, but with memory of 'winter', and with Marie's summer experience. It is not clearly spring rain in 'What the Thunder Said'. The implied rain is more like a summer storm than a spring shower. The poem seems to say, 'We retain the past without its opposite ideal, or even its pageantry.'[49]

The suffering of Philomel, leading to the spiritual exaltation of the bird's song, is to the waste landers a 'withered stump of time'. As in *Gerontion*, here also, history is incomprehensible; relics of the past are devoid of meaning and are used merely for decorating the drawing rooms. What creates the mood of horror is precisely the changelessness of this world. The futility of daily routine and its opposition to intense inner feelings are suggested by the next temporal images:

> 'What shall I do now? What shall I do?
> I shall rush out as I am, and walk the street
> With my hair down, so. What shall we do tomorrow?
> What shall we ever do?'
> The hot water at ten.
> And if it rains, a closed car at four.

As if the hot water at ten and a car at four could hold back chaotic emotion by concentrating on the outer crust of existence. The Pub-keeper's cry—'Hurry up please it's time'—is the central temporal image in the poem suggesting the time-ridden consciousness of modern man and his inability to transcend it. The image also reminds us of the 'still point' in the moving wheel of time in *The Gita* where Krishna tells Arjuna (11.3) that the warrior's time is up now. It is an ironical warning to turn from the degenerated way of life before reaching the whirlpool of death. The line 'Hurry up Please it's time' finds an ironical

---
49. Gish, Nancy K., *Time in the Poetry of T. S. Eliot*, p. 56.

parallel in the images of social time in 'The Fire Sermon', pervading the typist girl episode: 'At the violent hour . . . the human engine waits/Like a taxi throbbing waiting.' The time is now propitious as he guesses.

The moving wheel of time is also suggested in the image of ring in 'The Burial of the Dead'; 'I see crowds of people, walking round in a ring'. 'The Burial of the Dead' identifies the cycles of 'summer, winter, spring and autumn' with the great turning wheel of creation and corruption, growth and ruin. The temporal image in 'The Fire Sermon' makes the idea explicit:

> But at my back from time to time I hear
> The sound of horns and motors, which shall bring
> Sweeney to Mrs. Porter in the spring.

Fertility suggested by 'spring' — the cyclical time — is juxtaposed to unreal passion; the chastity and the myth of Diana in Marvell are juxtaposed to commercialisation of sex in *The Waste Land*. The historical (reference to Diana), spiritual (reminiscent of the wheel in *The Gita*) and cyclical time combine in these temporal images of 'ring' and 'spring'.

Bound to the wheel of time, Phlebas' drowning in 'Death by Water' re-enacts the rise and fall of temporal life in the 'flower garden' (symbolising the world of senses — lines 35–42) and the rise and decline through which,

> headed for death, he has passed his life:
> As he rose and fell
> He passed the stages of his age and youth
> Entering the whirlpool.
> Gentile or Jew
> O you who turn the wheel and look to windward,
> Consider Phlebas, who was once handsome and tall as you.

The rise and fall, youth and age, are temporal images suggesting the great turning wheel of time culminating in death and making life of temporal pleasures a matter of past as suggested by the use of 'once'. God is the 'still point', men in flux are wheel. So Tiresias and the forms populating his memory emphasise the dualism of eternity and time, duration and flux. This dualism intensifies the distortion of time in the poem. In the early poems time provides a deceptive facade of order, and the irony is that there is no order, only meaningless repetition of 'There will be time'. The significance of time in *The Waste Land* is that the cyclical images overlapping each other culminate or destroy any pretence of order. Time is coexistent and, being eternally present, it is unredeemable. So the modern typist and the girl in the canoe (Isolde) parallel Elizabeth and Leicester; the rape of Philomel acts as a motif by the repetition of 'jug jug'; Stetson is both ancient and modern; Tiresias watches the typist; the Hanged Man merges with the hanged God of Frazer and Christ and so on. All these references become images of historical time and consciousness by juxtaposing all times and similar events occurring in the context of different centuries. The horror is, thus, a combination of daily misery in personal life, similar to that in earlier poems, with a changelessness precluding salvation and renewal. Perhaps more than any other poem, *The Waste Land* embodies Eliot's remarks that 'The one thing time is ever sure to bring is the loss. Gain or compensation is always conceivable but never certain.'

Similarly, Eliot's play *Murder in the Cathedral* exists as a moment in time, a moment of choice which brings in something outside Time. 'The point of the intersection of Time with the Timeless ' is the point of Incarnation, and Thomas, after surmounting the temptation of the senses, of power, of private revenge and 'the last temptation' of pride makes his decision, on behalf of all. He is the one who sees, who has the responsibility of making the choice. This choice is presented through the imagery of time and nature in wider aspects.

The temporal image of wheel is the chief symbol in *Murder in the Cathedral*. It emphasises the idea of true martyrdom, of a 'moment out of time'. While the Chorus is the 'wheel' of active human life in the world, Becket is the 'still' centre for them; he is not to bear the yoke of time with them, but to break it. Timelessness can be attained only when Becket perfects his will so as to make it conform completely with the will of God. He has to purify himself of all selfish motives (temporal and spiritual) for martyrdom.

When he first supposes that he has the right to precipitate his sufferings he is aware that

> The wheel may turn and still
> Be forever still (1.216–217)

By a deeper intuition, he knows that the still wheel, as God beholds it, incorporates all the patterns of interlocking good and evil which men can only view as 'flux'. Confident that his cause is right, Becket proposes to act so as to vindicate the church by bringing good from the evil will of his foes.

But what he has forgotten is that he himself is easily able to object against a lesser temptation, that only the fool 'May think/ he can turn the wheel on which he turns'. For on the turning wheel of time, good as often produces evil as evil produces good; only with God are these resolved, without losing their peculiar character, into the perfection that man aspires to. In supplanting God's will, in electing to be the centre of the wheel without God, Becket would be inviting, on his own responsibility, whatever evils might ensue from his choice; he would be committing the Knights' sins of pride and murder.

Aghast, he exclaims: 'Can I neither act nor suffer/ without perdition?' While the Chorus, the Tempters, and the Priests counsel him to avert action, he comes to his awakening. The only way in which he can reach the stillness of the turning wheel is to yield to the mover, the point that is not himself. Those who act, all but God, and those who suffer are inescapably on the wheel, those who consent with the will of God are as God. Confessing that he has been about to 'do the right deed for the wrong reason,' to give a sinful turn to the wheel, he explains that this temptation sprang from his will for good. Only by extinction of self will can he avoid the mortal sin of pride at his moment of sacrifice. Accordingly, he is content that he 'shall no longer act or suffer, to the sword's end', for God, not he, is the only agent through whom good can proceed from evil, and what God will bring is neither pain nor suffering to one who accedes to it as to a vocation. We find an echo of Shakespearean philosophy in *King Lear*: 'As flies to wanton boys, are we to th' gods; they kill us for their sport'(Act 4, scene 1). The martyr, freeing himself from the wheel, can assist the ultimate redemption of time. 'He has made a decision,, he says later, 'to which my whole being gives entire consent', a decision taken 'out of Time'.t

The key temporal image of wheel is woven around the Chorus as deftly as around the protagonist Becket. They occupy a circumference, so to speak, of which Becket is the centre, for they rely on him as the source of the movement they participate in. When he is the point, they are the wheel, as he is the wheel, when God is the point. It is their dramatic function to comment upon the events they witness. They fit the role of sufferers by being ordinary hard working women with no pretence to power. They are like the crowds of people in *The Waste Land*, passively moved by what a Buddhist would call *Samsara* — the wheel of life.

Through most of the drama, the polarity of action and suffering finds correspondence in the temporal imagery of nature appertaining to the Chorus — the cycles of day and night, summer and winter, spring and autumn; these identify the Chorus with the great turning wheel of creation and corruption, growth and ruin. In the very first speech of the Chorus, the imagery from the seasons, repeated towards the end, insists upon the endless cycle of time and the returning years in which we live lives that are meaningless without relation to some eternal purpose outside time:

> Since golden October declined into somber November
> And the apples were gathered and stored, and the land
> Became brown sharp points
> Of death in a waste of water and mud,
> The New Year waits, destiny waits for the coming. (1. 10–14)

Much of Eliot's philosophy of Time underlies this speech. In *Sweeney Agonistes* (Second Fragment), *The Rock*, *The Family Reunion* and many other poems and dramas, Eliot reflects on the endless, cyclical return of year after year, season after season, from which there seems no escape:

> Birth, and copulation, and death . . .
> That's all, that's all, that's all, that's all,
> Birth and copulation and death .
> Morning Evening Noontime Night.
>
> *(Sweeney Agonistes)*

* * * *

> O perpetual recurrence of determined seasons,
> O world of spring and autumn, birth and dying!
>
> *(The Rock)*

There is no way (he seems at first to suggest) of breaking out of these meaningless cycles of time, but his answer to this is given first in *The Rock* (opening chorus of part II); then came, at a predetermined moment, a moment

> in time and of time:
> A moment in time but time was made through that moment.
> For without the meaning there is no time,
> And the moment of time gave the meaning.

Then in *Murder in the Cathedral*, Becket's submission to God transforms the temporal flow of the Chorus:

> Now I fear disturbance of the quiet seasons . . .
> Into
> We praise thee, O God, for Thy glory displayed in all the creatures of the earth   (II. 618)

* * * *

> Even in us the voices of seasons,
> The snuffle of winter, the song of spring,
> The drone of summer, the voices of beasts and of birds, praise Thee.
> Who hast given such blessing to Canterbury. (II. 628–630)

Becket's act makes the Chorus one with time and hence outside time. They achieve timelessness through the historical act of martyrdom. Becket's argument that 'It is not in time that my death shall be known' means that when an act is looked at in time, it can be assessed relatively to its motives and consequences, that is, it is a human action that partakes of both good and evil, as the world judges. To murder a man, not to say an Archbishop, is judged evil by the world, and therefore, it would seem wrong for Becket to make such a murder possible by opening the doors. But if martyrdom is 'made by the design of God', it is an act made beyond time, and bears an eternal witness. The Martyr, thus, achieves historical timelessness.

c) Time Spiritual

With *Ash-Wednesday* and *Ariel Poems*, Eliot's concept of time becomes more philosophical. He is less concerned with describing sordid reality and more prone to seeking some understanding of the reality. A timeless vision is asserted, while a temporal sorrow is felt. *The Journey of the Magi* and *A Song for Simeon* use specific historical images to describe human dilemma, discovering that one is between birth and death and that rebirth requires death of this life. By juxtaposing present and future, Eliot makes the incarnation a focal point to which all other things relate and Christ's birth and death become the model for all rebirth. In *Ash-Wednesday*, the theme of time finds one resolution; it presents the mystic way of escaping the bond of time. By *Ash-Wednesday*, Eliot has attained the certitude of 'time is always time' and prays 'redeem the time'. But in order to do so, one must traverse the 'time of tension between dying and birth', which troubles Simeon as well as the Magi who accept the death of temporal life in order to apprehend eternity. Time and eternity, opposed in *Ash-Wednesday* and *the Ariel Poems*, are reconciled in *Four Quartets*, where eternity is a quality or value experienced within time. This eternal moment, in and out of time, human yet transfigured, is woven into *Four Quartets*.

More than the other three *Quartets*, 'Burnt Norton' focuses on the transcendental moment, the fleeting ecstasy out of time defined as 'the still point of the turning world'. The epigraph from Heraclitus suggests that Eliot's concept of time is perhaps derived from Heraclitus, but in fact, Eliot's philosophy is rather a repudiation of the Heraclitean philosophy with its insistence upon the ultimate character of time as flux (or pure duree). There are elements from Heraclitus' Philosophy in Eliot, especially in *Four Quartets*, but these do not relate to Eliot's own positive theory of time. They are, rather, the notion of the logos in the flux; the contrast of wisdom and learning: the ultimate reality of fire; the generative-destructive character of the four elements: earth, water, air and fire. Eliot transforms these ideas into his own Christian philosophy which is essentially an *Immanence* doctrine, according to which the Eternal or Timeless is regarded as the creative source of flux or temporal. This is not to say that Eliot denies the reality of the flux, in some Parmenidean fashion. He is no dualist pitting the reality of the Eternal against the illusion of the flux. Instead, the flux, with all its reality, is sustained by the more ultimate reality of the Eternal. The flux is not an illusion, but it is an illusion to regard it as the only reality. Eliot's theory of time is neo-platonic, not Heraclitean. This notion of the Eternal or ultimate reality being immanent in the flux as the Logos which any one can discern, but which only few do discern, clarifies most of 'Burnt Norton'. We may consider the following lines:

> Footfalls echo in the memory
> Down the passage which we did not take
> Towards the door we never opened Into the rose-garden.
> My words echo
> Thus, in your mind.

The rose-garden is the key idea in the passage. Eliot has used this image in much of his poetry and plays and there is cogent conflicting opinion about its meaning. Here also it seems to function in a double sense, as an actual place—a rose-garden, and also as a symbol of those temporal experiences which reveal most poignantly the immanent character of the ultimately real. Like the Christian 'Kairos', the rose-garden symbolises those moments that show the meeting of the eternal and the temporal. The second movement of 'Burnt Norton' sharpens the immanence conception of time: that the Eternal or Timeless is the ultimate dimension of the flux and gives it whatever reality and meaning it has. So it is in the *Four Quartets* that the immanence theory of time is worked out fully in poetic terms as Grover Smith puts it:

> What Eliot did in the *Quartets* was to invoke the logos of Heraclitus as if it were this mover, in his own imagery, the center, round which the wheel of flux revolves for ever but which 'gathers' the movement into stillness . . . we each think that time passes, but in the logos it is eternal. We each think that the past endures in our memory, but in the logos it endures in immediate actuality.[50]

---

50. *Smith, Grover, T. S. Eliot's Poetry and Plays: A Study in Sources and Meaning*, p. 56.

The garden in 'Burnt Norton' provides a symbolic context for an apprehension of the ideal order. Eliot feels 'To be conscious is not to be in time'. Escape from time into consciousness is achieved in the transcendental ecstasy symbolised by 'The moment in the rose garden', so that all other time, unless it is a means to this end, is meaningless.

Eliot dramatically reiterates this new-platonic philosophy of time as the ultimate amalgam of temporal and spiritual, flux and logos in *The Family Reunion*. In this play, all major characters enact and symbolically represent different aspects of time. Amy lives in a pattern of timed moments, by the clock. At the start of the play, she grumbles that, now she is old, the clocks cannot be trusted; she fears that time will stop. As if in support of the characterisation, the physician, Warburton, is made to say of her, at the beginning of Part II:

> The whole machine is weak
> And running down. Her heart is very feeble   (110-111)

She laments her delicate health which keeps her housebound; it is autumn and summer seems a long way off. When young, she had no fears that life at Wishwood might come to an end; Time would flow perpetually on through the seasons, year after year, and nothing would change. Now she feels no assurance, so the normal self, patrician, stoical, practical, semi pagan, authoritarian, quivers for a moment with a lyrical feeling that the procession of the seasons, and the alternation of warm day and calm night may cease suddenly in darkness. Her last words as she dies in the final scene are:

> Agatha! Mary! Come!
> The clock has stopped in the dark!   (II, III. 258-260)

To Amy, time is any succession and a measure of succession; the past and the future do not exist even as determining forces. Thus, she is able to see life as order, controllable by the will. In her beginning is her end. Her philosophy of perpetuating the changeless cycle of life in her world of Wishwood— Wishwood for Wishwood's sake—is contrasted with the philosophy of detachment from the love of created things, which carries one beyond time into union with the eternal will of God; it is towards this detachment that Harry is being propelled, during the course of the play, by his sense of guilt, newly awakened. For his wheel of life, so to speak, is not the cold, precise pivot-wheel of the cosmic clock, but an organic 'burning wheel' of desire and memory. Like Lear, he is on a 'Wheel of Fire'.

Anne Ward has aptly pointed out that Harry's conception of time may well have come to Eliot from T. E. Hulme's modified concept of Bergsonian *duree*.[51] The view common to Hulme and Harry is a pessimistic one on the surface, of time in the natural order, not as succession or as an index of creative evolution but as destructive duration which bombards orders, preserving it only as the rubble of memory, still flaming with the suffering of the past. Just as Amy's perspective bears comparison with that of the Knights in *Murder in the Cathedral*, Harry's perspective resembles that of the Women of Canterbury when aroused to consciousness by Becket. In the same manner as they, Harry knows the suffering imposed by action. What distinguishes the two is Harry's more shrewd sense of the co-eternity of action and suffering, the sense awakened through the various images in 'Burnt Norton': He confirms Agatha's wise preliminary warning to the family:

> The man who returns will have to meet
> The boy who left. (I. 128–129)

He declares:

> I am the old house

---

51. Ward, Anne, 'Speculations of Eliot's Time-World: An Analysis of *The Family Reunion* in Relation to Hulme and Bergson,' *American Literature*, XXI (March, 1949), 26, FF.

> With the noxious smell and the sorrow before morning,
> In which all past is present, all degradation
> Is unredeemable. As for what happens
> Of the past you can only see what is past,
> Not what is always present. That is
> What matters.   (I. i.311–314)

Harry is a changed man, his innocence lost. His past will confront him at every corner on his return, to remind him of what he can never be again. And this will be no jolly home-coming. Agatha seems to show an intuitive knowledge of what is happening to Harry—that his real past (his childhood's innocence) is what his future must be built upon.

> When the loop in time comes— and it Does not come for everybody, The hidden is revealed, and the Specters show themselves.   (1. i. 134–135)

This echo from Henry James suggests that time is like an endless thread that may coil back and make a loop, and so two points of contact are formed that bring past and present together.

Through time, however, time is conquered. Harry gains the means of liberation from his nightmarish past by acquiring, in Wishwood, insight into a still earlier past which he had never comprehended. His father, a presence out of his first world, becomes intelligible to him, dignified, invisible, and his own crime, which he had been concerned to expiate in isolation, turns out to be simply the present cross-section of a family crime projected through generations. As he has willed to kill his wife, so his father, it turns out, had once willed to kill his.

> The trilling wire in the blood
> Sings below inveterate scars
> And reconciles forgotten wars

And Harry, the purpose of his visit to the great house with its garden now accomplished, takes his departure. It is easy to see the application to Harry's plight of the enigmatic epigraphs from Heraclitus which Eliot affixed to 'Burnt Norton': 'Though the law of things is universal in scope, most men act as though they had insight of their own'; and 'The way up and the way down are one and the same'. *The Family Reunion* Chorus proclaims:

> Whether in Argos or England
> There are certain inflexible laws
> Unalterable, in the nature of music   (11.i. 429–431)

Harry has assumed himself to be at the centre of a totally sick world which has arranged itself around his unique malaise. When Agatha awakens him to acceptance of his destiny, Harry remarks:

> I have thought of you as the completely strong,
> The liberated from the human wheel
> So I looked to you for strength. Now I think it is
> A common pursuit of liberation. (II. 1i. 60–63)

From her, Harry receives the commission, so to speak, to pursue his liberation from the wheel, not as his mother would have him do by denying his past and starting again as if nothing had happened, but by acknowledging with Agatha what he already believes, that past is irrevocable, 'the future can only be built/upon the real past'. To brood pessimistically on duration is tantamount to lunacy; to believe that duration can somehow be neutralised, as the turning wheel in *Murder in the Cathedral* can be stilled in the unmoved centre, marks the beginning of sanity. Harry's moment of deliverance from the temporal wheel is hinted at when he speaks of his transcendence:

> I feel quite happy, as if happiness
> Did not consist in getting what one wanted
> Or in getting rid of what can's be got rid of
> But in a different vision   (II. Ii. 145–148)

So purgation has been kept a mystery, though a future certainty, as the temporal images suggest that the past time is redeemable in so far as present knowledge redeems its memory. *The Waste Land* and *Ash Wednesday* shed some light on this notion. But they do not imply that because the past held the potentiality of this new meaning, now actualised, the redemption of the memory redeems the actual past, though ultimately 'out of time' and in the domain of eternity, where all things are perfected in God. Thus, Eliot offers a final solution to the terrible discrepancy between 'the idea and the reality'. In the last two *Quartets*, the concept is set forth with even greater clarity. 'The Dry Salvages' puts it this way:

> We had the experience but missed the meaning,
> And approach to the meaning restores the experience
> In a different form . . .

The redemption of wasted time is familiar from Shakespeare's *Henry IV, Part I*. But Shakespeare's Henry is characterised as deliberately redeeming time while ostensibly wasting it; Eliot's Harry redeems it, not only in reputation but in fact, after he has done harm. His new direction is to be in compliance with the past, not in resistance to it.

Thus temporal images in *The Family Reunion* work out a way for modern man from the agony of despair to the reality of belief. From the subjective realm of temporal time in *Prufrock*, Eliot moves to the spiritual time in *The Waste Land, Murder in the Cathedral* and more so in *The Family Reunion*. The latter poems and plays also offer an approach to historical existence and life in liberty, recognising that in transcendence alone lies self-realisation and a leap towards freedom.

Let us now concentrate upon the use of spatial images in the works of Eliot in the next chapter.

4

Spatial Images

The spatial images in Eliot's poetry and plays function as a persistent under-song to the macro and micro worlds of physical and metaphysical (spiritual) reality. They symbolise either a way to spiritual awakening or the attainment of the world of spiritual peace. So symbols like the two worlds (viz., the public world of material fact and the private world of a better spiritual life) — a journey through dry land, water or life and a door opening out into a garden or a better world form a linked set of spatial images in Eliot's works.

The spatial images in *The Love Song of J. Alfred Prufrock* present a sense of imprisonment in an empty, ugly and alien society, and the impossibility of escape from it. According to Elizabeth Drew:

> But it is apparent at once that the outward scene never exists for its own sake, that world which is being created from these sensory impressions and concrete objects is a world of emotional realities. The outward scene exists as a set of symbols, 'a thousand sordid images', through which the imagination senses the quality of a civilization, not of an environment.[52]

The social environment in which Prufrock is 'drowned' is 'brought home to us through (spatial) images

---
52. Drew, Elizabeth, *T. S. Eliot: The Design of His Poetry*, p. 26.

of the tortuous streets and the fog-cat . . .'[53] Indeed, after the urbane wit of the first lines, the 'certain half-deserted streets' impose their restless sordid impressions:

> Let us go, through certain half-deserted streets,
> The muttering retreats
> Of restless nights in one-night cheap hotels
> And sawdust restaurants with oyster-shells:
> Streets that follow like a tedious argument
> Of insidious intent
> To lead you to an overwhelming question

In the above lines, a desire to escape is suggested. The setting is upsetting. It is a landscape of nightmare, of half-deserted streets and muttering retreats. One wishes to take to the streets to get somewhere away from those streets of menace. The logic of streets is the logic of consciousness being drawn towards the nightmare, towards (as the epigraph so evidently warns) hell. The world of *Prufrock* is, therefore, inescapably ironic.

Prufrock's attention shifts from what it is to what it means to him; from perceptual metaphor to conceptual metaphor. After thinking of the women to be visited, he reverts to a vision of the 'streets':

> The yellow fog that rubs its back upon the window-panes,
> The yellow smoke that rubs its muzzle on the window-panes,
> Licked its tongue into the corners of the evening,
> Lingered upon the pools that stand in drains,
> Let fall upon its back the soot that falls from chimneys,
> Slipped by the terrace, made a sudden leap,
> And seeing that it was a soft October night,
> Curled once about the house, and fell asleep.

'Fog', 'smoke', 'window-panes', 'pools', 'drains', 'soot', 'chimneys', 'terrace', etc., are all spatial images. The smoke and fog are domesticated. The nightmarish and the seductive become confused. The cat is familiar, yet vaguely

---
53. Ibid., p. 28.

terrifying. The sordid images of the streets are eventually neutralised. According to Piers Gray:

> As the fog closes in on the soft October evening, the world is unfocussed: space, the distance through which Prufrock would travel, ironically extends into a profound obscurity and the self turns in upon itself and contemplates the extent of time available to make a choice. The more remote the world becomes, the world through which Prufrock would travel, the more intense becomes his self-consciousness.[54]

By concentrating on the twilight atmosphere of the 'streets' seen through 'smoke' and 'fog', Prufrock appears to have a twilight-zone in his mind which has blurred his articulation. As Elizabeth Drew puts it, the evening which is spread out against the sky like a patient etherized upon a table, is no placid, peaceful city sunset. The pervading atmosphere fills the imagination with thoughts of disease and helplessness. There is the smell of ether which is not the breath of the spirit, but the deadener of consciousness and volition. The first two lines of the poem present a contrast between the wide stretches of the sky and the vigour and vitality of the man reduced to the living death of anaesthesia. Prufrock's consciousness has been arrested in a moment. Like an etherized patient, he is living and yet not living. Elizabeth Drew goes on to say:

> The burnt-out ends of smoky days' are not the city dusk but the twilight of an epoch; 'the yellow fog that rubs its back upon the window panes', the dinginess, the stale smells, are the creeping, choking atmosphere of a spiritual miasma; the 'crowd of twisted things', the 'broken spring in the factory yard,/Rust that clings to the form that the strength has left' are emblems of moral, not material disintegration; the 'one-night cheap hotels' are not a reminder of the transient life of a great city, but of the homelessness of the human soul.[55]

---

54. Gray, Piers, *T. S. Eliot's Intellectual and Poetic Development, 1909–1922*, p. 61.
55. Drew, Elizabeth, *T. S. Eliot: The Design of His Poetry*, p. 26.

The hesitation and the lingering attitude are maintained throughout by the recurrent 'street' and 'smoke' images:

> And indeed there will be time
> For the yellow smoke that slides along the street
> Rubbing its back upon the window-panes
>
> * * * *
>
> Shall I say, I have gone at dusk through narrow streets
> And watched the smoke that rises from the pipes

But Prufrock's (of his split-self and will) approach to action generates its own automatic reversal and flight, conveyed through the grotesque spatial image central to the poem, which embodies Prufrock's recognition of what he is essentially:

> I should have been a pair of ragged claws
> Scuttling across the floors of silent seas.

He becomes a subhuman crustacean, doubly dehumanised by the synecdoche of claws even beyond identity as crab or lobster. As a cold solitary being, he moves in an armoured solitude on the sea floor. On one level, the claws suggest the longing for uncomplicated animal existence, which can clutch their prey and make off with it, without any preface of 'Do I dare?' or 'Shall I say?' But Elizabeth Schneider objects to such an interpretation, concentrating on the 'sea' image. She thinks that the image does not represent the desire for instinctual or predatory animal life; rather it is poetic equivalent for the commonplace metaphor of retreating into or being drawn out of one shell. Nevertheless, Prufrock's wish here is only to regress to a safe haven of sea where his inner universe is no longer disturbed by any tormenting human problem. The image 'silent sea' is in direct opposition to:

> In the room the women come and go
> Talking of Michelangelo.

The couplet gives an impression of automata, of agitated movement within a confined space, that is, 'in the room' which is ironically juxtaposed to the connotations of a genius like Michelangelo expressing himself in the still strength of marble. Thus, the 'room' becomes a corresponding spatial image. A.D. Moody substantiates that Eliot 'harmonises the very streets with the drawing room'.[56] By implication, then, both the streets and the room are 'tedious', hence antithetical to the 'sea' image. The seas are 'silent'. The women in the room talk. The sea is infinite. The room is confined (finite). The sea as a primordial symbol of both creation and destruction identifies Prufrock's psychological plight, revealed through the conflict raging in his mind. At the end of the poem, Prufrock hears the mermaids singing and has a vision of them:

> . . . riding seaward on the waves
> Combing the white hair of the waves blown back
> When the wind blows the water white and black.

Prufrock experiences love at a distance only, with its (love) back turned, for the mermaids, as he observes ruefully, are 'riding seaward'. Below in the chambers of the silent sea, he may still dream of 'sea-girls' wreathing him, but they are only dreams. He cannot stand the reality of a human relationship.

> We have lingered in the chambers of the sea
> By sea-girls wreathed with seaweed red and brown
> Till human voices wake us, and we drown.

The spatial image of undersea water here becomes a symbol of escape as well as realisation of reality resulting from the attempt to escape.

The spatial image of 'stairs' is another symbol of consciousness or awareness. This image recurs prominently in four poems, in the *Prufrock* group of poems, with similar

---
56. Moody A. D., *Thomas Stearns Eliot: Poet* (Cambridge: Cambridge University Press, 1979), p. 35.

associations and connotations in *Prufrock Portrait of a Lady, Rhapsody on a Windy Night* and *La Figlia Che Piange*. In every case, the 'stairs' are a literal reference, an image relating to space. In addition to the stairs, there is invariably a person present in a position in an activity relating to the stair. Having mounted the stairs, Prufrock contemplates a possible crisis of decision:

> And indeed there will be time
>
> To wonder, 'Do I dare?' and, 'Do I dare?'
> Time to turn back and descend the stair,
> With a bald spot in the middle of my hair

He is helpless and undecided. He has no courage to act. He is content with a bare reference to the room where women come and go talking of Michelangelo. He only resorts to lame excuses and malingers to avoid the unpleasant task of expressing his love. In *La Figlia Che Piange*, the lover leaves the girl standing at the stairs, grieving and cogitating. The protagonist in *Portrait of a Lady* mounts the 'stairs', turns the 'handle of the door' and feels as if he has mounted on his hands and knees, thus emphasising a human being dehumanised as also a sense of awareness rather than an actual posture. In the last passage of *Rhapsody*, the protagonist finally returns home. At the end of his wanderings, he mounts the stairs, sees the number on his door. The little indoor lamp lights the way past many floors of memory, and he ultimately reaches an empty bed to the trivialities and anguish of ordinary existence. So, in every case the image of stairs becomes a posture of awareness, and as such, it is a spatial as well as a psychological image.

Portrait of a Lady has three parts, or quasi-dramatic scenes, timed by seasons and spatial images. Each, constructing a different stage in the young man's attitude, takes its dominant tone from a particular pattern of imagery. There is first a foggy December afternoon of after-the-concert tedium: 'Among the smoke and fog of a December afternoon' and '. . . the darkened room,/ Four rings of light upon the ceiling overhead,/ An atmosphere of Juliet's tomb'. All the spatial images—'fog', 'smoke', darkened room', 'tomb'—are symbolic of boredom leading to death-in-life state of the lady. The image also suggests her emotional starvation. The first part ends with another spatial image indicating search for false joys: 'Let us take the air, in a tobacco trance.' The attempts at forgetting boredom end in failure. In the second part the image of 'the room with a bowl of lilacs' indicates the frivolous and deceptive nature of the lady's sentiments as do 'the smell of hyacinths across the garden' about the young man's evasive nature. Throughout, he is trying to elude emotional capture. Yet he is detained, if not by generosity or pity, then by his own inertia. In the third situation, the spatial image of 'stairs' (already mentioned) exposes the triviality of the whole situation as the self-possession of the young man flickers while mounting the stairs and then looking at his reflection in the glass to see if the smile is there on his face or not. They realise, 'we are really in the dark'. The image suggests his groping for a way to get out of confusion. However, unable to end the confusion, he seeks forgetfulness, like the waste landers: 'Let us take the air, in a tobacco trance'. But the haunting thoughts continue, 'what if she should die ./ With the smoke coming down about the housetops.' The spatial images, thus, melt with psychic process of the protagonists.

In *Rhapsody on a Windy Night*, the speaker, experiencing a 'vision of the street', soliloquises in response to spatial and visual images. His is the consciousness, corresponding to that of the woman in the *Preludes*, which marshals the flickering images into a pattern of subjective 'duree'.

In the poem there is also, it is true, a clock-time structure, which may be called a 'spatial' structure also divided by the hours announced at the beginning of the strophes—'Twelve o'clock', 'Half-past one', and the rest. This structure is spatial more particularly because the times are synchronised with the speaker's pauses at street lamps. But as each lamp mutters an 'incantation' to direct his gaze towards new spatial images, these pass into his memory and while with memories already there to make up subjective time where space is non-existent. The rhapsody of consciousness moves like a musical composition by introducing, abandoning and returning to set images scattered in time and space:

> Twelve o' clock
> Along the reaches of the street
> Held in a lunar synthesis,
> Whispering lunar incantations
> Dissolve the floors of memories.
>
> ....
>
> And the spaces of the dark
> Midnight shakes the memory
>
> ....
>
> Half-past one
> The street-lamp sputtered,
> . . . Regard that woman
> Who hesitates towards you in
> The light of the door.
>
> ....

All the spatial images emphasise the recurrent motifs of irrationality and decay or inanimation. Depressing images besiege the speaker's consciousness, for he cannot evade them: what is more dismaying, they constitute his soul. It is not surprising, therefore, that the *Rhapsody* ends bleakly. The withdrawal of the speaker into his solitary room, as the last lamp shows him the way, furnishes no escape from a world within. So here the spatial images relate consciousness to externality.

The spatial images in *The Waste Land* point out the way not of escape (as in *Prufrock*) but of salvation within the world. Elizabeth Schneider believes that the end of *The Waste Land* does suggest possible hope:

> In contrast to *Prufrock*, the answer at the end, after the Thunder has spoken, is 'perhaps'. There are uncertainties in the conclusion, uncertainties of chronology, with the order of events and tenses of verbs shifting back and forth bewilderingly. The life-giving rain appears to have come, yet at the end the land is still arid, London Bridge still 'falling down', and the message of the Thunder— *give, sympathise, control*—still I think hortatory rather than achieved. Nevertheless the end does clearly suggest possible hope.[57]

Emphasising the central spatial images in *The Waste Land*, Elizabeth Schneider further points out:

> Eliot's picture of the world is both unified and universalized by the recurring imagery of drought, of city superimposed upon city, river upon river . . . imagery that nearly all reflect the emphasis of Jessie Weston's study of the Grail myth.[58]

In *The Waste Land*, the universalising spatial images fall under the categories of earth, air, fire, water and ether. Of these elements, three are alluded to directly in the titles as well as in the imagery of the main division. 'The Burial of the Dead', with its earth covered in 'forgetful snow' and the embedded roots of the opening, 'handful of dust' and its 'corpse planted in the garden'; 'The Fire Sermon', with its sequence of the fires of lust and its double allusion to the fire sermon of the Buddha and St. Augustine's confession of youthful lust in Carthage, 'Burning, burning'; and 'Death by Water' with its drowned sailor, refer to the spatial images of earth, fire and water.

---

57. Schneider, Elizabeth, *T. S. Eliot: The Pattern in the Carpet* (Berkeley and Los Angeles, California: University of California Press, 1975), p. 60.
58. Ibid.

However, the second image 'air', is absent from the title of Part II, 'A Game of Chess', which is a variation of the earlier one, 'In the Cage'. The latter possibly becomes too obvious an allusion to the scenes of persons trapped in a sexual relationship. The 'air' may have alluded also to the poem's epigraph from Petronius: the Sybil of Cumae in her cage, hanging in the air, wishing to die. Whatever reasons there may have been for changing the title, the element of air is prominent in the imagery—in the odours of perfume 'stirred by the air/That freshened from the window' and in the dialogue:

> 'What is that noise?'
> The wind under the door.
> 'What is that noise now? What is the wind doing?'
> Nothing against nothing.

And in the last section, 'What the Thunder Said' the elements of sky/ether, symbolise spiritual preaching.

Under this universalising scheme, then, the present world is anatomised in the four divisions of the poem preceding the Thunder's message. Can life grow out of such stony rubbish as the poem presents? Reduced to its simplest terms, this is the theme of *The Waste Land* made concrete through spatial images. According to Helen Williams:

> It is through recurrent images ... that Eliot establishes the emotional and thematic unity of his apparently diverse fragments. It is also noticeable that these images seem to fall into patterned groups; for example, an underlying pattern of the four elements is discernible in *The Waste Land*, though in a far less schematic form than in the later *Four Quartets*.[59]

Helen Williams further argues that from earth comes the group of spatial images of aridity, stunted growth and mortal decay, 'dull roots', 'dried tubers', 'stony rubbish',

---

59. Williams, Helen, *T. S. Eliot: The Waste Land* (London: Edward Arnold, 1970), pp. 37–38.

'dead trees', 'dust', 'dry stone', 'bones', 'rattled by the rats foot', 'currents' (being shrivelled grapes), 'trains and dusty streets', 'Margate sands', all culminating in the extreme dryness of the desert in Part V where 'Sweat is dry and feet are in the sand', and we look into the 'Dead mountain mouth of carious teeth that cannot spit'. We hear 'dry sterile thunder' and meet people 'peering' from doors of 'mud-cracked houses', travel along a sandy road with 'dry singing grass' and desiccated trees that wait with 'limp leaves' meeting hordes 'stumbling in cracked earth' among 'empty cisterns' and 'exhausted wells'. Through these physical and spatial images emerges a pattern of the desiccated human encounters and relationships where both pains and pleasures are reduced and withered in the limbo condition, and the locked tower of selfhood prevents communication.

Linked with earth through the desert winds is again the second element, air. There is first the 'fresh' wind which was to blow Isle to land and which is clearly related to the air that 'freshened from the window' in Belladonna's closed boudoir. Belladonna is frightened by the noise of the 'wind under the door'. In 'The Fire Sermon', the same wind crosses the brown land but is silent, 'unheard', until it becomes the 'cold blast' of the terrified sense of mortality 'at my back'. A 'brisk swell', a south-west wind, carried Elizabeth and Leicester's 'gilded shell' down the Thames, and gets up again for its climax in the empty chapel, called 'only the wind's home'. The door swings and the cockcrow at last releases lightening and the damp gust. The fresh wind reappears, implicitly at least, in the third command where the sea was calm and propitious for a surrender of the heart, gaily, 'to controlling hands'.

Much more complex than the earth and air are the other antithetical pair, fire and water. Eliot draws upon every kind of association in these two elements. From Dante and from the Christian and Buddhist ascetic traditions, Eliot takes over the paradoxical symbol of fire as both the flame of lust and sensual attachment, and as the purifying flame of purgation. The purgatorial aspect of 'fire' is earlier established in the sun that beats upon the 'Son of Man' in the desert passage. The 'red rock' in whose shadow he is invited to take shelter has been variously interpreted as the rock of God of Israel, the rock being in the traditional landscapes of the Grail Knight's testing, as the red mountain of Dante's *Purgatorio*. It may well be an amalgam of all these and much more, but at the most immediate level of sensual apprehension it seems hot and fiery. Fire surrounds the sensual but sterile lady of situations in 'A Game of Chess'. She sits on a burnished throne beneath the flames of seven-branched Candelabra. Her hair is spread out 'in fiery points', like the flames surrounding the Souls in Dante's *Purgatorio* which glow as they speak; 'what the Thunder Said' opens with 'Torchlight red on sweaty faces'. Intense, vibrant heat is engendered by the suggestion in the trudge through the desert, surely a purgatorial journey. The sun is setting, the air violet, but the heat goes on until the flash of lightening releases the wind 'over Himavant' and the hot 'jungle crouched'. Thus fire combines with earth to cause the dust, red rock, and the nightmarish red faces and becomes a convenient traditional symbol for passionless human desires, which burn dryly, destructively.

Water is even more complex as a sustaining symbol, being the principal symbol in Jessie L. Weston's life cults as 'the modern variant of the universal parable of water, the river and the sea. According to Helen Williams:

> It is from this complex use of water-symbolism that the reader may derive a tentative sense of the significance of the total waste land experience. For the emotional weight in the poem seems to suggest that salvation from waste of man must lie more in the direction of ambivalent sea than of rain or river water.[60]

---

60. *Ibid.*, p. 43.

Eliot had once half-planned to write a book of childhood reminiscences to be entitled *The River and the Sea*, but, says Peter Ackroyd, he hardly needed to do so, for 'these natural forces run through all of his poetry, remembered even when they are absent from the landscape of desert or dry rock. The river was within him, a source of imagery and of feeling and the presence of the sea always instilled in him feelings of serenity and well- being.'[61] Eliot wrote in later life to a St. Louis newspaper, 'there is something in having passed one's childhood beside the big river which is incommunicable to those who have not'. The sea in Eliot is, indeed, a potent symbol expressive of the hidden depths of the mind.

The title, *The Waste Land*, itself is a powerful spatial image. The gap between 'waste' and 'land' evokes the distinct images of barren land and fertile land. Through this distinction, the gap in title seems to suggest a solution to the problem of infertility. A 'barren waste' can be transformed into a 'land'. There is a hope for renewal. The image of the wasteland has a wealth of possible references. It is the mythical land deprived of fertility by its ruler's weakness. It invokes the legendary England of Arthurian quest. It invokes a war-stricken Europe. And it may represent the spiritual state of modern civilisation. In each case, 'waste' suggests a state of depletion, barrenness and emptiness. According to Harriet Davidson:

> The title is exemplary. A barren place is a wasteland. The stricken land of legend, following Jessie L. Weston, is 'the land laid waste' or 'the waste land'. The definite article raises a common wasteland to a significant, perhaps symbolic one. And, diacritically, the separation of 'waste' from 'land' gives possibility to the noun form of 'waste', which must be defined in some degree of opposition to 'land'. The gap between 'waste' and 'land' maintains a fine distinction between a barren waste and a fertile land,

---

61. Ackroyd, Peter, *T. S. Eliot: A Life* (New York: Simon & Schuster, 1984), pp. 22–23.

as if in the blank space, that absence, were guarded the possibility for renewal without which the waste land could have no symbolic purpose.[62]

'The possibility for renewal' is suggested by the related image of water in the dry land. The water image, in fact, comes to symbolise man's metaphysical quest for regeneration and fertility. Though 'the river's tent is broken', 'Ganga was sunken', yet water itself becomes a source of liberation. This is suggested in the myth of fertility gods—Adonis, Attis and Osiris. These gods are drowned as effigies in the waters of the river Nile and they are believed to rise again in fuller and richer life of the corn. 'Water', thus, transforms the death-in-life state into life-in-death. Similarly, the dialectical meaning of 'Death by Water' emerges from the simple collision of death by water in the baptismal sense (as contained in the title) with death in the physical sense. The loss of self (that is death) required in the first instance is the vehicle through which one is born into higher life. So, in 'Death by water', the spatial image of 'sea' suggests both a sea of temptations (life) and a sea of spiritual enlightenment. Phlebas, rising and falling, is sucked up by the whirlpool of death:

> ... the deep sea swell
> And the profit and loss.
> A current under sea
> Picked his bones in whispers. As he rose and fell
> He passed the stages of his age and youth
> Entering the whirlpool.

Here there is a hint at the process of renewal and rebirth of a drowning man (drowned effigy of the fertility god) moving back from the point of death through all the stages of old age, youth, childhood to the moment of birth. By implications, Phlebas moves from death to birth, that is rebirth.

---

62. Davidson, Harriet, *T. S. Eliot and Hermeneutics: Absence and Interpretations in The Waste Land* (Louisiana: The State University Press, 1985), p. 2.

The Ganga passage in 'What the Thunder Said' sums up the cumulative development of the central spatial image of water—sea-water and rainwaters. Here again it is a spatial symbol, because Eliot is not concerned with buckets full of chlorinated water of a Municipal tap which has no capacity to fertilise or irrigate a vast tract of parched wasteland, but obviously, he is concerned with the water symbolising God's grace. In Hindu mythology, the Ganga represents Divine grace. So, in this passage Eliot uses spatial images exclusively without giving even a distant reference to the mental state of the denizens of the wasteland. But the images are rich in meaning suggestive enough to compress the entire theme of sterility versus fertility:

> Ganga was sunken, and the limp leaves
> Waited for rain, while the black clouds
> Gathered far distant, over Himavant.
> The Jungle crouched, humped in silence.
> Then spoke the thunder.

Here Eliot is using the graphic imagery of the physical wasteland. Ganga symbolises the continuous flow of life on earth, fertility. It is the home of faith and wisdom. Being an avid student of Sanskrit literature, Eliot rejects the anglicised forms 'Ganges' and 'Everest' in order to bring forth the wealth of spiritual, mythological and religious associations. Ganga, besides being the name of a holy river, the waters of which are sacred, is also the name of the divine consort of Lord Shiva. Himavant is the source of Ganga on earth. Mythologically, Ganga is also the father of Parvati, worshipped as divine mother, as also the abode of Lord Shiva and Parvati. Therefore, the sunken river symbolises, at once, the debased state of existence, the shrivelled stream of life and civilisation. And the black clouds, gathered far distant over Himavant, not only give the assurance of life-giving water but also indicate the goal of human aspiration and the promise of salvation. As such, thoughts and feelings are simultaneously realised in terms of spatial images: the cloud, hill, river and forest. And a whole climate of feeling is realised along with an apt, evocative setting for the message. The use of 'Thunder' (instead of Prajapati as in *The Chhandogya Upanishad*) suggests the natural revelation of God through the divine abode—the sky. 'Thunder' becomes the 'jagadguru', the 'Acharya' who not only guides and initiates the pupil into the mysteries of knowledge but also disciplines him and cultivates 'sanskaras' or 'values', curbing the negative elements of his personality. The teacher, here, takes the form of God speaking incognito through thunder; 'the voice of God' referred to in the Hindu scriptures is 'Akashvani'. Robert Minor points out:

> Manu 2.140 defines an acharya as a 'brahmin' who initiates a pupil and teaches him the Veda together with the Kalpa (the sutras which teach the rules described in the Veda) and the Rahasyas (the Upanishads).[63]

In this sense the message of the thunder is symbolic in its conception and execution. As a teacher it unfolds the 'Rahasyas' (secrets) of 'DA' to the deva, manushya and asura and echoes the 'conduct, rule, custom' to make life spiritually awakened. For Gods, the syllable 'da' conveys 'damyata' control yourself, for men 'datta' —give and for the demons 'dayadhvam' — be compassionate. What is significant here is that the same syllable 'da' conveys different messages to different beings.

It is, therefore, evident that the central ideas in *The Waste Land* correspond to the spatial images, and perceptual images correspond to conceptual ones. Eliot, thus, retains the fertility aspect of water symbolism only fleetingly in his poem. Nearly always it is overshadowed by the threat of the wasteland itself. The 'spring rain', a spatial image, becomes a part of April's cruelty, and a corresponding symbol of 'the dead land'.

---

63. Minor, Robert N., *Bhagvad Gita: An Exegetical Commentary* (New Delhi: Heritage Publishers, 1982), p. 4.

The lush associations of water (the Hyacinth girl with her wet hair, etc.) are set fleetingly against the powerful group of drowning, rotting and corrosive aspects of water. In *Tristan and Isolde*, the sea which should bring Isolde to Tristan is described as waste and void, signifying the hungry desolation bred by the surrender to the love potion by the two at sea, a craving which can only be assuaged by death. Madame Sosostris, finding the drowned sailor in her pack of cards, begins the whole train of drowning images. The terrifying aspect is recalled in 'Death by Water' where Phlebas' bones are picked up 'in whispers'. Ironically, the dwellers in the land, consultants of Madame Sosostris, are only aware of the physical terror. Hence, that 'fear death by water', and the 'currents under sea', the whirlpool that separates man forever from his body and from 'the profit and the loss' so important to his material existence. Eliot also uses the sea traditionally as the sea of life on which man is a bark afloat. Hence the image of the wheel. It is significant to note that fresh river waters, in *The Waste Land*, have dried up or suffered pollution by man so that the poem's rivers become an aspect of the waste itself. Even the full river at the beginning of 'The Fire Sermon' is presented in forbidding terms, suggestive of rape and drowning rather than of elemental vitality: 'The last fingers of leaf/Clutch and sink into the wet bank'. The river is polluted with 'testimony of summer nights', of casual love. The river banks are correspondingly rotten, a place for a rat to drag its slimy belly. Fishermen seek even the dull canal rather than the river as source of lively fish. Feet are washed not in holy water but in soda water, and the river 'sweats', as Eliot describes it in terms reminiscent of Conrad. The river in *Heart of Darkness*, like the Thames, is a symbol of corruption, and not vitality. When we reach the river Ganga, and the thunder breaks, it is sunken. The spatial image of 'ether' is reflected in the mental condition of the waste landers whose consciousness is arrested in a death-in-life state.

Thus, the five dominating elements of earth, air, water, fire and ether provide a background for the culminating spatial images in *The Waste Land*.

To point out the way to make the wasteland fertile again, Eliot employs the spatial metaphor of quest/pilgrimage. In *The Wasteland*, Tiresias/Fisher King and the entire modern mankind is undergoing the perilous journey of life, a journey which they sometime hope will be transformed into a pilgrimage. The landscape and action of 'what the Thunder said' define all that preceded in terms of a journey pattern. We move from the perilous ocean voyage ('Death by Water') to the journey on the dry-land. The faces, voices, and memories become parts of a whole. They all contribute to the 'continuous phantasmagoria' (Eliot's phrase for Dante's journey in the Inferno) through which the consciousness of the poet and the reader move towards the Chapel Perilous. As we follow 'the road winding above the mountains', the protagonist senses the presence of Him whose terrible absence seems confirmed by contemporary reality—'He who was living is now dead'; 'When I count, there are only you and I together'. The quest for the Grail culminates in a dizzying look backwards during the whole journey; the lines 367-385 of *The Waste Land* are a nightmarish echo-chamber recalling as well as distorting what has gone before. Suddenly the four lines (392-395) bring an abrupt turnabout—there appears a cock on the 'rooftree'. Its appearance at this crucial moment of journey is symbolic. Crowing of cock (a sign of resurrection, of putting wandering spirits to rest and in Indian tradition, the dawning of new day, of approaching light) is immediately succeeded by a flash of lightening instead of dawn's glimmer, and a 'damp gust' bringing rain. The quest for the Grail culminates not in a vision, but in the sounds of the fabled thunder.

Eliot has used the spatial metaphor of pilgrimage/quest in his plays also, sending Becket, Harry and Celia on a journey of 'dispassion' and renunciation towards sainthood. In *Murder in the Cathedral*, Becket's quest for timeless reality is presented through spatial images which reinforce the paradox of death and rebirth, the martyr's expiation for the sins of the world, and the fact that through that redemption comes the renewal of salvation for mankind. This pattern of death and rebirth, blood and redemption is woven into the spatial images of the sea and the wasteland:

> From where the Western Seas gnaw at the coast of Iona,
> To the death in the desert, the prayer in forgotten places by the broken
> Imperial column,
> From such ground springs that which forever renews the earth
> Though it is forever denied.
> (II: 633–636)

Grover Smith sees in Eliot's use of the river and sea-image an allusion 'to the Hindu Parable of the life cycle—the drop of water lifted as vapour from the sea, deposited as rain upon the Himalayas, and carried again seaward by the Ganges'.[64] In the *Upanishads* and *The Gita*, also, rain, river and sea are presented as symbols of life: 'From sea is the rain, from rain is the good, that sustains human life'.

As in *The Waste Land*, here too the images of earth and desert point out the way to salvation within the world: 'Except a grain of wheat fall into the ground and die, it abideth alone,/but if it die, it bringeth forth much fruit'. So the Chorus cries:

> We thank Thee for Thy mercies of blood,
> For thy redemption by blood,
> For the blood of Thy martyrs and saints
> Shall enrich the earth, shall create the holy places.
> For wherever a saint has dwelt,

---

64. Smith, Grover, *T. S. Eliot's Poetry and Plays: A Study in Sources and Meaning*, p. 278.

> Wherever a martyr has given his blood for the blood of Christ,
> There is holy ground . . .
>
> (II: 628–630)

The inevitability of Becket's death brings forth new hope for the Chorus Women who are terrified at the prospect of blood. 'Since . . . the land became brown sharp points of death in waste of water and mud'. (I: 9–11)

'The New Year waits, breathes, waits, whispers in darkness'. The image of the 'New Year' whispering in 'darkness' culminates at a key-point — the opening chorus of part II, when it reiterates the parallel between the cleaning of the earth, followed by the fruition of summer and harvest and the idea of redemption:

> What sign of the spring of the year?
>
> * * * *
>
> What signs of a bitter spring?
> The wind stored up in the East . . .
> And war among men defiles the world, but death in the Lord renews it,
> And the world must be cleaned in the winter, or we shall have only
> A sour spring, a parched summer, an empty harvest.
>
> (II: 3–16)

Hope of the renewal of the world prepares the Chorus Women for the advent of blood and death, though the dreadful reality is still a torture.

As the murderers hack at Becket's skull, the Women chant a tormented prayer for cleaning, for purification from defilement. Recalling that they 'did not wish anything to happen', they utter a cry of dread, reflected in a wealth of spatial images, an unimaginable 'instant eternity of evil and wrong' by which they are soiled, 'united to supernatural vermin'.

> Clear the air! Clean the sky! Wash the wind . . .
> The Land is Foul; the water is foul . . .
> It is not we alone, it is not the house,
> It is not the city that is defiled
> But the world that is wholly foul.
> Clear the air! Clean the sky! Wash the wind!
> Take the stone from the stone . . . and wash them
>
> (II: 397–422)

In this chorus of wild protest and amazement at the pollution of the natural order, all sense of time and place is lost and the immensity of cosmic evil overwhelms these poor Women of Canterbury, who are accustomed only to coping with their daily and parochial troubles, of which they can thankfully say 'sufficient to the day is the evil thereof'. But what they now suffer is universal, in abomination beyond imagination, endurance and redress. The world itself is wholly fouled, beyond anything that is possible for them to cleanse it. So they call for impossibilities, such as cleaning the sky or washing the wind. The spatial images effectively convey the idea of universal pollution hinted at in the images used earlier:

> I have felt
>   The heaving of earth at night fall, restless, absurd . . . .
> I have eaten
>   Smooth creatures still living, with the strong salt taste of living things under sea. . . . have lain on the floor of the sea and breathed with the breathing of the sea-anemone, swallowed with ingurgitation of the sponge.
>
> I have lain in the soil and criticized the worm. In the air
> Flirted with the passage of the kite . . .

Elizabeth Drew points out that here, 'Nature and Man seem part of an indestructible unity and harmony'.[65]

All the spatial images—'earth heaving', 'Sea', 'Air' and 'Kite' suggest horror, nausea, hysteria, monstrosity,

---
65. Drew, Elizabeth, *T. S. Eliot: The Design of his Poetry*, p. 123.

brute beastliness. Corruption in beautiful things symbolises death. The effect is to extend the power of evil to universal dimensions, and not simply to limit it to a handful of rude and brawling Knights with some shadowy king behind them. These images reinforce the impression of something more cosmic than a church-and- state squabble. In this tremendous aggregate of things intended to convey an imminence of evil, every spatial image strikes with a sick anticipation of the abomination about to take place.

Likewise, as in all the poems of Eliot, the image of 'stairs' becomes the most powerful spatial image of awareness and consciousness: 'Sometimes at you prayers, sometimes hesitating at the angles of stairs'. In its implication the image of stairs corresponds to 'the dark green light from a cloud on a withered tree' and 'the western seas gnaw at the cost of lona'. The images convey an acute sense of self-contamination which is destined to be the lot of the Chorus Women. But 'the stair' and 'steps' also illuminate the way out:

> If the blood is to flow on the steps,
> We must first build the steps,
> And if the Temple is to be cast down,
> We must first build the temple

Churches must always be built, not as part of a slow and ultimately triumphant penetration of the powers of darkness, but because churches are always decaying and we must bear witness. Man's duty is simple and single: 'it is to make perfect his will'. So the struggle of Becket to make perfect his will that is to purge himself of the last and most deadly manifestation of pride which is 'to do the right thing for the wrong reason' is paralleled with the struggle of the Chorus of poor Canterbury Women, the ordinary unsaintly mortal to nerve himself for the bloody working out of Destiny. The change in the spatial images from:

> Evil the wind, and bitter the sea, and grey the sky. Grey
> grey grey .... A doom on the house, a doom on yourself,
> a doom on the world

(I: 147-151)

To
And the world must be cleaned in winter
(II: 16)
And
Clear the air! Clean the sky! Wash the wind!

(II: 422)

is symptomatic not only of the acceptance of consciousness but also of the perception of the filth of the beast, or man without God. The blood of the martyr not only fertilises the world, but also cleanses the world of its ordinary filth. He has redeemed the crumbling faith, and now the Chorus are free to sing triumphantly of what before they had so dreaded, the act of death and the benediction proceeding from it:

> We praise Thee, O God, for the glory displayed . . .
> In the snow, in the rain, in the wind, in the storm . . .
> The darkness declares the glory of light (II: 618-621)

The spatial images in *Murder in the Cathedral*, thus, serve to highlight the motivation of Thomas and the reactions of the Chorus, two things which between them make up the real kernel of the play.

In *The Family Reunion*, the spatial images centre around the Wishwood set-up, and its feudal pretensions: in mocking the latter, Eliot is attacking the former and at the same time suggesting the way out through the imagist pattern. Wishwood is another spatial image for the death-in-life of Western civilisation that we see also in the 'Bloomsbury' background of *Prufrock*, the nameless London sub-demi-monde background of *Sweeney Agonistes*, the cosmopolitan background of *The Waste Land*, the fascist-communist shirt politics background of *The Rock*, and the despair of the Women of Canterbury in *Murder in the Cathedral*. Cleanth Brooks points out in his article *Sin and Expiation*:

> The work of few poets shows the intense continuity which we have learned to expect in the work of T. S. Eliot. It was to be predicted that *The Family Reunion* would contain a recapitulation of the symbols (and images) which dominated Eliot's earlier poetry. They are here: the purposeless people moving in a ring ('in an overcrowded desert, jostled by ghosts') of *The Waste Land*; the 'hellish, sweet smell' that accompanies the apprehension of the supernatural from *Murder in the Cathedra* . . .[66]

In fact, *The Family Reunion*, like *Murder in the Cathedral*, depicts two different worlds. The larger, the 'normal' world, is subdivided into different orders of reality according to the potentialities of the characters moving within it. Like the Knights, the people in this play, whose vision is circumscribed by purely natural law, are shallow, almost flat, lacking complexity. The second, or 'spiritual' world, has only one representative, Harry's aunt Agatha. Agatha's intuition tells her (and the audience) that a great moment, long predestined on a higher plane ('the world around the corner'), is about to come in Harry's life. The spatial images in her ironic speech, when the Chorus is getting ready (by preparing false faces) to receive Harry, are suggestive of those moments when experience of the normal world is suddenly heightened by a feeling of something coming to use from beyond it:

> The wind's talk in the dry holly-tree
> The inclination of the moon
> The attraction of the dark passage
> The paw under the door.

(Act I: Scene I. 119–220)

---

66. Clarke Graham, ed., *T. S. Eliot: Critical Assessment*, Volume III, p. 343.

Harry, the self-styled wife-murderer, belongs neither to the world of his mother and uncles, nor does he belong to the world of Agatha. He exists rather 'between sleep and waking'. Harry's birth into the spiritual world and his commitment to the purgatorial flame is supported largely by spatial images. The moment Harry enters, our minds are prepared to fasten on the blank dark space of the French window at the back of the stage, to which Harry's stare at his entrance directs us. The spatial images used by him suggest his guilt and the reflection of his own contamination staring back at him through the eyes of the Eumenides:

> How can you sit in this blaze of light for all the world to look at?
> If you knew how you looked, when I saw you through the window!
> Do you like to be stared at by eyes through a window?
> (I: i.222–225)

He immediately realises that his family has 'conspired to invent' a Harry as 'unchanged' as Wishwood; that people who have no experience of a supernatural reality cannot be expected to see how trivial the doings of drawing rooms and the ordinary world of births, deaths and marriages are to a man suddenly involved in 'the perpetual struggle of Good and Evil'. The moral stench of the corrupted world cannot be dealt with by the practical sort of means, the aunts and uncles understand. So he starts speaking in symbols, trying to convey to his hearers the nightmarish experience, to which he has awoken, in images that they would be able to understand. He pictures an old house (as it might be Wishwood) with drains that make it stink (but which no plumber can put right, in which you awake in the early hours, conscious of the haunting sadness in the ancient bedroom in which, perhaps, some terrible thing was done long ago)

> You do not know
> The noxious smells untraceable in the drains,
> Inaccessible to the plumbers.
>
> (I: i. 305–307)

> I am the old house
> With the noxious smell and the sorrow before morning,
> In which all past is present, all degradation is unredeemable.
>
> (I: i. 311–314)

This is his picture of the world (as he now perceives it) in which there is the pervasive degradation of sin (like a bad smell, like a great grief) that cannot be redeemed. It is also his picture of himself; he feels his own guilt (the impulse to kill his wife) is beyond redemption.

Caught in the web of self-disgust, Harry describes himself in the scene with Agatha as having been moving

> In and out, in an endless drift of shrieking forms in a circular desert.
>
> (II: ii. 195–196)

'Circular desert' is an important spatial image of Harry's nightmarish impressions. This is but a different picture of Agatha's insight into the same experience in her own earlier life:

> Up and down, through the stone passages
> Of an immense and empty hospital
> Pervaded by a smell of disinfectant . . .
>
> (II: ii. 201–203)

Harry proceeds to outline obscurely, 'in general terms/Because the particular has no language', his sense of damnation:

> The sudden solitude in a crowded desert
> In a thick smoke . . .
> One thinks to escape
> By violence, but one is still alone
> In an over-crowded desert, jostled by ghosts.

(I: i. 320-334)

Harry is suffering not because of the drowning of his wife but of something deeper:

> It is not my conscience
> Not my mind, that is diseased, but the world I have to live in.

(I: i. 365)

Harry has returned to Wishwood, without consciousness of personal guilt, in the belief that he can escape suffering; but this 'jolly corner' enshrines what he has all the time escaped. Almost as soon as he arrives, he understands this fact without being yet certain of it. His past, the house and family, and the Furies are all one. Before he is convinced, he carries on a dialogue with his cousin Mary, whom Amy has kept as a future wife for Harry. For him to do so would be to accept Amy's scheme of continued domination. The conversation discloses that Mary, having only an elementary idea of Harry's troubles, regards herself and Wishwood as supplying the solution. The temptation presents itself through her cryptic, trance-like plea that the flowers which spring the earliest, while the snow is still on the ground, suffer the least cruel of all painful births. Harry responds against his instinct that such escape is probably hopeless, by saying:

> . . . you seem
> Like someone who comes from a very long distance,
> Or the distant waterfall in the forest,
> Inaccessible, half-heard.

(I: ii. 239-242)

> You bring me news
> Of a door that opens at the end of a corridor,
> Sunlight and singing . . .
>
> (I: ii. 283–295)

Immediately, inducing in him an 'apprehension' like 'a sweet and bitter smell / From another world', the Furies stand revealed in the window. In a rage, he boorishly tells Mary that she is of no use to him, and the specters, their work done, vanish again. But Mary helps him to find out what is real in himself; he stands in sunlight once again. (I.II.310) But he is not to stay there, he is to start from there, from that innocence and sunlight of his real past, into the new life to be revealed to him by the angels of conscience.

The corresponding scene in Part II, between Harry and Agatha, awakens him to the real outside causes of his unhappiness. Through the explicit spatial image of rose-garden, the curse is revealed to have its cause in love and thus to be analogous to love. Harry with Agatha perfects in imagination his father's incomplete fruition of the 'rose-garden', and, whereas Agatha really 'only looked through the little door', they now figuratively commune in the garden itself. The terrible childhood is implicitly converted into a blessing. The wilderness has become the rose-garden. So while in 'Burnt Norton', 'moment' in the 'rose-garden' embodies the spiritual reality, 'out of time', here it is the crucial moment of fulfilment, or near fulfilment, which Harry and Agatha had together during childhood. She exclaims:

> I only looked through the little door
> When the sun was shining on the rose-garden.
> And heard in the distance tiny voices
> And then a black raven flew over.
> And then I was only my own feet walking
> Away, down a concrete corridor
> In a dead air.
>
> (II: ii. 183–189)

And Harry responds with:

> O my dear, and you walked through the little door And I ran to meet you in the rose-garden.
>
> (II: ii.216–217)

And Agatha adds:

> This is the next moment. This is the beginning. We do not pass twice through the same door or return to the door through which we did not pass. . . .
>
> You have a long journey.
>
> (II: ii. 218–224)

If the symbolic significance of these spatial images is examined, the same exhibitionistic motive which underlines the 'Burnt Norton' is discovered:

> And the pool was filled with water out of sunlight,
> And the lotus rose, quietly, quietly,
> The surface glittering out of heart of Light
> And they were behind us, reflected in the pool.
> Then cloud passed, and the pool was empty.

'They' are, indifferently, the adults, Agatha, or the Euminides when these last are 'accepted and accepting': 'they' see the lotus, which carries an obvious phallic significance. The episode is described from within 'our first world' and the manifold associations with childhood include the children in the leaves, 'hidden excitedly, containing laughter'.

They are excited because they are about to 'discover' themselves in a child's game of peek-a-boo. Just as 'Burnt Norton' presents the effort to recapture in later life, through spiritual discipline and art, the emotional state evoked by the moment in garden, similarly the play also seeks to objectify this deep connection by representing Harry's return home as an effort, finally successful, to get back to the sources of spiritual fertility.

Thus, the spatial images in Eliot's poetry and plays portray an existence in relation to time and place, torn between the highest spiritual vocation (symbolised by time in *Four Quartets*, *Murder in the Cathedral* and *The Family Reunion*) and the most trivial reality (symbolised by space in *Prufrock* and *The Waste Land*). Indeed, to recall Eliot's own words for Henry James, spatial images enhance the beauty of perception by making 'a place real not descriptively but by something happening there'. This is what transforms a place into 'space', for time is embodied in 'space'. The moments of the vanished past are revised in 'space'. These images make us aware of time's passage while immortalising certain timeless depths of time. Thus, time becomes an allegory of 'space', by uncovering the depths of a specific place and bringing permanence to a 'moment in time' by transforming it into a timeless, spiritual moment.

5

Psychological Images

Much of Eliot's poetry and plays are the expression of a certain kind of apprehension on the level of psychology. Instead of looking out upon the world, the poet turns away from the outer world of man to ponder over certain intimate personal experiences. Those experiences are reproduced through psychological images. The relation between psychology and image is obvious. The image, in psychology, means a mental reproduction, a memory, of past sentimental or pre-occupational experience, not necessarily visual. Ezra Pound defines the image not as pictorial representation but as that which represents an intellectual and emotional complex in an instant of time, a unification of disparate ideas. By implication, image, besides representing intellectual and emotional complex, presents psychic, super- sensuous, intuitional and supra-mental complex in the instant of time. It is not merely comparison or analogy, but it is also one with the substance of the experience, the embodiment, the living form of truth experienced in another world. It is materialisation of something not material: 'translucence of eternal through and in the temporal, of the universal through and in the individual and spatial'.

Therefore, the images—whether temporal or spatial—present the inner drama, reveal the inner perceptions and memories of the individual consciousness as confused and disjointed. Hence, the psychological images. By implication, the conjunction of temporal and spatial images is relevant to the psychology of Eliot's persona, for the sequence of perceptions described in his poems is of a world—a time-bound world—in which any action taken on the temporal level would be an action in a sinister world in which consciousness, seeking 'timelessness' within 'space', becomes disoriented. Such a disorientation is presented specifically through the technique of interior monologue, and psychological images become concrete devices of this stream of consciousness, that is, consciousness in flux. Here lies the integration and unity of Eliot's fragmentary poetry.

Since all of Eliot's poems are almost variants of the theme of the quest for a meaning, and spiritual and moral values in a materialistic society, much of his imagery is also drawn from more or less traditional archetypal symbols used by mystics and religious writers. Therefore, mythical and religious images abound in his poems. The unifying factor, however, is that these mythical images, like the temporal and spatial images, are used as devices to give life to an abstract idea of the unconscious.

The relation between psychology and religious archetypes is brought out by Eliot himself in *The Listener* (March 30, 1932):

> Psychology has very great utility in two ways. It can revive, and has already to some extent revived, truths long since known to Christianity, but mostly forgotten and ignored, and it can put them in a form and a language understandable by modern people to whom the language of Christianity is not only dead but undecipherable. . . . But I must add that I think psychology can do more than this, in discovering more about the human soul still; for I do not pretend that there is nothing more to know; the possibilities of knowledge are practically endless. Psychology is an indispensable handmaid to theology.

Jung's conception of the activities of the human psyche that symbols generated in dreams from the unconscious are psychic events of an independent nature, is more congenial to Eliot as a contribution to the 'mythical method'. Elizabeth Drew holds:

> The development of (Eliot's) poetry contains interesting parallel to some of the materials cited by Jung, and a confirmation of his belief that certain archetypal patterns of imagery which recur and interfuse in the myths of the human race are of great significance in the problems of the nature of the symbolizing process, as well as that of the nature of life in general.[67]

Therefore each of these mythical or archetypal images contains a piece of human psychology and human destiny, a relic of suffering or delight that has happened countless times in our ancestral story. According to C. Day Lewis:

> The poetic myth was created by a collective consciousness; the poetic image returns to that consciousness for its sanction. It is not merely that, time and again, we find in the images (of Eliot) forms and impulses derived from the myths; but the very nature of the image — of poetry in its metaphorical aspect — invokes that consciousness.[68]

However, in the matter of dealing with the unconscious or the psychic state, Eliot is indebted to Bergson and Laforgue, especially to Bergson's book *Matiere et Memoire*. Memory, indeed, is significant in Eliot's poetry. For Bergson, the planes of consciousness are always pushing the past towards present action, and the past enters the present, and accordingly affects the action.

According to Bergson, there are two memories, which are profoundly distinct: the one, fixed in the organism, is nothing else but the complete set of intelligently constructed mechanisms, which ensure the appropriate reply to the various possible demands. The manifestation

---
67. Drew, Elizabeth, T.S. Eliot: *The Design of His Poetry*, p. 6.
68. Lewis, C. Day, *The Poetic Image* (London: Jonathan Cape, 1949), p. 32.

of this extreme is the man of impulse, one who, given any set of circumstances, reacts immediately: habit rather than memory is at work. The man who proceeds in this way is a man of impulse. Eliot plays with this extreme of consciousness in his early poetry:

> Half-past two,
> The street-lamp said,
> 'Remark the cat which flattens itself in the gutter,
> Slips out its tongue
> And devours a morsel of rancid butter.'
> So the hand of the child, automatic,
> Slipped out and pocketed a toy that was running along the quay.
> I could see nothing behind that child's eye.
> I have seen eyes in the street
> Trying to peer through lighted shutters,
> And a crab one afternoon in a pool,
> An old crab . . .
>
> *Rhapsody on a Windy Night*

This passage is intentionally drab, because the darkness here is expressive of life below reflective consciousness. The lower animals and the automatic hand of the child are systems reacting to impulse. Eliot's purpose here is to imagine the world without imagination, below thought and memory, hence non-reflective. The lower animals — cats and crabs — reappear in *Prufrock*. Here feline qualities are metaphorically attributed to a befuddling fog, while crabs are creatures to be envied. The image 'ragged claws' is the ironic play with psychological impressions.

Bergson explains the other kind of memory in the following words:

> But he who lives in the past for the mere pleasure of living there, and in whom recollections merge into the light of consciousness without any advantage for the present situation, is hardly better fitted for action: here we have no man of impulse, but a dreamer.[69]

---

69. Bergson, Henri, *Matiere et Memoire (Matter and Memory)*, trans. Nancy Margaret Paul and W. Scott Palmer (New York: The Macmillan Company, 1913), p. 198.

He who lives in the past, thus, is he who lives in the realm of pure memory. The realm of pure memory is, for Bergson, synonymous with the unconscious. The memory might be of the Freudian past (individual past) or the Jungian past (inherited past of the species—collective unconscious). This is the state when memory does not support any action. The mind simply drifts into a state of potentially total recall; random memories are brought out of the unconscious into consciousness. Thus, the farther we move from action, the more do we realise our past.

Besides the self's consciousness, the psychological images in Eliot's poetry can be divided into the following categories:

i. Zoological imagery
ii. Sexual imagery
iii. Sense and smell imagery
iv. Religious or archetypal imagery
v. Imagery relating to music

The world of Bergsonian consciousness is most beautifully expressed in *Prufrock*. It encompasses the self's consciousness which displaces the ordinary comprehension of language through the dislocation of personal pronouns within a seedy and distressing environment.

The first line 'Let us go . . .' is a psychological image, which presents the drama of the poem through interior monologue, the action being limited to the interplay of impressions, including memory, in Prufrock's mind. A rather curious device complicates his reverie. By a distinction between 'I' and 'you' he differentiates between his 'unconscious' (sensitive, thinking and dreaming character) and his outward self (conscious character). It seems Prufrock is addressing, as if looking into a mirror, his whole public personality. In a strict sense it is ego supervising the interior monologue. The ego alone 'goes' anywhere, even in fantasy. The other conscious self, at the risk of being rebuffed with 'Oh, do not ask, what is it?' merely raises objections.

The projection of Prufrock's psychological plight is presented in the next image: 'Like a patient etherized upon a table'. Notably there is no distinct pause in the preceding (second) line: 'The evening is spread out against the sky' — a qualifying line for the image in the third line. It comes as a single extended phrase, a flight of feeling-in-perception. But in the third line, however, sound, phrasing and sense together enforce slight but distinct pauses — which also emphasise 'patient' and 'etherized'. Thus the flow of feeling associated with the evening sky is broken. There is the shock of 'patient etherized upon a table'. This gets intensified into a new idea by the immensity of the pun, for in this context 'ethereal' may just lie beyond 'etherized'. Are the ethereal emotions generated by the evening sky so powerful that they become a drug or ether to the mind? Or are they a decadent form of something more remote and genuinely of heaven? Certainly, Prufrock has found an image to express his own state. For the calm and serene emotion that 'the evening sky' produces is identical to the emotion of happiness which Keats feels when he listens to the song of the Nightingale. And such intense emotion psychologically has a numbing effect on a mind already entangled in suffering or indecision indicated by 'you' and 'I'. Numbness leads to inertia. Bergson argues that it is in a state of greatest inertia that the mind is at its most active in so far as it is engaged with the deepest memory. To be etherized is to be indifferent to one's environment; also, it is to be potentially open to one's past life.

The shock of paralysed faculties is further intensified by the next zoological image — of a cat — which is a figurative image for the stagnant smoke and fog, which are literal, and the afternoon that 'malingers'. The cat image presents the Bergsonian hypothesis of degrees of consciousness. Eliot suddenly turns the two extremes of consciousness upon each other, as the fog, figuratively the cat,

> . . . made a sudden leap,
> And seeing that it was soft October night,
> Curled once about the house, and fell asleep.

Cat is the essence of unthinking reaction, of movement or impulse (first extreme of consciousness), and sleep is the essence of inertia, the destructive play of memory and of dream (the second extreme of consciousness). We have, on the one hand, automatism, and on the other, inertia. Between them, in varying degrees, is the realm of consciousness attuned to the decisions and choices of ordinary day-to-day activity. It is a realm of choice. Conscious within shifting realm, the mind discriminates.

Indeed, as the fog closes in on the soft October evening, the world becomes more remote. The more intense becomes Prufrock's self-consciousness, the more aware he becomes of time's duration.

The most violent psychological images in the poems are related to the senses of sight and smell. The image of 'eyes' conveys the extremes of self-consciousness, of fear of being looked at and not looked at: 'the eyes that fix you' like a specimen insect impaled, to be stared at in its death agony. Thus, Prufrock, in speaking of himself, combines the zoological and sense images:

> The eyes that fix you in a formulated phrase,
> And when I am formulated, sprawling on a pin,
> When I am pinned and wriggling on the wall,
> Then how should I begin
> To spit out all the butt-ends of my days and ways?

'The wriggling on the wall' implies movement arrested — like a patient etherized upon a table — a reflection of his psychological inactivity contaminated and distorted by dread of reproach. The effect of distress, dejection and sexual anxiety is further accentuated by the psychological image of smell:

> Is it perfume from a dress
> That makes me so digress

The image of female perfume and other images of sex draw upon a rich experience of social catastrophes by bringing forth the past memories:

> For I have known them all already, known them all —

*   *   *   *

> So how should I presume?
> And I have known the eyes already, known them all —

*   *   *   *

> And I have known the arms already, known them all —
> Arms that are braceleted and white and bare
> (But in the lamplight, downed with light brown hair!)

Prufrock's attitude to women oscillates between two extremes. On the one hand, as a bachelor of some standing, he professes to be bored with them: 'I have known them already,' but on the other hand, he gives himself away in the next line: 'But in the lamplight, downed with light brown hair'. His minute observation of the 'arms' he professes to be bored with, however, tells an altogether different story.

According to A. D. Moody, Prufrock is not in love with these women. His passions, if declared, would be closer to boredom and terror. It is interesting to note that one of the alternative titles Eliot had in mind for the poem was 'Prufrock Among the women'.[70] It indicates Prufrock's sexual insufficiency, the lack of strength to force the moment to its crisis.

To highlight the awareness of consciousness with dramatic vividness, Eliot often uses the image of music. Leonard Unger remarks: 'The images of music . . . relate to the idea of awareness'.[71] Unger's view is substantiated by the

---

70. Everett, Barbara, 'In Search of Prufrock', *Critical Quarterly*, XZI, No. 2, Summer, 1974, p. 107.
71. *Leonard Unger, T. S. Eliot: Moments and Patterns*, p. 171.

key line in one of the earliest poems of Eliot, *Conversation Galante*:

> . . . music which we seize
> To body forth our own vacuity.

The music is a particularised representation of the mental emptiness of the listeners. In *Prufrock*, there are only two references to music: 'I know the voices dying with a dying fall/ Beneath the music from a farther room'; and 'I have heard the mermaids singing, each to each'. In each case, the music is overheard. This observation is relevant to the fact that Eliot often indicates the degree of awareness and the kind of awareness with which the music is heard. The images of 'Music with a dying fall' and 'Mermaids signing each to each' put a concluding note to Prufrock's whole vision of the women's world as muted and powerless. He is the victim of music he would parody, and his song becomes a form of homage to the world, which is too much for him.

But the recurring thought of women leads him to speculate on their reaction to him, to his baldness and ill-disguised thinness of his arms and legs. Significantly, Prufrock is occupied throughout, rather obsessed, with sexual images, which emphasise, paradoxically, his impotence. At this point he admits his first doubt, whether he 'dare/disturb the universe', thus highlighting his terrified self-consciousness. Rejecting the voices, the eyes, and the arms, (all impersonal, monotonous, hostile, delusive), he can think of no formula of proposal but one humiliating to himself—a presumptuous obsequiousness:

> Shall I say, I have gone at dusk through narrow streets
> And watched the smoke that rises from the pipes
> Of lonely men in shirt-sleeves, leaning out of windows?

His horror of being dissected, of being 'pinned' makes him recoil to the wish that he had been 'a pair of ragged claws'. With this image, just before the climax of the dramatic structure, Prufrock perceives his lack of instinct, of mindless appetite, which would have given him a realisable aim and which, of course, would have made him at home in those depths where at present he exists abnormally.

He has already spoken of the fog and smoke as if it were a cat curling round the house. He now refers to the drowsy afternoon (which correcting himself, he realises is evening after all), saying it 'sleeps so peacefully':

> Smoothed by long fingers,
> Asleep . . . tired . . . or it malingers,
> Stretched on the floor, here beside you and me.

The image suggests that Prufrock is again confronting difficulty of action rather than its unpleasantness.

The next psychological image shapes the climax of his reverie as he compares himself to John the Baptist. The religious image sharpens the whole effect of triviality. Yet at once he disclaims the dignity of a prophet, seeing himself instead as the butt of a lackey's derision, as the butt of snickering death:

> I am no prophet—and here's no great matter;
> I have seen the moment of my greatness flicker,
> And I have seen the eternal Footman hold my coat, and snicker,
> And in short, I was afraid.

The mythical image of John the Baptist suggests, crudely, Prufrock's split-self. Having confessed his cowardice, he knows that it is too late for him to go, and indeed that it always was. The mocking voice of his rejected self can be heard again in the second Biblical image of Lazarus, as his buried life is reduced to a mock-heroic counterfeit of the miracle of history: 'I am Lazarus, come from the dead,/ Come back to tell you all'. What has the dead man to communicate that the living could understand?

Moreover, the answer of the lady might have been a casual rebuff. So, towards the end of his monologue, the central psychological image of 'screen' appears which sharpens the fear of exposure, that of seeing one's own nervous system projected in patterns on a screen. In order to say 'just what I mean', Prufrock must render the essential man himself; he must throw, as it were ('But as if'), the nerves in patterns on screen.

His final state is inward reverie. In the six lines from 'I grow old', his romantic soul dreams of transformation. The sea in Eliot is always a metaphor of the hidden depths of mind, the 'unconscious'. The ministering sea nymphs are simply the actuality reinterpreted according to feeble desires, and the actuality is stronger than the dream. Dream causes him to forget the intolerable human voices until they 'wake us, and we drown'.

So Prufrock returns to the chain of his event-less life and resumes the time-ridden existence. Since his ego cannot survive the disgrace of his personality, at the end of the poem, it is 'we' who drown. All the psychological images in *Prufrock* show that his world is a closed one. Various oppositions of images convey Prufrock's sense of impotence, inferiority, isolation and awareness: the evening against the sky and the patient on the operation table; the streets and the room; the fog and the house; the women's transfixing eyes and the victim wriggling like a stuck bug; the white, bare arms of cold day and the sensuous arms of lamplight; the proper coat and collar and the informal shirt and sleeve; the clothing and the feeble limbs; the prophet and the ignobly severed head; the resurrection and the grave; the prince and the emotional pauper; the bright world of singing mermaids skimming the waves and the buried world of death in the sea-depths of fantasy. These psychological images set down a record of Prufrock's longing to reach out, like grasping claws, and take life into his embrace, as also of his inhibition.

Martin Scofield observes in his book that 'Eliot does not write about the "unconscious" in these poems, but he frequently presents its working.'[72]

The mind turns again and again inwards towards its inner images, towards an unconscious life. *Portrait of a Lady* also examines the Prufrockian world, and to some extent the Prufrockian type (in the narrator), but with a more dramatic sense of conflict, and perhaps in the end with greater penetration. The music of the poem (the verbal music which complements and is complemented by the 'music' which is one of the poem's recurrent psychological images) is subtler than in *Prufrock*.

The poem opens with the man and woman having just arrived at the woman's room after attending a concert of Chopin's 'Preludes':

We have been, let us say, to hear the latest Pole . . .

With the words, 'let us say', the occasion is presented as typical as well as specific. The phrase also serves to intimate that the entire poem is recited within the memory of the man, who is the narrator of the poem, rather than simply narrated according to the indeterminate occasion of literary convention. So considered, the poem approaches the kind of 'interior monologue' which is fully developed in *Prufrock*. The perspective of memory and typicality of the mode of interior monologue are decidedly resumed in the final passage of the poem.

Returning to the first section, it is significant that as 'the conversation slips', the sounds of violins and cornets echo in the mind of the man, thus indicating a diffusion of awareness and a quality of strain and distress in the man's relation with both music and woman. Since Chopin's 'Preludes' are exclusively for piano, the shift in reference to violins and cornets contributes to the diffusion of awareness. Finally, to the mingled sounds of these instruments and the

---

72. Scofield, Martin , *T.S. Eliot: the Poems* (Cambridge: Cambridge University Press, 1988), p. 63.

woman's conversation there is added an actual headache, which is represented in musical terms:

> Inside my brain a dull tom-tom begins
> Absurdly hammering a prelude of its own,
> Capricious monotone
> That is at least one definite 'false note'.

The second section of the poem contains two images of music, both of which present music as unwelcome invasions of awareness. In the first of these the voice of the woman is again associated with the irritating sound of a musical instrument:

> The voice returns like the insistent out-of-tune
> Of a broken violin on an August afternoon . . .

The second image comes in the final lines of the section at the end of a passage of interior monologue where the speaker describes himself as he might be found reading the newspaper 'any morning in the park';

> I keep my countenance
> I remain self-possessed
> Except when a street-piano, mechanical and tired
> Reiterates some worn-out common song
> With the smell of hyacinths across the garden
> Recalling things that other people have desired,
> Are these ideas right or wrong?

In this passage the speaker tells us of one kind of awareness being displaced by another. While reading the newspaper, he is self-possessed, a spectator standing aside from the commotion of the world, of other people until the common song of the street-piano and the smell of hyacinths provoke an awareness of 'things . . . desired', desired by the speaker himself as well as by 'other people'. The speaker loses his self-possession when he becomes aware of the desires, which are common to man-kind, including himself. This dichotomy between desire and the newspaper is the same as that between 'the appetites of life' and the Boston Evening Transcript.

The third section of the poem contains a single image of music. This comes in the very last line of the poem, at the end of the passage already noted as being decidedly in the mode of an interior monologue. The passage opens with the speaker speculating on the possibility of the woman's death and on how that event might affect him, and the poem ends:

> Would she not have the advantage, after all?
> This music is successful with a 'dying fall'
> Now that we talk of dying-
> And should I have the right to smile?

The words in quotation marks are so put, presumably, because Eliot intended an allusion to the opening lines of *Twelfth Night*, where Duke Orsino says, 'if music be the food of love, play on! . . . That strain again! It had a dying fall . . .' But the music in Eliot's poem is not the food of love. With the speaker's reference to the poem as 'music', the identity of the speaker merges with that of the poet. *Portrait of a Lady* is primarily a portrait of the person who narrates the poem, just as *The Love Song of J. Alfred Prufrock* is a portrait of Prufrock. Both poems are concerned with problems of love, including self-love. Each is a dramatic representation (especially in its conclusion) of an awareness which is contemplating itself, contemplating not only narcissistically, but also:

> . . . like one who smiles, and turning shall remark
> Suddenly, his expression in a glass.

The imagery in part III also effectively highlights the psyche of the protagonist—especially the figurative mounting on hands and knees, the smile falling, 'heavily among the bric-a-brac' and the mental shape—shifting to bear to parrot to ape—suggests a kind of dehumanisation, as if through his abashment the crestfallen young man had become a bungling animal.

Another psychological image that is significant enough to require 'special consideration' [73] is that of 'the smell of hyacinths across the garden'. The image tells of an invasion of awareness, whereby the speaker of the poem is distracted from his newspaper by the street-piano and the hyacinths. These provoke him to recall 'things that other people have desired'. It is the evocative fragrance of the flowers which contributes to the intimations of poignancy suiting to the occasion on which the street-piano is heard. In the larger context of Eliot's work, the image of hyacinth recalls the 'hyacinth girl' of *The Waste Land* and thus the entire body of rose-garden imagery with all its familiar details and meanings. As an invasion of awareness, the 'smell of hyacinths' is also comparable to the distracting 'perfume from dress' in *Prufrock*. The two images also contrast with each other, thus representing the characteristic polarities of Eliot's female references. On the one hand, the idealised figure is ruefully lost and/or poignantly remote, and on the other hand, a female presence which is repulsive in its physical immediacy. The imagery of spring flowers also objectifies the lady's frustration and the young man's own pricked certitude.

In the *Rhapsody on a Windy Night*, there is also a catalogue of such images: 'old nocturnal smells'. Of particular significance are 'a paper rose,/ that smells of dust and eau de cologne', and 'female smells in shuttered room'. The latter conveys the theme of sexual anxiety.

The poem represents the mood and thoughts of a dry brain in a dry season, strung upon the continuity of a solitary walk through city streets from street lamp to street lamp and from hour to hour in the hours past midnight. Temporal and spatial images merge into psychological images. Objects seen and objects remembered slide into each other. The walker sees a whore and remembers unrelated trivia, sees a cat and remembers a young child and an old

---

73. Tate, Allen, ed., *T. S. Eliot: The Man and His Work* (New York: Dell Publishing Co. Inc., 1966), p. 225.

crab. Presiding over the night, the moon, ancient mistress of madness and imagination, dissolves the 'floors' of rational, ordered memory, subjectivising in her 'lunar synthesis' objects seen and objects floating up from memories shaken free of rational order by the lunar dissociation, 'as a madman shakes a dead geranium'. This dazzling psychological image is from Laforgue's *Dernieres Vers X*. It is a city moon, a moon disfigured that is beheld by the walker. The key to her synthesis of his mood lies in the psychological images of the crooked and the twisted, both literal and symbolic: crooked eye, crooked pin, crooked tear in the woman's dress, twisted branch and broken rusty spring; automatic meaningless grasping after what is worthless, offspring of the twisted: cat reaching for butter that is rancid, child for a toy not his or scarcely desired, voyeur reaching for others' lives, crab for a dry stick. Twisted images of present and past have drifted together and soon the moon and the whore, too, drift together; they are one and she is mad. As whore she had reached out automatically for a customer, but she is alone. From these phantasmal floating images of the distorted and the worthless is crystallised a deep sense of disgust, synthesising the 'crowd of twisted things' and their stale smells.

> Through the psychological images Eliot has related consciousness to externality, thus deviating from Bergson's optimism at the outset.

The Waste Land, certainly a development on *Prufrock*, is not the unique sensibility playing on an object, for here neither sensibility nor object seems defined. It is, to quote A. D. Moody, 'the poetry of dream or vision'[74]. The poetry of dream is a refinement and recreation of the objective substance (what Tiresias sees) in image and music. The intellectual 'content' is digested and incorporated into the mode of feeling. Such a fusion of many ideas into a single

---

74. Moody, A. D., ed., *The Waste Land in Different Voices* (London: Edward Arnold, 1974), p. 98.

state of consciousness and feeling occurs in the introduction of various myths. Eliot's mind responds to and relives certain symbols of imaginative experience recurrent in the whole human history.

These dream-symbols and archetypal myths are related by Eliot to the element of blindness and numbness of the external contemporary consciousness which is partly and agonisingly aware that the possibilities of rebirth cannot be dismissed as a historical anachronism; that the truth of experience is eternally present and that the living of this truth plunges one into a process of disintegration and conflict. It is this aspect of the poem which can be related to Jung's 'archetype of transformation'. So, by weaving the suggestive myths into the matrix of *The Waste Land*, Eliot seems to point out that the kind of devastation caused during the World War could only have been caused by human beings suffering a spiritual draught. Obviously, the twentieth century poet-seer is holding a mirror, as it were, to the moral wasteland in human personality. In *The Waste Land*, the central psychological images are related to the myths of King Fisher, Tiresias and Fertility gods. The myth of King Fisher implies that the dry-land of moral depravity can be fertilised only by taking the arduous journey of purgation and suffering (thereby purifying consciousness) and giving the right answers. This later stage can be reinterpreted in terms of Dante's view. Dante considered human actions and their cumulative consequences or karma, against a vertical scale of values in terms of personality in human beings. This potentiality he saw in three stages of consciousness (*gunas* and fields of actions) in the broad divisions of *Inferno, Purgatorio* and *Paradiso*, corresponding in his work *The Comedia* to *Tamas, Rajas, Sattva*, respectively.

Tiresias' myth in *The Waste Land* is relevant to the theme of the poem. Its two features are the combination of two sexes in Tiresias and his blindness, both of which are integral to the poem. He combines all the characters, male and female. One character of the poem melts into another, but all ultimately melt into old Tiresies. The melting of two sexes in him also suggests the sterility of person. Secondly, Tiresias with his long life surveys past, present and future. The whole poem is a projection of the consciousness of Tiresias. Through this strategy, what Leavis calls 'an inclusive consciousness' in Tiresias, Eliot projects a variety of correlated images of spiritual waste and death, drawn from the past and present.

Tiresias, in escaping the limitations of finitude, can see anything and everything the absence which human errancy ('Errancy' is a key term in Heidegger which implies the inevitable human condition of being able to know only particular beings and never seeing as a whole) obscures. This fact distinguishes Tiresias from other narrators or voices in the poem. Eliot himself says: 'What Tiresies sees, in fact, is the substance of the poem.' F. R. Leavis notes that in *The Waste Land*, Eliot realises a maximum of impersonality in order to apprehend the maximum of reality. The self he explores here is not the individual self, but the human self, ideally constructed. Harriet Davidson, talking about Eliot's creation of a universal consciousness which is a central psychological feature, says:

> The frequent use of 'I' by both dramatized characters with specified voice (Tiresias, the Lithuanian, Marie, the hyacinth girl, Madame Sosostris, the nervous woman, the woman in the pub, the three Thames-daughters) and unspecified narrative voices (which include the non- human category — the nightingale, 'Twit twit twit/Jug jug jug jug', and the Thunder 'DA') remind us of the impossibility of escaping finite particularity — Eliot's finite centre or point of view — which is not, however, a coherent or controlling self.[75]

The vegetation myth symbolises the death of body and renewal of soul, or the death of ego or self and rebirth of soul. There the image used is that of the drowning of

---

75. Davidson, Harriet, *T. S. Eliot and Hermeneutics: Absence and Interpretation of The Waste Land*, p. 107.

the fertility gods who die only to rise again with fuller and richer life. The myth of the death and resurrection of the corn-gods, according to Sir Frazer, was originally assimilated into the Christian myth of crucifixion, martyrdom and resurrection of Christ to make the world spiritually fertile.

Thus, the common pattern in all these 'archetypal images' is the motif of death and rebirth, the loss of life and its subsequent renewal. These images are not employed in the poem one after another, but simultaneously. Interwoven with these mythical images are the images on the psychological level, concerning conflicts and contrasts of mood, which ultimately interpenetrate and interfuse. The conflict is present in the opening lines where the line 'Memory and desire' has serious psychological overtones. Memory checks desire; it disrupts the existing conscious pattern. April is echoed and altered in 'cruelest'; the lilacs hurt. The poem is full of anxiety about death and regeneration, and is aching with a desire for a separation from out limitation and finitude. But every separation from memory is sterile and barren, a fate worse than death. Like the Sibyl in her prison of immortality, with lack of death there remains no desire, except for death: 'I yearn to die'. Throughout the poem, the worst horror is reserved for the barren, changeless environment devoid of a human life of pain and death. The waste-landers fear the return of life.

Eliot uses various images to suggest this over-riding image of fear in 'The Burial of the Dead'. The word itself appears three times: 'And I was frightened', 'fear' in a handful of dust, and 'fear' of death by water. Madame Sosostris is afraid lest she should be discovered, and brings the horoscope herself because 'one must be so careful'; the speaker is afraid of having the corpse dug up. The corpse suggests a sinister and hidden death and fear of discovery.

The self-awareness, sexual experience and spiritual awakening of the protagonists are often presented in Eliot through the psychological image of flowers. In *The Waste*

Land the memories of Tiresias as the Fisher King contain no more important event than his failure with the hyacinth girl. She is the Grail-bearer, the maiden bringing love. As in the legend, the quester has met her in a place of water and flowers, the hyacinth garden. The psychological implications of the image of hyacinths can be better understood when it is examined along with the image of hyacinths in *Portrait of a Lady*. In the *Portrait*, the flowers provoke the protagonist to recall 'things that other people have desired'. According to Leonard Unger:

> In the larger context of Eliot's work, the hyacinths recall the 'hyacinth girl' of *The Waste Land* and thus the entire body of rose-garden imagery with all its familiar details and meaning.[76]

The smell of hyacinth, thus, becomes an image of an invasion of awareness like the distracting 'perfume from a dress' in *Prufrock*. The hyacinth girl, with her peculiar fragrance, is a symbol of sex. At his meeting with the hyacinth girl, Tiresias as the quester has failed to ask the indispensable question of the Grail initiation. But the failure of communication is inevitable here. He merely stood agape while she, bearing the sexual symbol—the spike-shaped blossoms representing the slain god Hyacinth of *The Golden Bough*—awaited the word he could not utter:

> Yet when we came back, late, from the hyacinth garden,
> Your arms full, and your hair wet, I could not
> Speak, and my eyes failed, I was neither
> Living nor dead, and I knew nothing
> Looking into the heart of light, the silence.

The verbs in the above lines are retrospective. For the girl the event has faded to a fact no longer directly felt; she remembers it as others saw her. It is significant that the section on the hyacinth retains all the psychic echoes of Conrad's *Heart of Darkness*. 'Heart of Light' is an

---

76. Unger, Leonard, *T. S. Eliot: Moments and Patterns*, p. 180.

Psychological Images

inversion of 'Heart of Darkness', for it suggests Marlow's encounter with Kurtz's 'Intended', the noble nature who, in the final scene, seems to gather all the light around her smooth, white forehead. She has mourned in silence and her words, 'love him', silence Marlow into an appalled dumbness. In the end he cannot speak Kurtz's words, being unable to share with her the truth of the horror he has seen. This image of hyacinth, in this sense, unites the failure of communication.

Lack of communication is also conveyed through psychological images throughout the poem. The upper class characters in 'A Game of Chess' cannot speak to one another and are obsessed with nothingness: 'I could not/ Speak, I can connect / Nothing with nothing.' The image of smell is also used with psychic overtones. The theme of sexual anxiety is presented through the elaborate imagery of the 'strange synthetic perfumes' which 'lurked', odours 'ascended', flames 'flung their smoke into the laquearia'. The perfumes are finally associated with the woman whose 'nerves are bad tonight'.

The image of eyes frequently occurs in *The Waste Land* symbolising awareness of a hideous self, spiritual confusion and barrenness. The lover in the hyacinth garden is not the only one whose eyes 'fail'; Madame Sosostris with phoney prophecies is forbidden to see into mysteries: 'I do not find / The Hanged man'; the crowd avoids seeing. 'and each man fixed his eyes before his feet'. Belladonna's flirtatious Cupidon 'hid his eyes behind his wings', and her own eyes are deceived by the delusions of art so that she cries to her lover: 'You know nothing? Do you see nothing?' and what he remembers is the tag of visual transformation, 'Those are pearls that were his eyes'. In the last section, actual sight can no longer be distinguished from what is either vision or hallucination: 'Who is the third who walks always beside you', and the 'doors of perception' are broken as part of a total dissolution of the mind.

The use of the image of music heightens the desolation which is the end of passion. In Wagner's music the lovers' end is as ambivalent as 'the heart of light, the silence'. The song of the sailor has been rendered in English as:

> The wind blows fresh to the homeland,
> My Irish girl where are you lingering?

The passion that was lying suppressed seems to have been released at death into pure lyricism.

The music in the typist-girl episode is also a psychological image:

> . . . alone,
> She smooths her hair with automatic hand,
> And puts a record on the gramophone.

The 'lovely woman' is reduced to 'automatic hand', while any pathos in 'alone' is mocked at by the mechanical 'gramophone'. A.D. Moody remarks:

> As it were in counterpoint to the witty dismissal of the typist, the music gives another and inward account of her, and we sense what she might feel and suffer. That is, the verse moves us beyond Tiresias' cold study towards a felt and immediate experience of her state.[77]

That suggestion of direct response defines the limits of Tiresias. He sees but does not feel; criticises but does not live its experience. His seeing, without love, passion or pathos, is the dead heart of *The Waste Land*. Only the music of the Thames-daughters expresses a common predicament as a new order of sensibility in the common speech.

Thus, all the psychological images in *The Waste Land* present the paradox most basic to human nature and existence, the absolute interdependence of life and death. A transformation is possible only by surrendering to the will of God. The sea becomes a symbol of man's own subconscious mind into which he must make a terrifying

---
77. Moody, A. D., *Thomas Stearns Eliot: Poet*, p. 92.

Psychological Images

descent, surrendering the wheel of control by personal will to the unknown power of the sea, control from without:

> . . . your heart would have responded
> Gaily, when invited, beating obedient/
> To controlling hands.

The Sea and Fishing are, thus, central psychological images of mysterious wisdom.

Murder in the Cathedral, like *The Waste Land*, conveys a movement of the mind in the form of mental exploration with a subtle interweaving of suffering, striving and acceptance. The dramatic conflict, therefore, is an inner one, of a sort that shows Eliot even more clearly than ever in the tradition of Henry James and more especially here of Hawthorne. For the conflict is Becket's struggle against pride and his final transcendence over it. His struggle to make perfect his will before the events and to purge himself of pride runs parallel to the struggle of the Chorus Women. The dual conversion of Becket and the Chorus Women, which is at the heart of the play, is dramatised through psychological images.

The choric function of setting a mood of fear and doom is achieved by what seems the natural reaction of the poor Women of Canterbury expecting more trouble; they seem dimly aware of some rumour of the Archbishop's return:

> Are we drawn by danger? Is it the
> knowledge of safety that draws our feet towards the cathedral? . . .
> The new Year waits, breathes, waits, whispers in darkness . . .[78]

Eliot uses a seeming contradiction, characteristically, to stress a point. We are aware at once that there is both danger and safety and that, though hyperconscious of it,

---

78. Eliot, T. S., *Murder in the Cathedral* (Delhi: Oxford University Press, 1963), p. 23.

the Chorus know that the danger only indirectly threatens them. 'There is no danger for us'. They have an intuition that all will not be well if Becket does come, however much they need his presence. It is natural for them to crowd together for comfort, and seek the cathedral for sanctuary, perhaps for prayer, while knowing that even a cathedral can be desecrated. But they also realise that in any case such folk as they are need fear nothing for themselves, since nobody bothers about them; they are too unimportant.

'For us' is emphasised twice at the beginning of a line. The Chorus are, as they realise, initially presented merely as lookers-on, and they put accent on their own insignificance by speaking of their limbs and organs as if these were out of their direct control:

> Some presage of an act
> Which our eyes are compelled to witness,
> Has forced our feet
> Towards the cathedral.[79]

Quickly the atmosphere of strain and expectancy is evoked, a simple visual image being loaded from line to line with more and more psychological significance:

> While the labourer kicks off a muddy boot and stretches his hand to the fire,
> The new Year waits, destiny waits for the coming.
> Who has stretched out his hand to the fire and remembered the Saints at All Hallows,
> Remembered the martyrs and Saints who wait? And who shall Stretch out his hand to the fire, and deny his master?[80]

The interest shifts from Peter (and Christ) to Thomas. It is indicated that he 'was always kind to his people' but that 'it would not be well if he should return'. It becomes clear that it is he whom the danger threatens. So the position of the Chorus and their working of mind also clarifies through the image of the 'Labourer'.

---
79. *Murder in the Cathedral*, p. 23.
80. Ibid.

Psychological Images

Since the women see the intrusion of Becket's struggle as a disturbance, they want to be left alone. The chorus has prophetic intuition vaguely apprehended, of the crossing of the sea by the Four Knights; 'winter shall come bringing death from the sea'. The Chorus affirms this intuition metaphorically swaying 'I have seen these things in a shaft of sunlight'. The visionary fears grow with the scene and take more certain shape in their minds, as the image of 'death' suggests when Becket comes: 'You come bringing death into Canterbury'.

With Becket's arrival they are again overshadowed by the premonition of something catastrophic, even nature is ominous to them:

> Here is no continuing city, here is no abiding stay.
> Ill the wind, ill the time, uncertain the profit, certain the danger.
> O late late late, late is the time, late too late, and rotten the year;
> Evil the wind, and bitter the sea, and grey the sky, grey grey grey.[81]

They have been helpless victims of poverty and exploitation, of extortion and violence and destitution and disease, but now they apprehend a greater misfortune, as the images of 'fear' suggest:

> But now a great fear is upon us, fear not of one but of many,
> A fear like birth and death, which we see birth and death alone In a void apart. We are afraid in a fear which we cannot know,
> which we cannot face, which none understands,
> And our hearts are torn from us, our brains unskinned like the layers of an
> onion, ourselves are lost lost
> Ourselves are lost lost
> In a final fear which none understands.[82]

---
81. *Murder in the Cathedral*, p. 29.
82. Ibid., pp. 30–31.

As Becket's destiny—their doom, as they regard it—becomes perspicuous, the Chorus starts using animal imagery. Patricia M. Adair observes in her article about Eliot's *Murder in the Cathedral* that:

> Mr. Eliot also uses animal imagery which is less explicit than the season image but has a terrifying power. It seems to suggest the forces of evil let loose upon the world like beasts of prey and the terrible powers of cruelty and evil in man himself, when restraints are broken and the animal in him is set free.[83]

The animal images, thus, reveal the fear of the Chorus and become psychological imagery. The Chorus cries in unnamed terror to Thomas, whose spirit alone can save them from the evil that is coming and the evil in themselves:

> The forms take shape in the dark air:
> Puss purr of leopard, footfall of padding bear,
> Palm-pat of nodding ape, square hyena waiting
> For laughter, laughter, laughter. The Lords of Hell are here.[84]

Later just before the murder, the Chorus cries again:

> I have heard
> Laughter in the noises of beasts that make strange noises:
> Jackal, jackass, jackdaw; the scurrying noise of mouse and jerboa;
> The laugh of the loon, the lunatic bird.
> I have seen Grey necks twisting, rat tails twining . . .[85]

Animal imagery is used to convey a sense of the unnatural, a general terror.

Leonard Unger emphasises the image of stairs as the most important psychological image as it is 'an image of awareness',[86] though visually it is a spatial image as

---

83. Clarke, Graham, ed., *T.S. Eliot: Critical Assessments*, Volume III (London: Christopher Helm, 1990), p. 487.
84. Eliot, T. S., *Murder in the Cathedral*, p. 52.
85. Ibid., p. 73.
86 Unger, Leonard, *T. S. Eliot: Moments and Patterns*, p. 168.

mentioned already. There are two references to stairs with psychological implications. The first reference comes in a stichomythic set of lines spoken by the Chorus, Priests and Tempters near the end of Part I.

> Chorus: A man may walk with a lamp at night, and yet be drowned in a ditch
> Priests: A man may climb the stair in the day, and slip on a broken step
> Tempters: A man may sit at meat, and feel the cold in his groin.[87]

The image, here, has both literal and symbolic aspects. Climbing the stair by day, like walking with a lamp by night or sitting at meat is a characterised or typical activity and as such also symbolic. The image of slipping on a broken step implies the ideas of awareness and of unawareness. The second image comes a few moments earlier and it is the most interesting. It is spoken by the Fourth Tempter, the only genuine Tempter because he offers what Thomas himself has desired — martyrdom, sainthood, heavenly grandeur. In the passage containing the image, the Tempter is revealing his knowledge of Thomas's own thoughts that the shrine and the fame of sainthood will decay or be destroyed, and that the only part of sainthood worth desiring is the 'heavenly grandeur'. The Tempter says:

> Your thoughts have more power than kings to compel you.
> You have also thought, sometimes at your prayers,
> Sometimes hesitating at the angles of stairs,
> And between sleep and waking, early in the morning,
> When the bird cries, have thought of further scorning. . . .
> That the shrine shall be pillaged . . .

Murder In the Cathedral, p. 47

The activities mentioned here, like those in the stichomythic set above, are meant to be characteristic and

---
87. *Murder in the Cathedral*, p. 51.

typical, and they are also much more highly specialised. While the others are things which any man may do, these activities have a special appropriateness for Thomas, the Archbishop. The detail of prayers has a specific relevance to the play and to the immediate context, but the other details have a more striking poetic quality and are otherwise of particular interest. The stairs, the time between sleep and waking, the early morning, the cry of the bird, all of these occur a number of times in Eliot's works and they invariably signify a special moment of awareness. The last three details—sleep and waking, morning, bird cry— are all descriptive elements of the same movement. So, the image of stairs is the central image of the series here, just as it is in the stichomythic set. And, thus, 'the stairs' images receive in each case this same kind of emphasis. The clearest and most important fact about the stairs image here is that it is also an image of hesitation (another kind of awareness). The Tempter has already said that these are occasions of 'thought' and the 'hesitating'—along with the detail of the 'angle'—gives dramatic emphasis to the nature of the occasion. The image here is, indeed, the posture of awareness, the symbol of awareness, and in so being it relates with marked significance to the images of the *Prufrock* poems. Each of those images is wholly circumstantial and literal in its own context, but when we observe that they share a common quality, then in their collective aspect they yield the paradigm of the posture of awareness. Hence they all become psychological images with sharp symbolic connotations.

Similarly, the images of smell, used by the Chorus, express a deep sense of evil, since the sense of smell represents the deepest and most intense kind of awareness. This device is first used briefly in each of the last two speeches spoken by the Chorus toward the end of Part I:

> There is no rest in the house. There is no rest in the street. I hear restless movement of feet. And the air is heavy and thick.

Psychological Images

> Thick and heavy the sky. And the earth presses up beneath my feet.
> What is the sickly smell, the vapour? . . .

> * * * *

> God is leaving us, God is leaving us, more pang, more pain
> Than birth or death.
> Sweet and cloying through the dark air Falls the stifling sense of despair . . .[88]

In Part II, following Thomas' first encounter with the threatening Knights, this thematic imagery is developed with elaborate detail in a long speech delivered by the Chorus. The figurative references to the senses are worth quoting:

> I have smelt them, the death-bringers, senses are quickened
> By subtle forebodings; I have heard
> Fluting in the night time . . . have seen at noon
> Scaly wings . . . I have tasted
> The savour of putrid flesh in the spoon. I have felt
> The heaving of earth at night fall . . . I have heard
> Laughter in the noises of beasts . . . I have seen
> Grey necks twisting . . . I have eaten
> Smooth creatures still living . . . I have tasted
> The living lobster, the crab, the oyster . . . I have smelt
> Death in the rose . . . I have seen
> Trunk and horn, Tusk and hook, in odd places;

> * * * *

> . . . I have felt
> The horn of the beetle . . . I have smelt
> Corruption in the dish, incense in the latrine,
> The sewer in the incense, the smell of sweet soap in the woodpath,
> A hellish sweet scent in the wood path,
> While the ground heaved . . .
> I have smelt them, the death bringers . . .[89]

---
88. *Murder in the Cathedral*, p. 49.
89. *Ibid.*, pp. 73–74.

In this rhapsody of grotesque and nightmarish sensory images, it is the sense of smell, opening and closing the series, which is the dominant motif.

Since the centre of the play is the consciousness of the martyr, all the images springing from the two-fold conflict (the internal conflict of Becket with himself and his temptations and the external conflict between spiritual and temporal) become psychological images. Becket himself describes his struggle in imagistic terms:

> Meanwhile the substance of our first act
> Will be shadows, and the strife with shadows.
> Heavier the interval than the consummation
> All things prepare the event. Watch.[90]

'The strife with shadows' is, of course, the struggle with the Tempters, with the unrecognised evil in himself. The Fourth Tempter says to Becket what Becket has already said about the Chorus:

> You know and do not know, that it is to act or suffer.
> You know and do not know, that action is suffering,
> And suffering action.
> Neither does the agent suffer
> Nor the patient act.
> But both are fixed
> In an eternal action, an eternal patience
> To which all must consent that it may be willed
> And which all must suffer that they may will it,
> That the pattern may subsist, that the wheel may turn and still
> Be forever still.[91]

When Becket speaks to the Chorus, he thinks of himself as the actor, the source of will, and of the Women as passive recipients of sorrows and benefits resulting from his choice of martyrdom. The Fourth Tempter becomes a psychological image of his own inner longing to be a

---
90. Ibid., p. 33.
91. Ibid., p. 49.

martyr, almost his 'Doppelganger' when he flings the same words back in his teeth. Suddenly, Becket seems to realise that unless the sufferer refrains from willing to suffer and thus soiling his hands with his own blood, he cannot be a true martyr. After nearly blundering, Becket recognises that not only the women but he himself must be passive.

Aghast, he exclaims: 'Can I neither act nor suffer / without perdition?' While the Chorus, the Tempters, and the Priests counsel him to avert action, he comes to his awakening. In his concluding speech of the first act, Becket has moved forward spiritually into an area of lucid consciousness. The Fourth Tempter, echo of his own wishes (and perhaps his angel), has shown him his own heart's way to purge his soul of impure motivation:

> Now is my way clear, now is the meaning plain;
> Temptation shall not come in this kind again.[92]

The first three Tempters are now seen as psychological images of the past, 'ghosts' (like Gomez and Mrs. Carghill in *The Elder Statesman*). They are the occasion for a review of his past as friend of the king, and of confrontation with the fact that spiritual authority puts the soul in even deadlier danger than temporal power:

> For those who serve the greater cause may make the cause serve them,
> Still doing right: and striving with political men
> May make that cause political, not by what they do
> But by what they are.[93]

Thomas, addressing out of his past a 'modern' audience, knows that his history will seem to most of those onlookers futility, the lunatic self-slaughter of a fanatic. His aim is further elucidated in the sermon which he preaches in the Cathedral on Christmas morning, 1170:

---

92. *Murder in the Cathedral*, p. 52.
93. Ibid., p. 53.

A Christian martyrdom is never an accident, for
Saints are not made by accident. . . .
A martyrdom is always the design of God, for his love of men, to warn them and to lead them to bring them back to His ways. It is never the design of man; for the true martyr is he who has become the instrument of
God, who has lost his will in the will of God . . .[94]

So, all the psychological images springing from the struggle of Becket and his purgation point to the fact that religious life and its reality creates living values.

In psychological terms, the Four Knights, agents of the King, who come to murder Thomas and who explain at considerable length, in a style that owes something to Shaw's St. Joan, their reasons for doing so correspond to the Four Tempters. They, indeed, are images of the Tempters, not of Thomas but of the Chorus in seeking their approbation of the murder. They are also, just as much as Thomas, instruments whereby Thomas perfects his own will within that of God.

In *The Family Reunion* the central imagery springs from the resolution of the play—a wish-fulfilment of impulses which cannot be openly expressed, since they have no accepted place in social life. What takes place in the mind of the personae involved is dramatised through the psychological images. C. L. Barber suggests psycho-analytical approach towards the understanding of the play's content in the article, 'Strange Gods in T. S. Eliot's *The Family Reunion*' :

One must employ psychoanalytic interpretation to get at the content— interpretation that is appropriate to non-communicative, asocial, psychic products. In pursuing the meaning of the play, gaps appear which cannot be bridged except by following out unconscious symbolic associations.[95]

---
94. Ibid., p. 57.
95. Clarke, Graham, ed., *T. S. Eliot: Critical Assessments* (London : Christopher Helm , 1990), p. 463.

The play attempts to express two socially incompatible motives without sacrificing either, according to the pattern Dr. Karen Horney has made familiar in *The Neurotic Personality of Our Time*.[96] On the one hand, the action is the vehicle for hostile impulses towards wife and mother, and towards the world in general as represented by the family. Yet on the other hand, the representation is also arranged to satisfy the need to feel secure while being hostile. In Harry, the neurotic necessity of finding reassurance and safety is finally achieved by being perfect and by being loved. Harry is provided with a higher destiny to justify his superior hostility; and at the reunion he rediscovers in his aunt Agatha a 'real' mother who gives him her affection and approval. Although Harry suffers in general he doesn't suffer for his sins. He says, 'It is not my conscience / Not my mind, that is diseased, but the world I have to live in.'[97] The Euminides become, therefore, the psychological images which justify Harry's ruthlessness and shift the hero's guilt from himself to the compulsion of the curse upon the house. The unintelligibility of the curse and the Furies who convey it forces us to look for unconscious symbolic meanings. Grover Smith remarks:

> The imagery of *The Family Reunion* is designed largely to support
> Harry's nightmarish impressions.[98]

Afflicted with horror because of the duration of his anterior life like the murderer's cancer mentioned by Warburton, he objectifies his feelings by talking of stench and contamination, of 'the slow stain', 'Tainting the flesh and discoloring the bone'.

As in *Murder in the Cathedral*, in *The Family Reunion* also, Eliot uses sense and smell imagery to represent the deepest and most intense kind of awareness. In *Murder in the Cathedral*, Eliot has the Chorus use an imagery of

---
96. Ibid., pp. 464–465.
97. Eliot, T. S., *The Family Reunion* (Delhi: Oxford University Press, 1963), p. 84. All subsequent citations are from this edition.
98. *Smith, Grover, T. S. Eliot's Poetry and Plays: A Study in Sources and Meaning* (The University of Chicago Press, 1950), p. 199.

all the senses but especially smell to express its sense (or awareness) of evil. Similarly, here Harry tells the members of his family, shortly after the opening of the play, that he is alienated from them because they do not share his awareness of evil and guilt:

> I tell you life would be unendurable
> If you were wide awake. You do not know
> The noxious smell untraceable in the drains,
> Inaccessible to plumbers, that has its hour of the night;
> you do not know
> The unspoken voice of sorrow in the ancient bedroom.
> At three o'clock in the morning. I am not speaking
> Of my own experience, but trying to give you
> Comparisons in a more familiar medium. I am the old house
> With the noxious smell and the sorrow before morning,
> In which all past is present, all degradation
> Is unredeemable.[99]

There are two occasions when comparisons are made in the familiar medium of smell. In Part I, Scene II, after an extended dialogue with his cousin Mary, Harry arrives at a moment of unexpected elation—'Sunlight and Singing'—which is almost immediately dispelled by his sudden awareness of the presence of the ghosts. He describes the awareness:

> That apprehension deeper than all sense,
> Deeper than the sense of smell, but like a smell
> In that it is indescribable, a sweet and bitter smell
> From another world. I know it, I know it!
> More potent than ever before, a vapour dissolving
> All other worlds, and me into it.[100]

The unintelligible and 'indescribable' ghosts are the psychological images of his guilty conscience, his all-consuming awareness of guilt. The image of sunlight and singing is an intimation of the rose garden experience

---
99. *The Family Reunion*, p. 82.
100. Ibid., p. 110.

which emerges fully in part II, Scene II, where Harry and his aunt Agatha speak with shared knowledge of this experience and of the prolonged suffering which is in contrast to it. Each in turn refers to this suffering with an image of smell—first Harry, with 'contagion of putrescent embraces / On dissolving bone'[101] and then Agatha with 'an immense and empty hospital / pervaded by a smell of disinfectant. . . .'[102] After such references Harry and Agatha speak again of the rose garden and then Harry is suddenly aware of the presence of the ghosts—the awareness, as before, compared to the sense of smell:

> Do you feel a kind of stirring underneath the air?
> Do you? Don't you? A communication, a scent
> Direct to the brain . . . but not just as before,
> Not quite like, not the same . . .[103]

'Not the same' since the restored moment of the rose garden leads immediately into a scene of recognition and reversal, where Harry sees the ghosts whom he has been fleeing—the Eumenides—as 'bright angels', whom he now wishes to follow. He tells Agatha in a moment of clarity, 'I know there is only one way out of defilement / Which leads in the end to reconciliation / And I know that I must go'[104] Harry, with Agatha, perfects in imagination, his father's incomplete fruition of the 'rose garden', and, whereas Agatha really 'only looked through the little door', they now figuratively commune in the garden itself. The terrible childhood is thus implicitly converted into a blessing, so that the Eumenides, now projected from the new 'mother' Agatha, are 'bright angels'.[105] This episode symbolises Harry's learning the truth about his father, and more important his learning for the first time what the Eumenides are: the bearers of a curse, something outside

---
101. Ibid., p. 151.
102. Ibid.
103. Ibid., p. 152.
104. *The Family Reunion*, p. 154.
105. Ibid., p. 157.

him, which he must endure and turn. So the Furies are only symbols. As Helen Gardner comments in *The Art of T.S. Eliot*:

> Although the symbol of the 'powers beyond us' is the Eumenides, they are employed in a way no dramatist would have used. They are purely symbols and have no dramatic life. They neither act nor speak, but simply appear, or do not appear.[106]

A crucial statement which throws light on the psychological character of the images of 'furies' is Harry's remark when he decides to follow the Furies.

> I know that you are ready,
> Ready to leave Wishwood, and I am going with you.
> You followed me here, where I thought I should escape you —
> No! you were already here before
> I arrived.
> Now I see at last that I am following you . . .[107]

If the Eumenides have the symbolic character of voyeurs in an exhibitionistic dream or fantasy, and if Harry's experience corresponds to that of the dreamer, then his at once fleeing and pursuing them can be understood as ambivalent. At one level to be looked at by them is horrible; at another deeper level it is something he seeks. Before the decision to follow them, the anguish alone is expressed in consciousness, while the positive element is repressed, appearing only in his obsession with the pursuers: the 'grip' they have on him. Because their attraction is repressed, they seem to come from outside, independent of the will. In fact, Harry's repeated insistence that they are outside is a way of confirming the repression. Freud describes this ambivalence in connection with his discussion of exhibition dreams:

---

106. Gardner, Helen, *The Art of T. S. Eliot* (Faber and Faber, 1949), p. 140.
107. *The Family Reunion*, p. 152.

> According to our unconscious purpose the exhibition is to proceed; according to the demands of the censorship, it is to come to an end.[108]

The anguish or embarrassment felt by the dreamer is the feeling of inhibition. It represents 'the reaction . . . to the fact that the exhibitionist scene which has been condemned by the censorship has nevertheless succeeded in presenting itself'.[109] With Harry's decision to pursue the Eumenides, the positive element of his ambivalent attitude emerges into consciousness in the recognition that he has been following them all along. His decision itself consists in accepting the subconscious wish; the impulse to exhibitionism is fulfilled symbolically by following the Furies. With the decision goes a reintegration of Harry's personality which can now be understood. The conflict between the perverse or infantile impulse and the social morality requiring its repression has been resolved by embarrassing the perversion. Of course, this can be done only because the Furies are elevated and spiritualised, and their subconscious content is heavily disguised.

The specific symbolic content of the Eumenides must be submerged when they have become bright angels whom Harry is following. It can come closer to the surface when he is pursued, because then the conscious emotion of horror serves as a disguise. It is in these encounters that the experience of being looked at is made concrete in sensual imagery. When Harry enters, he stops suddenly at the door and stares at the window, catching a glimpse of his pursuers. His first words are:

> How can you sit in this blaze of light
> For all the world to look at? . . .
> Do you like to be stared at by eyes through a window?[110]

---

108. Graham Clarke, ed., *T. S. Eliot: Critical Assessments* (Christopher Helm, London 1990), p. 171.
109. Ibid., p. 171.
110. *The Family Reunion*, p. 78.

This utterance is followed almost at once by an agitated reference to apparitions looking at him:

> Can't you see them? You don't see them, but I see them,
> And they see me. This is the first time that I have seen them.[111]

The poetry which expressed this feeling about being seen is distinguished by a special quality of its own from the staple verse of the play:

> In Italy, from behind the nightingale's thicket,
> The eyes stared at me, and corrupted that song.[112]

The constrained but intense quality of this, its combination of an emotional form of statement with the substratum of strong feeling, recurs later when the Eumenides first directly confront Harry:

> I tell you, it is not me you are looking at,
> Not me you are grinning at, not me your confidential looks
> Incriminate, but that other person, if person
> You thought I was: let your necrophily
> Feed upon that carcase.[113]

The images of eyes, thus, highlight Harry's awareness and, at times, his repression of awareness. It is notable that when the avengers actually appear, their character is not that of avengers. Their grinning and their confidential, incriminating looks suggest rather partners in an illicit relationship from whom the hero struggles to dissociate his conscious personality.

The success of the inner action in *The Family Reunion* depends on Eliot's use of symbols and images. The rose garden where all loves end, which Eliot uses in *Ash Wednesday*, is made central (Psychological image) to the play. In 'Burnt Norton', made from fragments of *Murder in the Cathedral*, Eliot explores the coexistence of past and

---
111. Ibid.
112. Ibid., p. 79.
113. Ibid., p. 111.

future in a timeless reality, the experience of the moment out of time in the innocence of Eden, the perfection of Divine love in the garden:

Footfalls echo in the memory
Down the passage which we did not take
Towards the door we never opened
Into the rose garden

> These are the footfalls heard by Agatha when she speaks of walking down endless corridors, and this experience becomes
> Both a new world
> And the old made explicit, understood In the completion of its partial ecstasy
> The resolution of its partial horror.

Eliot develops his images in the central scenes with Mary and Agatha, the two lyrical scenes which comprise in themselves the whole action and meaning of the play.

Harry's conversation with Mary opens with his explanation of the sudden comprehension of the death of hope. The question in Harry's mind is whether there were two ways of life, an innocent and a guilty one, or whether there was really only an innocent one that turned inevitably into guilt, with no way back or out, and brought with it a total loss of hope (I. ii. 119). You do not know what hope is (Harry says) until you have lost it (I. ii. 167). In the intimacy of this conversation with Mary, as it moves towards its lyrical duet (I. ii. 250. 78), Mary suggests that he is still capable of hope; he must have hoped for something in returning to Wishwood, she argues (I. ii. 188–9); he had expected to find his real self there (I. ii. 195–6). For Mary, footfalls echo in the memory of the hollow tree by the river, of those moments of spiritual liberation experienced by children, the laughter in the trees of 'Burnt Norton'.

From this arises the lyrical apotheosis of suffering as a means of bringing life to the spirit. For Harry this is a revelation:

> You bring me news
> Of door that opens at the end of the corridor,
> Sunlight and singing, when I had felt sure
> That every corridor only led to another . . .[114]

Mary has, in fact, set him on the path of spiritual regeneration. He calls himself 'the terrified spirit/compelled to be reborn'.[115]

But, when the Furies appear, Harry is once more plunged into despair. Eliot has commented on this scene in a letter to Martin Browne:

> The scene with Mary is meant to bring out the conflict inside him between . . . repulsion for Mary as a woman, and the attraction which the normal part of his, that is left, feels towards her personally for the first time. This is the first time since his marriage ('there was no ecstasy') that he had been attracted towards any woman. The attraction glimmers for a moment in his mind, half consciously as a possible 'way of escape' and the Furies (for the Furies are divine instruments, not simple hell hounds) come in the nick of time to warn him away from this evasion though at that moment he misunderstands their function.[116]

As always, here too 'the rose-garden is Mr. Eliot's constant image of the ecstasy — the illusory ecstasy — of love between man and woman'.[117]

The corresponding scene in part II between Harry and Agatha awakens him to the real outside cause of his unhappiness. Agatha brings the illumination that he has inherited his father's guilt for wishing to kill his mother, but more important is her insight that he is the conscience of his family sent through the purgatorial flame. Harry turns away, like the murderer is *Sweeney Agonistes*, from the things of sense, the warm human relationship sustaining

---
114. *The Family Reunion*, p. 109.
115. Ibid.
116. See introduction by Nevill Coghill to *The Family Reunion*, p. 32.
117. Clarke, Graham , ed., *T. S. Eliot: Critical Assessments*, Volume III (London: Christopher Helm, 1990), p. 566.

Psychological Images

other men, and perpetrates one final unrepented crime in order to sever himself wholly from the love of created beings. Although he has experienced what the mystics would technically call an 'awakening' through Agatha in the rose-garden of reconsidered passion, it is doubtful whether he takes with him even the image of their shared emotional experience. The eyes he shall face are no longer human, the eyes of inhibition or love; they are divine, 'the judicial sun / Of the final eye', under whose gaze the awful purging 'evacuation / Cleanses'. He has dared to cross from the 'dream kingdom' of *The Hollow Men* into 'death's twilight kingdom'. In that realm alone, by the quasiredemptive sacrifice of Harry as the family's Isaac, will occur the true birthday and the true family reunion.

Agatha remarks about Harry with the same phrase Eliot used long before in *Eeldrop and Appleplex*:

> Harry has crossed the frontier
> Beyond which safety and danger have a different meaning.
> And he cannot return. That is his privilege.
> * * * *
> Harry has been led across the frontier: he must follow;[118]

He follows the bright angels to a place on the other side of despair:

> To the worship in the desert, the thirst and deprivation,
> A stormy sanctuary and a primitive altar,
> The heat of the sun and the icy vigil . . .[119]

These images recall the final Chorus of *Murder in the Cathedral*. His exit is not an end but a beginning, as the images seem to suggest.

Thus in the artistic world of Eliot 'most of the crucial action is primarily on the mental plane with the final striving towards illumination being shown through

---

118. *The Family Reunion*, p. 162.
119. Ibid., p. 157.

spiritual dilemmas, inward battles and mental conflicts.'[120] The psychological images 'remove the surface of things, expose . . . the inside of the surface appearance'.[121] In other words, psyche or the mental awareness is the coordinating factor in the works of Eliot for which all the other images exist.

By relying on psyche, Eliot has found a solution to the problem of the long meditative poem.

---

120. Naik, M. K., *Mighty Voices: Studies in T.S. Eliot* (Delhi: Arnold Heinemann Publishers, 1980), p. 99.
121. Empson, William, *Seven Types of Ambiguity*, (London: 1947), p. 2.

6

Classical Images

Eliot's art is a meld of classical and modern modes as he is an innovator as well as a traditionalist. The surface of each of his works is modern, with all the attendant images and symbols being modern in concept and effect (as substantiated by the temporal, spatial and psychological images), but the background is rooted in classical heritage. That Eliot is consciously using classical images as structure and under-pattern of the modern theme and setting is established by his remarks scattered throughout his writings. In 'The Possibility of a Poetic Drama' (*The Sacred Wood*, p. 67.), he speaks of adapting 'a true structure, Athenian or Elizabethan, to contemporary feeling'. For him, true art involved 'a constant process of hard and clear thinking, a constant adjustment, in other words, of the experience of the past to the changing needs of the present' (*Tradition and the Individual Talent*). It is a 'completion and enrichment of present experience by that of the past'. In his search for a 'neutral' style he is neither too modern, nor in the wrong way archaic. His method of dealing with literary traditions and his reasons for so doing can be traced to the influence of Sir James Frazer whose work made an impact on his poetry and drama.

By presenting the modern audience with ancient Greek and Indian forms, myths and images wrapped in a modern disguise, Eliot tends to recreate, with all its archetypal resonance, a model for this 'community of all men'. Thus, in order to fulfil his artistic intentions, he chose to follow not only Aeschylus, Sophocles, Euripides, etc., but also Indian Upanishads and the Vedas. Eliot's artistic mind adapted itself easily to Greek literature since all the classical artists concentrated on the restrained, self-contained and economical effect of language. As C. M. Bowra has commented:

> Greek poetry achieves its effect through the sustained rhythm of words chosen for their imaginative power, and Greek prose through the persuasiveness and clarity which are essential to eloquence. Greek writers avoided the sentimental and the purely decorative. They seem to have felt that poetry must be intimately allied to common experience and be shared with most men.[122]

This is what Eliot has done by using language to convey the primary emotions, instead of 'the twilight corners of sensibility and the fleeting shades of sentiment'.[123] That is to say that both in Eliot and major Greek writers the function of language is utilitarian. So what Leo Aylen has said about Aeschylus' plays is applicable to Eliot's art as well:

> The structure of the plays is a system of images, and in the same way that the images used are both themselves and represent many other things as well, so the events also are both particular events in themselves, and represent many other events as well. If this is so, we may more easily understand the structure of the plays by thinking of the actions as subordinated to the pattern of images.[124]

---

122. Bowra, C. M., *Ancient Greek Literature* (London: Oxford University Press, 1967), p. ix.
123. Ibid., p. x.
124. Aylen, Leo, *Greek Tragedy and the Modern World* (London: Methuen and Co. Ltd, 1964), p. 38.

Eliot's poems and plays also have a structure which is 'subordinated to the pattern of images'. But the ingenuity of Eliot's art consists of an attempt to tap the traditions of classical masters and Indian scriptures not merely to reshape it according to modern attitudes, but to create a new embodiment of those traditional attitudes which he considers crucial to the maintenance and development of Western culture.

Eliot's poems and plays deal with the modern themes within the conventional forms. So while 'atmospheric' images express modern mood and content, the classical images provide universal perspective to the modern content and create conventional aura. The imagery springing from this classical heritage in Eliot's work is a meld of rituals, myths, motifs and conventional structural patterns. Therefore, his plays and poems can be studied under the following working areas of classical images:

I. Structural Images (Images of Reversal)
II. Mythical Images
III. Ritualistic Images

I. Structural Images (Images of Reversal)

Traditionally, 'tragedy' and 'comedy' are the forms that include patterns of action with conventional meanings. When tragedy is looked at from a distance, the pattern emerges stripped to its essential framework: the tragic action is a movement or journey from guilt through suffering to purgation and insight. Each dramatisation of the conventional tragic pattern finally makes a statement through the specific experience of the individual play about the relationship of the guilty individual to his society. The pattern reflects a basic human desire to be free from guilt—as the specific culture may define it—and to join and re-join a purified society. So tragic structure is a progress by which the guilty individual is reconciled to society and in which society itself is renewed. The way in which this pattern is filled out differs considerably from age to age and culture to culture and even playwright to playwright, but its outlines persist in western drama. Whether the play is *Oresteia* or *Oedipus* or *Hamlet* or *Death* of a *Salesman*, the structure is a progress from guilt to purgation. Eliot has used these three stages of guilt, suffering and purgation both in his poems and his plays and the classical images emanating from the three levels of psychic movement externalise the working of the protagonist's mind as he gradually moves towards insight and illumination as do Prufrock, Tiresias, Becket, Harry and Celia. These protagonists correspond to the classical heroes— Agamemnon, Oedipus, Agaue—in their progress toward purgation. Oliver Taplin establishes:

> We feel an overwhelming compassion for these people who undergo the tribulations, pain and waste which are the stuff of the tragedy.[125]

But the sense of guilt they harbour and the willingness to do penance evoke other feelings as well:

> We pity Agamemnon, Oedipus, Agaue; yet at the same time we feel horror, alarm (phrike) and at the same time we want Agamemnon to be murdered, Oedipus to find out the truth, Agaue to recognize her son's head. The important point is that the emotions of the tragic experience are complex, and they are of course ever-shifting.[126]

The only medium to convey such ever-shifting emotions is symbolic language.

Eliot's use of classical images, whether in plays or in poetry, aims at arousing these 'ever-shifting emotions' for the protagonists as they are holding a conflict on the psychic plane. As G. S. Amur observes in his article 'The Poetry does not Matter-Progress of the Self in T.S. Eliot's Poetry':

---

125. Segal, Erich, ed.., *Oxford Readings in Greek Tragedy* (London: Oxford University Press, 1983), p. 10.
126. Ibid.

> Eliot's central concern, namely his concern with the Self, is the most important single source of unity in his poetry. . . . Perhaps even a closed affinity may be discovered between Eliot and Whitman in terms of their concern with self-exploration and self-affirmation and the roles of the quester-prophet which they often assumed.[127]

Eliot's Prufrock is apparently a 'tragic figure' going through all the three stages. Negligible to others, he suffers in a hell of defeated idealism, tortured by unappeasable desires and guilt of inability to act resulting into self-mockery:

> I should have been a pair of ragged claws
> Scuttling across the floors of silent seas.
> * * * *
> Should I, after tea and cakes and ices,
> Have the strength to force the moment to its crisis?
> * * * *
> And in short, I was afraid.[128]

This is his tragic flaw: through timidity he is incapable of action. In contrast to the lady in the *Portrait*, who feels that she might come alive with lilacs in the spring, he has descended, because of his very idealism, into a winter of passivity. To pursue the tragic analogy, one might call Prufrock's idealism the 'curse' which co-operates with his flaw to make him wretched.

Prufrock is a Sophoclean protagonist in a mock-heroic fashion. 'Sophocles' deities offer no comfort to man, and when they lead his fate to a point where he recognizes what he is, it is his discovery that he is abandoned and alone. This makes him realize his human condition,' remarks Karl Reinhardt.[129] Similarly, Eliot's Prufrock, by yearning for the impossible, confirms his human limitations and his fate as trapped victim of those earthly limitations. In both cases

---

127. Narasimhaiah, C. D., ed., *Asian Response to American Literature* (Delhi: Vikas Publications, 1972), p. 62.
128. Eliot, T. S., *Selected Poems* (London: Faber and Faber, 1954), pp.12–13.
129. Reinhardt, Karl , *Sophocles (Oxford*: Basil Blackwell, 1979), p. 2.

'the protagonists' sole freedom is in being conscious of their fate which they cannot master. This is the predicament of Prufrock . . .'[130] and Eliot's criticism of Prufrock may be read as a criticism of Sophocles also.

Prufrock's guilt is dramatised through the violent images which convey the extremes of self-shattering consciousness: 'the eyes that fix you' like a specimen insect impaled, to be stared at in its death agony as it ejects its insides at both ends:

> The eyes that fix you in a formulated phrase,
> And when I am formulated, sprawling on a pin,
> When I am pinned and wriggling on the wall,
> Then how should I begin
> To spit out all the butt-ends of my days and ways?

The image of 'eyes' presents a contrast of Tiresias' prophetic speech to that of Oedipus which combines a prophecy of the future with an interpretation of the present:

> You have your eyes but see not
> Whether you are in sin, nor where you live, nor whom you live with.
> A deadly-footed, double-striking curse,
> . . . shall drive you forth out of this land, with darkness on your eyes,
> That now have such straight vision.

In Prufrock's case the eyes do not see but 'perceive' while in Oedipus's case it is vice-versa. Mind and senses are dissociated.

In both the cases (Prufrock and Oedipus), what is described is the abject loss of control of bodily functions in the extremity of terror, agony and ignorance. Only less violent is the other image of exposure and split consciousness, that of seeing one's own extravagantly in that of the split self of John the Baptist: Prufrock has 'seen'

---

130. Moody, A. D., *Thomas Stearns Eliot: Poet* (Cambridge University Press, 1979), p. 19.

his own head brought in upon a platter. And finally, there is the figure that recalls the epigraph from Dante; just as Prufrock is thinking once more of how it might have been had he attempted to establish an intimacy:

> Would it have been worth while . . .
> To say: 'I am Lazarus, come from the dead,
> Come back to tell you all, I shall tell you all'
> *   *   *   *
> She would not understand:
> *   *   *   *
> 'That is not it at all,
> That is not what I meant, at all.'

The classical image of 'Lazarus' gives the doom of Prufrock a tone of finality.

Prufrock's guilt of indulging in day dreams leads to his sufferings, for his ideal conception of woman (the sea-girls at the end) dominates his transactions with reality. His self-detraction when he confesses that he is only a pompous fool, a Polonius instead of a Hamlet (and recognising this fact, partly a wise fool too), accompanies his realisation and insight that the dream itself has been only a snare, though he cannot get out of its meshes:

> I have heard the mermaids singing, each to each.
> I do not think that they will sing to me.

Paradoxically and ironically, the mermaids have a reality that the ladies among the tea-cups do not possess. The ladies are not really alive but exist in a kind of half-way state between life and death. The Greek poet Hesiod, in his poem *The Theogony*, relates that once he himself heard the nine muses dancing and singing together. Is Eliot making an oblique reference here to Hesiod's experience? It is impossible to say with certainty, but the ironic contrast between the ancient Greek's experience and the modern American's does make a point. Hesiod's Muses and Prufrock's mermaids sing to each other, but the Greek poet was able to profit from the muses' inspiration to write his poems, whereas Prufrock presumably was not. Though he can hear their singing, he cannot himself utter any love song. More important than this, the possibility of an echo of Hesiod is the contrast between these fabulous creatures of the imagination and the human beings sipping tea. The mermaids are more 'real', symbolic of supernatural energy and elemental power; they fairly surge with vitality as they ride the sea-waves. Aphrodite, the Greek goddess of love and fertility, was fabled to have been born from the sea-foam. Life itself, we are told, first began in the sea. Prufrock is aware that the fabulous and the mythical have a life that his 'fin de siecle' world does not have. Unfortunately, he cannot attain to this source of power; the very conditions of his 'civilized' existence render it unavailable to him.

The closing lines of the poem ironically sum up his situation. Prufrock feels the sea's attraction; for a moment, he shakes off his languor and has a vision of beauty linked with power. But 'human voices' soon shut out the songs of the mermaids, wake him up from his dream of freedom and energy, and cause him to 'drown'. The truly suffocating element for Prufrock is the world in which he normally draws his breath. But since he accepts his responsibility for not having forced his way out of his enervating prison, his purgation thus commences with this realisation. His tragedy remains that of a man for whom love is beyond achievement, but within desire. And desire is the road to achievement.

In *The Waste Land*, Eliot employs the anthropological and classical framework of three stages — guilt, suffering and purgation — to present the substratum beneath the 'horror, boredom and glory' of life. The title itself recalls to mind the setting of *Oedipus* which starts with the Chorus of the Thebans beseeching the king to redeem them of the plague that is destroying the city :

> For the city, as thou thyself seest, is now too sorely vexed, and can no more lift her head from beneath the angry waves of death; a blight is on her in the fruitful blossoms of the land, in the herds among the pastures, in the barren pangs of women. . . . For if thou art to rule the land, even as thou art now its lord, 'tis better to be lord of men than of a waste . . .

The city, 'blasted with barrenness' is not different from Eliot's waste land which is suffering the curse due to the guilt of its inhabitants. But the wastelanders still harbour a hope of renewal as the gap in the title of *The Waste Land* suggests. The land laid waste by impure acts and consequent guilt can be redeemed if genuine penance is performed.

The act is so unclean in both the wastelands that 'neither the earth can receive it, nor the holy rain nor the sunshine endure its presence'.[131] Therefore, 'April is the cruelest month' which reminds one of all that is fertile, fruitful, living, vibrant. Just as 'Oedipus mutilated himself because he can face neither living nor the dead'[132], the protagonist of *The Waste Land* also wails: 'my eyes failed, I was neither living nor dead, and I knew nothing looking into the heart of light, the silence.' So the inhabitants of the modern wasteland don't wish to rouse themselves from the death-in-life in which they live. They are afraid to live in reality, as were Prufrock and Oedipus. They have lost all contact with reality. Their timidity, lack of courage to face it makes even April, the month of rebirth, the cruellest. Winter, at least kept them warm in forgetful snow. In *Murder in the Cathedral* also, the Chorus says:

> We do not wish anything to happen
> Seven years we have lived quietly,
> Succeeded in avoiding notice,
> Living and partly living.

---

131. Segal, Erich, ed. *Oxford Readings in Greek Tragedy*, (Oxford University Press, 1983), p. 184.
132. Ibid., p. 183.

And in another passage: 'Now I fear disturbance of the quiet seasons'. So all the initial images suggest an inclination to escape the unnecessary turbulence which might (they realise later-on) bring about their salvation.

The image of the desert reflects both guilt as well as the suffering of the protagonists. If *The Waste Land* is compared with *Ash Wednesday*, we find desert-like scenes in the first, but the term itself appears in the second: 'the quiet of the desert' where the bones lie scattered (II), and 'the last desert between the last blue rocks; the desert in the garden, the garden in the desert' (V). But in *The Waste Land*, the relevant scenes are infertile places partly lamenting a vanished fertility. The connotation is opposite to that suggested by the image in *Ash Wednesday*, where the scriptural references identify the deserts as metaphors for the spiritual life, and the poem's protagonist actively seeks the condition they imply. 'The red rock scene' in 'The Burial of the Dead' comes close to *Ash Wednesday*, but the lesson it teaches ('fear in a handful of dust') is very unlike the ascetic calm welcomed by the scattered bones of the later poem. In 'The Fire Sermon', the 'brown land' is an image of a regretted sexual and cultural failure implying the desirability of renewal. And in 'what the Thunder said', while the journey through barren mountains amounts to a search for spirituality, its culmination in the ruined chapel is only one of several indications that it has taken the wrong direction. Graham Martian establishes:

> *The Waste Land* 'deserts', then it is no surprise to discover, are elusive, self-contradictory places, linked to shifting ambiguities of feeling which the poem leaves unresolved.[133]

While 'desert' is an image of suffering, 'water' image seems to suggest a way to salvation, purgation and insight. But paradoxically enough, the character of Madame Sosostris seems to suggest the destructive power of water.

---

133. Martin, Graham, ed., *Eliot in Perspective: A Symposium* (London: Macmillan Press, 1970), p. 115.

The suggestion implies that the way into life may be by death itself. The drowned Phoenician sailor is warned against death by water, not realizing the purgatorial effect of water. The subsequent images—Belladonna, the Lady of the Rocks, the Fisher King, the Hanged Man—suggest the way to salvation by accentuating the intensity of suffering. Madame Sosostris's 'cards' remind us of the riddling leaves of the Sibyl of Cumae in the sixth book of the *Aeneid*, whose injunction to Aeneas, when he wanted to visit the underworld, required him not only to locate the golden bough but to perform for a drowned companion the rite of the burial of the dead.

The keystone of the tragic architecture, the model which serves as matrix to its tragic organisation and to its language, is reversal. All the Greek tragedians had recourse to ambiguity as a means of expression and as a mode of thought. This resulted into images of reversal, like Shakespeare's witches in *Macbeth* chanting 'Fair is foul, foul is fair'. Eliot's use of the images of reversal, can best be exemplified by the first three lines of *Prufrock* where 'evening is spread out against the sky,' unlike Wordsworth's 'evening sleeps like a nun'. The beautiful image of evening immediately gives way to the horrific image of 'like a patient etherized upon a table'. The reader's imagination does suffer a shock, but soon the beauty of realism sets in.

Thus, Eliot's conceptual and perceptual metaphors, when studied on the level of his use of structural images, can be termed as 'images of reversal' which are recurring throughout his poems and plays. In the *Agamemnon* of Aeschylus, we find the best example of such images of reversal. Welcoming Agamemnon at the threshold of his palace, Clytemnestra uses ambiguous language, with double meaning. It sounds agreeably like a token of love and of conjugal fidelity in the ears of her husband. But already equivocal for the Chorus, which has a presentiment of an obscure threat, it reveals itself as completely sinister to the spectator, who early deciphers in it the plan for death which she has contrived against her husband. The ambiguity does not mark the conflict of values but the duplicity of a character. It is an almost demonic duplicity: the same discourse, the same words which entice Agamemnon into the trap by concealing the danger at the same time proclaim to the world the crime about to be perpetrated. To the ambiguity of the discourse of the queen corresponds exactly the ambiguity of the image of 'the purple carpet' spread out by her in front of the king and on which she persuades him to walk. When he enters into his palace, as Clytemnestra invites him to, in terms which evoke at the same time quite another dwelling, these are indeed the doors of Hades through which, without knowing it, Agamemnon passes. When he places his bare foot on the 'sumptuous fabrics' with which the ground has been strewn, the road of purple given birth beneath his steps is in no way, as he imagines it, an elevated consecration of his glory. But it is instead a way to deliver him over to the infernal powers, to pledge him to death without remission, that 'red' death which comes to him in the same 'sumptuous fabric' prepared by Clytemnestra for taking him in trap as in net. The purple colour turns out to have an affinity with death. So images of reversal change their associations under the impact of character as do all the images of Eliot.

In the 'nightingale' image Eliot has presented such connotations of suffering that it seems to denote contrary meaning to the common place mind and so becomes an image of reversal. As A. D. Moody suggests:

> What is not felt in the common place mind, and was unfelt in the associated literary tradition, does find surprising expression in the painted nightingale. She could be as inertly decorative as the other unfortunate women. Yet just here the rhythm quickens and perception clears.[134]

What the image suggests in no longer the lifeless sensibility, but directly we are made aware of:

---
134. Moody, A. D., *Thomas Stearns Eliot: Poet* (London: Cambridge University Press, 1977), p. 86.

The change of Philomel, by the barbarous kind
So rudely forced; yet there the nightingale
Filled all the desert with inviolable voice
And still she cried . . .

David Moody observes pertinently in his book *Thomas Stearns Eliot: Poet*:

> This is what has been missed: a natural music, expressing the reality of evil and suffering, the compelling need for a release from it, and a possible mode of transformation. But that mode of pure lyrical being is out of this world. If the woman's nervous suffering associates her with Philomel, it is still far from a final transformation. The chair she sits in reminds us of Cleopatra's 'burnished throne' and the stately room of Dido's palace. The image of Philomel also denotes that the lady is seductive, but that she is also, like Cleopatra with Anthony and Dido with Aeneas, one of those who is in the end violated and abandoned by a man. But here the association with Philomel strikes, ironically, at the reality of her situation. She is beside herself with irrational fears; and could be moving towards complete dissociation or madness, the antithesis of the nightingale, though not unlike Dido running wildly through Carthage, or Cassandra before the palace in Argos where Agamemnon is being killed. The man sees the horror, but feels nothing; while she feels it without knowing why. As she is going out of her mind, his blank basilisk stare is fixing their desolation into a waking nightmare. These are only the negative elements from the Philomel myth, and they imply only suffering, no saving change or song.

The way to release from sufferings and to purgation is suggested in the Upanishadic message of thunder. The message is symbolic in its conception and execution. The message which each group derives is born out of an instinctive consciousness on the part of that particular group.

From the message of thunder, the protagonist realises the true ideals that make life meaningful. Each ideal sets him to an uncompromising introspective self-scrutiny.

After *Datta*, the inevitable question, 'what have we given?' follows. It is not ironical as Leavis thinks, because the question leads to the knowledge that he had yielded to desires of sterile lust, not to the demands of love essential for preservation of life and race, the fall which cannot be redeemed by human prudence:

> The awful daring of a moment's surrender
> Which an age of prudence can never retract

The second command, *dayadhvam*, makes him recognise his incapacity to transcend the circle of his experience. He was like a person condemned to the prison of his own self and pride. His awareness of his self-imposed confinement, the closed circle on the outside, reminds him of the way out, the ultimate release through the breaking of the citadel of pride, guilt and suffering:

> We think of the key, each in his prison
> Thinking of the key, each confirms a prison
> Only at nightfall, aethereal rumours
> Revive for a moment a broken Coriolanus.

The third command, *damyata*, drives the protagonist to recognise the need for self-control, the necessity of submitting himself to the universal law. To lead a meaningful life one has to regulate his individual impulses in accordance with the laws of eternity. That is, to reach the shore safely, the person has to steer the boat of his life according to the laws of eternity, the sea, its tide, current and wind, 'beating obedient to the controlling hands'. Thus Eliot has combined all the three commands into a single message and imparted a full human significance to the entire image of the thunder. The image is based on high philosophical truths as provided by Sankara. Commenting on the Upanishadic passage, Sankara says,

> Other than men, there are neither Gods nor demons. . . . Those who are predominantly selfish are men. In the same way, men who are inclined to cruelty and to inflict pain

are demons. The same men if they acquire self-control and overcome the other two defects, are eligible to be styled as Gods.[135]

The benediction of peace symbolised by the word *shantih* at the end reflects a state of mind attained after a complete resolution of all disturbances, anxieties, doubts, and feelings of guilt. Hence, it figures as 'the end' of a variety of chants, scriptures and literary classics. The word *shantih* is purposefully repeated thrice to indicate the absolute three-dimensional peace resulting from within (*adhyatmikam*), from above (*adi-daivikam*), from around (*adi-bhoutikam*). Its rich, evocative power communicates a state of mind akin to, but far richer than, the calm of mind, all passion spent, of Greek classics. Aristotle terms it as a state of 'catharsis' which means 'purgation'. It is with this note of peace and humility resulting from insight and enlightenment that the poem, like the Upanishads, ends. Thus, the classical images revolve around the journey from guilt to purgation.

Murder in the Cathedral is a drama of such symbolic relationships that the ingredients of tragedy are all present, but apportioned allegorically among the different characters rather than confined to Becket himself. There is a moral (fatal) flaw, original and particular sin; there is (in the external view) a catastrophe, affecting the victim destined to expiation; and there is justification. The first is manifested in the suggestions of the Tempters, the will and act of the Knights, and the suffering of the Chorus; the second, the martyrdom, is executed upon the sufferer, Becket; the third is fulfilled in the damnation of the Knights, the potential salvation of the Chorus, and the exaltation of the saint. The late Theodore Spencer aptly pointed out that:

> The characters live on different levels of moral refinement: that is, Becket, the Priests, the Chorus of the women of

---

135. Radhakrishnan, S., ed., *The Principal Upanishads* (Allen and Unwin), p. 290.

Canterbury, and the murderers have, on a descending scale, distinct ideas of reality, ranging from the acute spirituality of Becket to the depraved worldliness of the Knights.[136]

The accumulation of these, with a distributive allotment of dramatic functions, makes up the total movement called 'tragic'. The different functions here co-exist: the Knights are sin incarnate, the Chorus is suffering, Becket is martyrdom. But sin (guilt) and suffering are attributed to Becket and Chorus equally. There is an overlapping of these functions, as the images suggest.

The images employed to dramatise three-dimensional guilt: Becket's vision of conscious glory in martyrdom; guilt of the Chorus women's participation in act, despite their fear and finally the murder 'which has a peculiar horror by the addition of sacrilege to the guilt of murder'[137] become classical images. The isolated elements are meant to coalesce, the Chorus and Becket to come together in the redemption of one by the death of the other.

Becket's guilt is reflected, in the images of the Tempters; in the perfunctory temptations of worldly pleasure as well as in the lure of conscious glory in martyrdom. Though Becket rejects it, yet this act is only an intensification, a validation of his status as an appointed martyr. When Eliot chooses to adapt his imagery closely to character, the results are striking: the imagery of the speeches of the Four Tempters is eminently in character, though the Tempters themselves are personified abstractions or, more so, images of Becket's hidden desires and guilt. The First Tempter represents the temptation of worldly pleasure. The images of 'Fluting in the meadows, viols in the hall,/Language and apple-blossom floating on the water,/ singing at night fall, whispering in chambers' in his argument are, hence, more appropriate. This is true also of

---
136. Spencer, *Harvard Advocate*, CXXV, No. 3, 21–22.
137. Gardner, Helen, *The Art of T. S. Eliot* (London: Faber and Faber, 1949), p. 133.

his homely analogies of 'The easy man lives to eat the best dinners' and 'or your goose maybe cooked and eaten to the bone'. The Second Tempter stands for worldly power, and the most striking images used by him are those from hunting 'the old stag circled with hounds', and hawking 'your sin soars sunward, covering King's falcons'. The Third Tempter's pose is of 'a rough straight-forward Englishman'. His words are, naturally, bereft of all imagery, the best he can do in the line being the extremely trite, 'We, not the plotting parasites/ About the king.' The subtlest of the whole group is the Fourth Tempter whose privilege it is to tempt Becket with his strongest desires. Hence, he alone uses the wheel image used by Becket himself.

The images of angling and trapping such as 'hooks have been baited with morsels of the past' and 'you would wait for the trap to snap' (corresponding to the reversal image of 'net'[138] in the *Agamemnon* of Aeschylus, the first play of his trilogy *Oresteia*) are also suggestive of his own efforts to entice Becket. Both the images, 'The Wheel' and 'the hooks' or 'trap', make Becket confess that he has been about to 'do the right deed for the wrong reason', to give a sinful turn to the wheel. 'Sin grows with doing good', he says, like Milton in *Areopagitica* ('Good and evil we know in the field of this world grow up together almost inseparably'). It leads to his insight that he has been guilty of presumption, like Antigone, as her sister (the embodiment of ordinary womanhood) tells her. Thus all the images centred around the Tempters symbolise an introspective process: from guilt of desires through suffering horror to purgation of will.

It is with the clamorous hopelessness of the Chorus Women, suggested through the images of beasts— 'Lords of Hell'—that resolution breaks across his hesitancy:

---

138. Leo, Aylen, *Greek Tragedy and the Modern World* (London: Methuen and Co. Ltd,1964), pp. 56-57.

O Thomas Archbishop, save us, save us, save yourself that we may be saved;

> Destroy yourself and we are destroyed.
> Thomas: Now is my way clear, now is the meaning plain . . .[139]

The Archbishop realises that his decision is no longer personal or autonomous. Involved in the integrity with which he must resolve the struggle in his own conscience is the spiritual integrity and well-being of the whole church, and particularly of these members of it, the Women of Canterbury. His moral struggle teaches him the meaning of martyrdom as the perfection of will. In like manner the Chorus is to learn the meaning of suffering. In discovering that his grandiose will to be martyred is sinful, he allows the wheel of fortune to bear him materially down and morally up. Thus he rises to a greater good. Eliot, here, has adopted the 'imminent horror' type of discovery praised by Aristotle with reference to *Iphigenia in Tauris*.

The fluctuations of the Chorus are the true measure of Thomas' spiritual conquest. The ambivalent guilt of the Chorus Women is dramatised through the classical images of reversal which bring home the full import of their psychic movements. At first they are simply the poor Women of Canterbury, immersed in the routine of existence and fearful lest anything should occur to upset that routine. John Peter observes:

> It is in terms of the modification of this attitude that much of the significance of the 'murder' is embodied and expressed. Salvation is presented . . . by showing it operating in the consciousness of the Chorus.[140]

The play opens with the Chorus Women emphasising their own impotence by speaking of their limbs and organs as if they were out of their direct control:

---

139. *Murder in the Cathedral* (Delhi: Oxford University Press, 1963), p. 52. All subsequent citations are from this edition.
140. Clarke, Graham, ed., *T. S. Eliot: Critical Assessments*, Volume III (London: Christopher Helm, 1990), p. 515.

> Some presage of an act
> Which our eyes are compelled to witness,
> Has forced our feet towards the cathedral.[141]

The Chorus becomes increasingly aware that experience is the doorway of hell, and as the murderers move closer, the Women of Canterbury are haunted by images of beasts of prey, filth and corruption. Grover Smith regards the zoological imagery as reflecting the guilt and corruption of the Chorus Women:

> Perhaps the most prominent imagery is zoological; it has two purposes, to characterize the murderers, in which application it joins with the imagery of sensation, and to associate the passive Chorus with unredeemed, elemental nature. But not less important is the imagery of nature in wider aspects — the cycles of day and night, summer and winter, spring and autumn; these identify the Chorus with the great turning wheel of creation and corruption, growth and ruin.[142]

There is an undercurrent of sexual imagery, often springing up in the Choruses. The antithesis between violence and passivity becomes one between male and female. The Women see the intrusion of Becket's struggle as a disturbance, a strain. They want to be let alone. They speak of 'births, deaths and marriages,' of girls who 'have disappeared/Unaccountably, and some not able to,' of 'private terrors' and 'secret fears.'[143] The images, by conveying suffering through guilt, also become psychological images. Gradually, as Becket's destiny, their doom as they regard it, becomes perspicuous, the terrors increase until in the last chorus of Part I they have heightened their imagery to the point of speaking of 'oppression and torture,' 'extortion and violence,' 'Our labour taken away from us,/Our sins made heavier upon

---
141. *Murder in the Cathedral*, p. 23.
142. Smith, Grover, *T. S. Eliot's Poetry and Plays: A Study in Sources and Meaning*, p. 191.
143. *Murder in the Cathedral*, p. 51.

us,' 'the young man mutilated,/ The torn girl trembling by the mill-stream.' And at this juncture they begin to name the beasts—leopard, bear, ape, hyena—the 'Lords of Hell'. They 'know and do not know', for they feel the danger but mistake where safety lies:

> God is leaving us, God is leaving us,
> More pang, more pain, than birth or death.
> Sweet and cloying through the dark air
> Falls the stifling sense of despair;
> The forms take shape in the dark air:
> Puss-purr of leopard, footfall of padding bear . . .
> The Lords of Hell are here.[144]

Animal images are used here to produce a general terror to give a sense of the unnatural. It is a moment of crisis.

As the play lengthens toward its *denouement* (after the opening chorus of Part II, where the Women balance against the retrospective autumnal imagery of the start of the play an imagery that looks to the coming spring, still buried in winter) they reach the extremity of having to accept an overt embrace of the bestial. In the extraordinarily moving passage just after Becket's first wrangle with the Knights, they acknowledge that death has violated them through every sense—smell, hearing, taste, touch, and sight— whereby they have known, almost in the intimacy of beast with beast, the creatures of the earth and sea. This sensation of suffering, this identification of guilt, finds unequivocally sexual language when the women succumb to 'the shamed swoon/Of those consenting to the last humiliation,' subdued, violated, mastered, 'Dominated by the lust of self-demolition . . ./By the final ecstasy of waste and shame.' The Chorus, when it resumes, faces the dread of being 'fully united for ever, nothing with nothing', of being no longer human, of being cast out into the void behind the judgment. Between Becket's submission to the

---
144. Ibid., p. 52.

acts of his murderers and the anguish of the Women's resignation to the Divine will, of which the Knights are sinful instruments, this astounding imagery stands as a precise symbol of both. The passion of the Women comes later in Part I than the consent already ordaining Becket's tribulation; here in Part II, however, their spasm of suffering leaves him behind, and they have died in will before his blood spouts under the sword.

As the murderers hack at Becket's skull, the Women chant a tormented prayer for cleansing, for purification from defilement. Recalling that they did not wish anything to 'happen', they utter a cry of dread at the unimaginable 'instant eternity of evil and wrong' by which they are soiled, 'united forever to supernatural vermin',

> It is not we alone, it is not the house, it is not the city that is defiled,
> But the world that is wholly foul.[145]

Nature itself, as at the moment of Adam's fall from paradise, becomes contaminated by the Knights' re-enactment of the Primal Sin. They identify themselves with a whole world of groaning and wailing. The images of suffering springing from the monstrous act, they are about to witness, are an expression of the universal malice and corruption, which it is man's burden and glory to be conscious of. Helen Gardner observes in *The Art of T.S. Eliot*:

> We identify ourselves with the Women of the Chorus; their experience communicates itself to us, and gives us the feeling we have not been spectators but sharers in a mystery. We live through a 'Peripeteia', we experience a great discovery. We pass with them through horror, out of boredom, into glory.[146]

---

145. *Murder in the Cathedral*, p. 83.
146. Gardner, Helen, *The Art of T. S. Eliot*, pp. 137–138.

The sequence of events that concludes the play, beginning with the moment the Knights attack Thomas in the cathedral, testifies to the Chorus Women's share in the guilt of murder. Thomas cries out at length, and the murder continues throughout the entire chorus which begins, 'Clear the air! Clean the sky! Wash the wind! Take stone from stone and wash them.' The drunken Knights, then, hack Thomas to death, while the Chorus chants in terror. Beyond the insistent terror of the act itself there is further effect of juxtaposition achieved between the murder and the action of the Chorus. Properly acted, the choral text suggests that in its terror the Chorus is somehow egging the murderers on, that the continuing blows of the Knights are accomplishing what the violent, physical, heavily accented cries for purgation call for: 'Clear the air! Clean the sky!' The chorus brings to a flooding climax the ambivalent current of fear that has haunted the Women of Canterbury from the opening scene—attraction toward Thomas and a powerful aversion from him, fear for and of the martyr. The murder is felt not only as a protracted physical horror but as an action in which the Chorus has participated.

But to the Women, Becket has spoken earlier of the reconciling joy that shall replace their pain:

> Peace, and be at peace with your thoughts and visions.
> These things had to come to you and you to accept them.
> This is your share of the eternal burden,
> The perpetual glory. This is one moment,
> But know that another
> Shall pierce you with a sudden painful joy
> When the figure of God's purpose is made complete.[147]

The lines are reminiscent of the Chorus in Aeschylus' Agamemnon which expressed similar hope of wisdom through suffering:

---

147. *Murder in the Cathedral*, p. 75.

> Men shall learn wisdom, by affliction schooled
> In visions of the night, like dropping rain,
> Descend the many memories of pain
> Before the spirit's sight: through tear and dole
> Comes wisdom o'er the unwilling soul —
> A boon, I wot, of all Divinity.

The birth of peace is to follow the ravishment of will; a sword has pierced their hearts only that death may give life, as Becket knows it must. It is in obedience to his own words that the doors have been opened to the eruption of merciless force.

With the prospect of assured beatitude, recompense, redemption of time, the Women raise their voices once more at the end of the play in a 'Te Deum' beyond resignation. They have learned that all things, and even their loss, are for the Divine glory and that even in denial there is affirmation. Yet not only in 'both the hunters and the hunted' is the glory manifested, but in both resides the guilt of Primal Sin: in those who act and in those who suffer. The song of praise, therefore, which has acclaimed the goodness of creatures that a little earlier would have symbolised bestiality, ends with a supplication for personal forgiveness. The Women assume the burden disclaimed by the Knights. This paradox that the Knights should have affirmed by denying and that the Chorus should have denied by affirming is but contributory to the more central paradox of the wheel turning and remaining still. Now at the price of humility all is appeased and adjusted. Catharsis is complete.

The dramatic action of *The Family Reunion* consists in Harry's liberation from his sense of guilt and defilement, from his imprisonment in a private, curse-haunted and intolerable universe. He is, like the Women of Canterbury, haunted by a sense of latent evil hiding behind his life. His wife has drowned at sea, and he says that he pushed her overboard but nobody believes him. He says that he can express his feelings only in symbols of guilt. The imagery, therefore, is designed largely to support Harry's nightmarish impressions and his subsequent insight.

Harry's liberation is gradual and progressive. The first stage is one of utter despair, when Harry, looking through the window on to the assembled family party, realises that the release he hoped for is not there. The imagery of smell shortly after the opening of the play is significant. Harry tells the members of his family that he is alienated from them because they do not share his awareness of evil and guilt:

> . . . I tell you, life would be unendurable If you were wide awake.
> You do not know
> The noxious smell untraceable in the drains,
> Inaccessible to the plumbers, that has its hour of the night;
> You do not know
> The unspoken voice of sorrow in the ancient bedroom
> At three o'clock in the morning. I am not speaking
> Of my own experience, but trying to give you
> Comparisons in a more familiar medium. I am the old house
> With the noxious smell and the sorrow before morning,
> In which all past is present, all degradation
> Is unredeemable.[148]

Here, for the first time, Harry 'sees' his pursuers, the Eumenides as objective presence: 'Can't you see them? You don't see them, but I see them, and they see me'. This is a paraphrase of Orestes' cry at the end of *Choephori*. The Eumenides are only dark shadows to Harry before he has diagnosed his own malady; as soon as he does so they become 'the bright angels'.

Eliot has employed the images of light and darkness beautifully. Light and warmth have been associated with pleasure, comfort, spiritual enlightenment and purgation symbolised by 'the bright angels' after Harry's awakening.

---
148. *The Family Reunion* (Delhi: Oxford University Press, 1963), p. 82.

And darkness and cold have been associated with guilt, despair, misery, spiritual confusion, Hell.

The play, which opens with the shades of darkness closing in upon the quiet country house of the Monchenseys and closes with Agatha and Mary gyrating round the birthday cake, blowing out its lighted candles, 'so that their last words are spoken in the dark', employs the images effectively.

Images of disease and filth in *The Family Reunion* indicate symbolically what is rotten in the house of Monchenseys. Harry calls his sense of guilt 'the cancer / That eats away the self'.[149] He hopes to 'clean my skin / Purify my life . . ./ But always the filthiness, that lies a little deeper'[150]. He further objectifies his feelings by talking of stench and contamination, of 'the slow stain', 'Tainting the flesh and discoloring the bone'[151]. His guilt is so overwhelming that he describes himself in the scene with Agatha as having been moving, 'In and out, in an endless drift / of Shrieking forms in a circular desert'.[152] He describes his sense of damnation as 'The sudden solitude in a crowded desert / In a thick smoke . . .'[153] This is but a different picture of Agatha's insight into the same experience in her own earlier life, 'Up and down, through the stone passages of an immense and empty hospital'.[154]

The desert and hospital are the images of temptation, guilt, solitude, persecution and godlessness. After the dastardly murder of Becket, the Chorus in *Murder in the Cathedral* wanders 'in a land of dry stones'. One of the possibilities open before Harry after he has come to terms with the Eumenides is 'the worship in the desert'. For as Agatha (not Harry) has already learned that within the

---

149. *The Family Reunion, p. 84.*
150. Ibid., p. 138.
151. Ibid., p. 83.
152. Ibid., p. 151.
153. Ibid., p. 82.
154. Ibid., p. 151.

insane hell of solitude and despair exists, in potentiality, a state of reconciliation, of transcendence, and that suffering is the means for its attainment.

The world of spiritual peace can be reached only after an arduous journey, which indicates self-discipline, suffering and penance. Harry is encouraged to undertake such a 'journey' by Agatha who is his spiritual preceptor; she is a kind of analyst who helps Harry to discover in his loveless relation to his parents the reasons for the failure of his marriage, and to rid himself, therefore, of his obsessive feeling of guilt. Agatha explains:

> It is possible that you have not known what sin
> You shall expiate, or whose, or why. It is certain
> That the knowledge of it must precede the expiation.
> It is possible that sin may strain and struggle
> In its dark instinctive birth, to come to consciousness
> And so find expurgation. It is possible
> You are the consciousness of your unhappy family,
> Its bird sent flying though the purgatorial flame.
> Indeed it is possible.[155]

> Harry answers:
> Look, I do not know why,
> I feel happy for a moment, as if I had come home . . .
> The things I thought were real are shadows, and the real
> are what I thought were private shadows
> O that awful privacy
> Of the insane mind! Now I can live in public. Liberty is
> different kind of pain from prison.[156]

When Harry hears of those summer months when his father plotted to murder his mother, while Agatha thought of him as her child coming to birth, his obsession becomes 'true in a different sense' and slips from him. At this juncture, the rose garden image is used to symbolise transcendence both for Harry and Agatha, since 'it is a

---
155. *Ibid., p. 148.*
156. Ibid., pp. 149-150.

Classical Images

common pursuit of liberation': 'I only looked through the little door/when the sun was shining on the rose-garden'.[157]

Harry's liberation has commenced; he has come out into the light under the eye of God or conscience that gives final judgment; he feels himself cleansed by knowledge, as a body is cleansed by vomiting or excretion (evacuation). He is in a state of excitement in which he cannot be explicit, and can only think in images:

> The chain breaks,
> The wheel stops, and the noise of machinery,
> And the desert is cleared, under the judicial sun
> Of the final eye, and the awful evacuation
> Cleanses. . . .
> O my dear, and you walked through the little door
> And I ran to meet you in the rose-garden. [158]

The 'rose-garden' image symbolises a mystical moment which follows Agatha's confession of love and renunciation. It has opened Harry's eyes to the reality that the 'he' and 'she' which had passed through the hells described now seem mere phantasms (semblance) of their true selves. But now the chains are broken and the prisoners are free. They run towards each other, almost like lovers in this new-found intimacy. The wilderness becomes the rose-garden in preparation for the second visit of the Eumenides, when the Avengers become the Bright Angels. They are no longer Furies of their first appearance (which was to call him back to recognition of his sin). The Eumenides are not images or projections of Harry's sense of guilt, any more than the sin he has to expiate is an unreal sin. The sin remains: it is his birth sin, the 'sin where he began, which is his sin, though it was done before'. Conceived and brought forth in hatred, not in love, he bears the sins of his parents, at once their victim and their perpetuator for he has been incapable of love. Agatha, by showing him

---
157. *The Family Reunion*, p. 150.
158. Ibid., p. 151.

the nature of love, has transformed 'wilderness' into 'rose-garden', 'furies' into 'Bright Angels'. He now 'sees' that he must pursue these 'Bright Angels', that he cannot escape the guilt they symbolise but must accept it as the basis of a wider understanding. He must think, not 'there they are', but 'here they are', The Furies, like Becket's Fourth Temptation, are really a gift of grace. They are hounds of heaven. They will lead him to an unknown destiny.

Thus, each of Eliot's protagonists, like classical characters, is not a deliberate sinner; 'sinless in my crime' as Antigone tells her sister. Guilt and crime may be unwitting, but punishment is deliberate. It is a painful progress toward enlightenment and transcendence.

II. Mythical Images and Motifs

Eliot's approach to art rests on his conviction that literary tradition is the life and blood of art. The Greek tragedians also drew predominantly on literary sources, on myths about the distant heroic age of Greece. But it was not just a repository of myths. There was limitless variation. Each myth was subjected to innovative treatment. What matters, for the dramatist and his audience, is the way he has shaped the story, the way he has turned it into drama. Eliot has been under the influence of the Greek practice of mythical methods and their tendency to perceive myths and rituals as potential means of ordering and transforming contemporary experience into significance. The very title of his review in *The Dial* of Joyce's *Ulysses* makes the point: 'Ulysses, Order and Myth'[159]. He sets out to answer the challenge of the readers who saw Ulysses as 'an invitation to chaos; an expression of feelings which are perverse, partial and a distortion of reality'. Eliot, in answer to this, calls the work 'classical' and complains that people have underestimated the importance of the *Odyssey* as a parallel structural device: 'In using the myth, in manipulating a

---

159. Eliot, T. S., 'Ulysses, Order and Myth', *The Dial* (1923), pp. 480–483.

continuous parallel between contemporaneity and antiquity, Mr. Joyce is pursuing a method which others must pursue after him'.[160] He observes that 'it is simply a way of controlling, of ordering, of giving a shape and a significance to the immense panorama of futility and anarchy which is contemporary history'.[161] Eliot's own technique for presenting the 'immense panorama' is different from Joyce's. By compression and allusion, he condenses it, where Joyce expands the moment almost to infinitude, but both resort, like classical masters, to a back-cloth of mythical images to hold their material in a shape

In *Prufrock*, the private hell of the protagonist gains significance when associated with the myth of Dante's visit to Hell with Vergil. The epigraph from Dante's *Inferno* relates that Dante, allowed to visit Hell in the company of Vergil, has come upon the spirit of Count Guido de Montefeltro encased in a tongue-like flame for the sin of fraud through evil counsel. He replies to Dante's question about his identity:

> If I thought my answer were to one who ever could return to the
> World, this flame should shake no more;
> But since no one ever did return alive from this depth, if what
> I hear be true, without fear of infamy I answer thee.

His crime has been to pervert human reason by guile; like Ulysses, he is wrapped in a flame representing his duplicity in his former life, when he knew and practiced 'wiles and covert ways'. This reply is applicable to Prufrock's own life. He, like Guido, is in hell, though, unlike Guido, he has never participated in the active evil of the world, so that this resemblance is as ironic as the resemblance to Hamlet. But Prufrock is similar to Guido in having abused intellect; he has done so by channelising it into profitless fantasy.

---
160. Ibid., pp. 480–483.
161. Ibid.

The image of Guido's hell expands the context of Prufrock's frustration. The mythical images of 'John the Baptist' ('I am no prophet'), the 'eternal footman' and 'Lazarus', suggest an order of things vaster than Prufrock's pitiably enclosed universe. The images also present Prufrock as the mere fool of banalities whose wit is so easily diminished by the mere reflection of what one might say. So like Guido, Prufrock's hell is to be enclosed in the flame of self knowledge or, perhaps, the lack of it. He believes, having abandoned hope, that he has no way out. His psychological plight reveals itself in the identification of both the positive and negative elements of his conflict with images of the sea, primordial symbols of both creation and destruction

La Figlia Che Piange finds a way out of these failures (the related failures of *Prufrock* and the young man of *Portrait*) in the examples of Dante, and of Vergil, Dante's guide. The epigraph is from Aeneas' meeting with Venus near Carthage: she appears disguised as a maid of the country, and only reveals her divinity as she leaves him. That meeting is echoed in his later encounter with Dido in Hades; his duty to found Rome has compelled him to leave her, renouncing her love; now she turns from him coldly, disdaining his regrets. The title may echo *Inferno* 126; and in any case the whole poem gains from a comparison with that most moving meeting with Francesca who could not constrain desire, and is forever bound to her lover in the wind of Hell. Then there is a positive general relation with the visions and separations of the *Vita Nuova*, and the meetings with Matilda and Beatrice in the Earthly Paradise at the summit of Purgatory. The common meaning which the poem draws from these images and allusions is that the passion for an ideal can be fulfilled only by passing through and going beyond the immediate occasions of love.

All the finest poems in the 1920 volume are concerned with the dramatic opposition of the world of today to the sources of vitality and order from which it is now cut off and of which it has the most urgent need.

In *Sweeney among the Nightingales* the emphasis is upon the distinction between two atmospheres, two attitudes towards reality. After the setting of the first two verses the drama sweeps in one long sentence of descriptive vision to the climax which links Agamemnon with the contemporary scene. That, and the epigraph from Aeschylus, 'Alas, I have been smitten deep with a mortal blow', lead us to seek a parallel in the action between the murder of Agamemnon and the scene in the poem. But it seems more characteristic that the relationship should be symbolic; that it is everything that Agamemnon and his story (and myth in general) stands for, that has been killed by Sweeney and his like.

The link between the two worlds, that of myth and of the immediate actuality, are the nightingales. They are present in both, but Sweeney and his companions do not hear them. They are as deaf to their song as to the story behind the song; it is a horrible story of cruelty and revenge, just as the Agamemnon myth is, and the story of the 'bloody wood'. Here Eliot is using a favourite device of his: the telescoping of associations of mythical images to get greater intensity. Agamemnon, after all, was not killed in a wood. The wood is that from which Frazer named his great work *The Golden Bough,* and from which Eliot took the title for his first essay, *The Sacred Wood,* where he uses it as symbol for the immortal poetic tradition, always dying and being reborn. The opening chapter of Frazer's book traces the story of the wood of Nemi, which was the scene of the bloody ritual by which the old priest of the grove was slain by a younger one, who succeeded as both priest and king until he in turn was slain. Frazer shows how this ritual is the basis for all the oldest symbols of the concept of the fertility god and his resurrection every spring, and extended in to the larger theme of the death and resurrection of the human spirit. Eliot's purpose is to emphasise that pattern. Philomel is raped, but magical powers render her voice inviolable and immortal. It lives on in a bird, linking together man and nature, the animal and the spiritual. Agamemnon is murdered, Clytemnestra is murdered, and Orestes is pursued by the Furies, but the end of the trilogy is the transcendence of revenge by reconciliation and mercy. All these stories create a pattern of reality which gives meaning to human hate and horror, sacrifice and suffering, because they are related to an order and value beyond the temporal and immediate.

> In the words of David Ward (*T. S. Eliot: Between Two Worlds*): The basic ironic contrasts of the poem *Sweeney among the Nightingales* are those between the suggestions of the significance of life seen in such terms of value and order and the complete insignificance of the modern scene.

These people have not even vitality to have violent passions of any sort. Their 'murderous paws' tear only grapes; their sexual passion is that of a drunken prostitute trying to sit on Sweeney's knees; the outcome of the assault is only to pull off a tablecloth and overturn a coffee-cup. They move in the clearest pictorial outline, but there is no point at which the images suggest organic relationship with the worlds of spiritual value, of nature, or of human fellowship, no point at which they touch the patterns suggested by the worlds of classical myth, of heroic tragedy, or of the convent. They are indeed barely human. They are largely designated in animal terms, and thus dehumanised, and as men and women they have neither identity nor community. They do not even speak. Sweeney himself is simply a laugh in a body which otherwise suggests an ape, a zebra or a giraffe. In the images of gesture also, Eliot suggests the disintegrated quality of life they symbolise. They 'sprawl', they 'gape', they show 'fatigue'. The woman 'slips' in her tipsy efforts to seduce Sweeney: even her reorganization' upon the floor is only to yawn and pull up a stocking, and is an ironic comment on the concept of organisation. The mythical images joined with contemporary associations, thus, underline the deathless reality of the eternal and the

Classical Images

sordid face of the temporal. The stormy moon is blurred; it 'slides' to its setting towards the shallowest of rivers with the ominous 'drift' of doom about it. All the myths linking man and the heavens and the gods and so drawing them all into one pattern, are 'veiled'. The sea itself, symbol of life, is 'hushed' and 'shrunken'. The images of the convent, the nightingales, the wood and the memory of the dead Agamemnon bring out the relationship of man and nature, mortality and immortality, death and resurrection, the temporal and the eternal, nature and spirit.

In *The Waste Land*, Eliot has used material from Frazer's cultivation rituals and Jessie L. Weston's Fisher King and Grail myths. He confesses to having been influenced by James Frazer's *The Golden Bough* (1922) and Jessie L. Weston's book *From Ritual to Romance* (1920). The Fisher King of Miss Weston, the barrenness and sterility and the quest for the Holy Grail acquire a new aesthetic dimension when reflected through the conceptual images of Eliot. The symbolic meaning of the mythical associations with the modern world can be comprehended through the epigraph [a prose original] which has been versified by D. G. Rosetti as follows:

> 'I saw the
> Sybil at Cumae'
> (one said) with mine own eye.
> She hung in a cage, and read her rune
> To all the passers-by.
> Said the boys, 'What wouldst thou, Sibyl?'
> She answered 'I would die'.[162]

The Sibyl of Cumae was a classical prophetess who, besides being the guardian of a sacred cave from which she delivered oracles, was a gatekeeper of the underworld, as in the *Aeneid*. Aeneas' descent into hell by way of a cavern can be identified with the initiation ordeal to which novices were subjected in the mystery cults. The trials of

---
162. Rossetti, D. G., *Works* (London: 1911), p. 240.

spiritual initiation included a progress through a cavern, labyrinth, or maze. Natural or artificial labyrinth is the central image, both in the myths and *The Waste Land*, of spiritual initiation. Candidates descended and had a combat with death; that is, 'they were led through labyrinthine wanderings, and afterwards were permitted to return, as of boon again, to the light of day'.[163] A labyrinth is actually mentioned in Vergil's description of the 'temple of Daedalus', which stands outside the Sibyl's cave. In Eliot's *The Cocktail Party* the image occurs along with the desert, the symbol of spiritual trial. An 'archetypal' pattern of descent and ascent is symbolised in the *Aeneid* not only by the episode of the Sibyl but by the entire quest of Aeneas from Troy to Italy. The ocean-voyage pattern of the hero myth, thus, accompanies and dominates the narrower detail of his visit to hell and serves to unify the themes of sea-trial and grave-trial, necessary for symbolic rebirth. So the image of labyrinth and Sibyl in the epigraph unifies all the mythical symbols of initiation, spiritual trial, death and rebirth, sterility and fertility. As Alfred Nutt remarks:

> Since *The Waste Land* employs the primordial imagery of death and rebirth in accordance with the Grail legend, the Sibyl belongs to the machinery of initiation in the poem; appearing in one of the Grail romances, she links the medieval legend to classical myth.[164]

But her misfortune to be shut in a cage and to wither away indefinitely, being preserved from death but condemned like Tithonus to grow old, symbolises the motif of the waste land. The feminine power which should enable the protagonist to complete his quest for initiation cannot do so, and Tiresias himself, whom success would benefit, remains blind and impotent. The failure, however, is owning to him, so that the Sibyl and the

---

163. Frazer, Sir James, *The Golden Bough*, 3rd ed., (London: 1906-15), IV, p. 75–77.
164. *Nutt, Alfred, Studies on the Legend of the Holy Grail (London, 1888), p. 28.*

people in the poem itself are victims of his weakness. The Sibyl here is the image of death-in-life because the land is dead, and it is dead because Tiresias, the Fisher king, has been wounded and has not achieved, in the person of the quester, the goal of the quest. The Sibyl (Madame Sosostris), the youthful Grail-bearer (the hyacinth girl), the quester (variously characterised, for example, 'the young man Carbuncular'), and the Fisher King embody facets of the one personality struggling to attain salvation. It is a spiritual quest undertaken by classical and mythical figures reflected in and identified with contemporary protagonists, exhibiting similar psychic complexes and aspirations.

The Waste Land summarises the Grail legend, not precisely in the usual order, but 'retaining the principal images and adapting them to a modern setting'. [165] Identification of the Grail-story with the common myth of the hero assailing a devil-dragon underground or in the depths of the sea completes the unifying idea behind *The Waste Land*. The Grail legend corresponds to the classical hero epics; it dramatises initiation into maturity, and it bespeaks a quest for sexual, cultural, and spiritual healing. Through all these attributed functions, it influenced Eliot's symbolism.

In the myths Miss Weston deals in her book, the land is under a curse and the Fisher king, the lord of the land, is either maimed or rather rendered impotent. Eliot effects an easy transmogrification of the perspectives of the myth and the images reflect a transition from the physical to the spiritual plane: 'April is the cruelest month, breeding / Lilacs out of the dead land'; 'what are the roots that clutch, what branches grow / Out of the stony rubbish?'; 'A heap of broken images, where the sun beats / And the dead tree gives no shelter, the cricket no relief.' Through such images it is possible to see the waste land as a metaphoric internal landscape of the mind as well as an external imagistic projection of a dead land.

---

165. Nuhn, Ferner, *The Wind Blew from the East* (New York and London: 1942), p. 221.

This perception is made intrinsic in the sustained imagery of eyes and seeing within the poem. All the paradoxical possibilities of perception, seeing and knowing, earthly and spiritual sight are explored. The subsuming Tiresias, seer though blind, 'can see' and is an instance of the mysterious transformation of eyes into pearls; his loss of earthly sight being compensated by prophetic vision. The images of 'sight' springing from the classical and mythical figure of Tiresias traverse to the prophet Ezekiel who will 'show' fear to man, through dust, the visible symbol of mortality. The lover in the hyacinth garden is not the only one whose eyes 'fail'; Madame Sosostris, the phoney prophetess, is forbidden to see into mysteries: 'I do not find / The Hanged man.' The crowd avoids seeing: 'And each man fixed his eyes before his feet.' Belladonna's flirtatious cupidon 'hid his eyes behind his wing', and her own eyes are cheated by the delusions of art so that she cries to her lover: 'You know nothing? Do you see nothing?' And what he remembers is the tag of visual transformation: 'Those are the pearls that were his eyes.'

The poem's women look vainly or indifferently at their own reflection, seeing nothing; 'Her brain allows one half-formed thought to pass' and in the last section, actual sight can no longer be distinguished from what is either vision or hallucination,' 'who is the third who walks always beside you', and the 'doors of perception' are broken as part of a total dissolution of the mind. The whole 'experience' in the poem, then, is born out of the myth of Fisher King and the images contain, through Tiresias' observations, many apprehensions of the vision of desolation and aridity.

The aridity in the waste land is symbolic of perverted natural rhythms. From the moment of the distortion of natural attitudes to season, April cruel and winter kind, the images suggest that man can no longer expect a natural restoration of lost vitality, erotic or spiritual. We remember *Gerontion* which Eliot once intended as a preface to *The Waste Land*:

> I have lost my sight, smell, hearing, taste and touch:
> How should I use them for your closer contact?

In *The Waste Land*, the loss of natural vitality is not dependent on old age; it is part of the blight of youth. The quest for rain, symbol of natural growth, is doomed from the beginning in such a world. The river is symbolically polluted by civilisations whose vitality cannot be restored merely by natural means. There is a suggestion of this loss in the recurrent images of rain and water. Marie, who sheltered summer rain in the colonnade and 'reads much of the night' and goes 'south in winter' represents the aristocratic boredom and insomnia, even madness. In the case of Belladonna, the futility of the quest for rain is made explicit. She and her lover reiterate their stale routine:

> The hot water at ten
> And if it rains, a closed car at four.

If the rain falls, they will be protected. Lil's perversion of nature is more drastic. The abortion pills have aged her prematurely and drained her of all vitality. Although water is the principal symbol in Jessie L. Weston's life cults as 'the freeing of the waters', here the image is always overshadowed by the threat of the waste land itself, as in the Ganga passage. Therefore, when water is absent, it is strongly desired. It is lamented that amongst the dry stones there is 'no sound of water' and later in the last desert extremity, the marvellously conjured aural mirage of water intensifies this craving:

> It there were rock
> And also water
> And water
> A spring
> A pool among the rock
> If there were the sound of water only.
> Drip drop drip drop drop drop drop.

The images suggest parched longing which, through the association of rock and water, alluding to Moses' smiting of the rock in the desert to bring forth waters of salvation, is of spiritual as well as physical significance. The poem's moments of nearly missed ecstasy are associated with moisture. Marie in the mountain snows, the Hyacinth girl with her wet hair and the very succulent lushness of her flowers are contributing as much to their sexual symbolism as the allusion to the Hyacinth myth.

The sapped vitality of these inhabitants of the waste land is reflected in the mythical figure of Tiresias whose perception provides the overall framework for the poem's parallels with its source myths. As the framed observer within the poem, Tiresias declares his identity and refers to his own bi-sexual nature:

> I Tiresias, though blind, throbbing between two lives,
> Old man with wrinkled female breasts, can see.

Tiresias' bi-sexuality corresponds to the sterile state of the Fisher King and the aridity of the land in terms of the perversion of nature. He adds to his prophetic vision a historical perspective: 'I who have sat by Thebes below the wall and walked among the lowest of the dead'.

He recognises an eternal archetype of living death in the waste land, because the same act was to be seen in Thebes where Tiresias had seen and fore suffered the blind sexual pollution of Oedipus. It has been re-enacted through history, by Dido, Cleopatra and Elizabeth I whose gorgeous trappings have not blinded the prophet to the essence of their acts. Tiresias sees too that it is the anti-thesis of the fertile ecstatic love-encounter which all lovers have sought and which, in the Grail myths, precedes spiritual initiation. But his inward sight gives him a comprehensive despair rather than knowledge which he can use. Ironically, he, and we through him, will recognise parallels with the sanctified Grail situation.

Classical Images

The chief images of 'A game of Chess'—the sexual violation, the fiery hair, the chess game and the blindness, as well as the silence—are all consonant with the Grail legend or other fertility myths. The fiery points of the woman's hair present a Medusa-like contrast to the wet hair of the hyacinth girl; fire here is a symbol of lust; water, of love. The game of chess, likewise, is an image taken from the Grail romances where the hero occasionally visits a chess board castle and meets a water-maiden. In addition, chess has often been a symbol of man's life and government in the world. So we may detect in Eliot's use of the image a suggestion that the people in the waste land belong to a drama they do not understand, where they move like chessmen toward destination they cannot force.

Through Tiresias' perceptions, the mind responds to the intricate range of thematic links formed through mythical images and echoes. A subtle echo of this process comes in the nightmare sequence of the falling towers and 'unreal' cities which shatter and crumble before the thunder speaks. Many images of this nightmare recall those endured traditionally by the questers at the Chapel Perilous, in particular a curious half-light, the sounds of lamentation, and the visions of death, a meeting with a woman and the finding of a belfry. The sudden close-up which follows the fall of the distant cities contains such images:

> A woman drew her long black hair out tight
> And fiddled whisper music on those strings
> And bats with baby faces in the violet light
> Whistled, and beat their wings
> And crawled head downward down a blackened wall
> And upside down in air were towers
> Tolling reminiscent bells.

The image of 'the long black hair' drawn out tight sends us back to the woman in 'A Game of Chess', her nerves now cracked into madness. There, her hair was 'spread out in fiery points', and there too it was made as if to speak: 'Glowed into words, they would be savagely still'. The savagery is now fulfilled in mad music. Then, she had neurotically threatened to rush out into the street 'with my hair down, so', hair dry and fiery with the frustration of love, sharply contrasted with the life-promising Hyacinth girl. 'Your arms full and your hair wet'. And somewhere between the two, indifferent, neither dry, nor lush and wet, is the hair of the typist who, looking momentarily into a glass, just as Belladonna gazed into hers: 'smoothes her hair with automatic hand'.

It is significant that the mad music is played upon female hair, the sustained image offering the theme of thwarted or perverted love which all these women exemplify. Only bats have 'baby' faces in the whole poem, there is no 'laughter of children among leaves', and the bats' upside downiness reminds us of Lil's despairing perversion of birth through abortion. Moreover, the upside-down vision of falling towers—even the Grail belfry is inverted like a reflection in water—takes us back to the visual imagery of the lady's boudoir:

> Doubled the flames of seven branched candelabra
> Reflecting light upon the table as
> The glitter of her jewels rose to meet it.

Everything in the boudoir is an example of man-made luxury, ornate to the point of decadence.

It is through recurrent images, such as hair, eyes, water which link these mythical episodes, that Eliot establishes the emotional and thematic unity of his apparently diverse fragments. Each image emphasises the leading motif of the Fisher King myth—the perversion of Nature and humanity.

When Eliot wrote *Murder in the Cathedral*, he said:

> I had the advantages for a beginner, of an occasion which called for a subject generally admitted to be suitable for verse. Verse plays, it has been generally held, should either take their subject matter from some mythology, else should

be about some remote historical period, far enough away from the present characters not to need to be recognizable as human beings, and therefore for them to be licensed to talk in verse.[166]

So Eliot drew not only from historical events but also from myths.

Murder in the Cathedral is built around the Christian myth of fall and regeneration symbolised by Christ and Adam. Atonement is symbolised by Becket. As martyr in Part II, Becket is a type of Christ, who also suffers temptation before entering upon the drama of action through suffering. The Tempters are the images of whispering Adversary; as sinners and sufferers, the Women of Canterbury are images of fallen Adam, enacting the inward strife in imitation of Becket, who enacts it in imitation of Christ; and as persecutors, the Knights are images of Satan going to and fro on the earth and walking up and down in it. Becket, like Christ, is tested, slain, and exalted, not for his sin but for the sin of others. So Part I presents the motif of suffering, through Becket's decision not to act. Part II presents the motif of action, through Becket's suffering, the acts of others. Therefore, all the images in relation to the myth of fall and regeneration and the motif of action and suffering, turn out to be mythical images (besides being temporal, spatial and psychological) as well.

The 'murder', in the cathedral primarily is not a murder at all, but an act of redemption. This redemption is presented by showing it operating in the consciousness of the Chorus. At first they are passive sufferers. Then they prepare us for developments, rousing us, with their passionate dithyrambs, (like their equivalents in Greek tragedy), to participate in the emotional crises that arise. In this second role, they now speak of moments of vision 'in a shaft of sunlight' and it is in a flash of clairvoyance that their concluding apostrophe to December is made:

---

166. Hayward, John, ed., *T. S. Eliot: Selected Prose* (Harmondsworth: Penguin Books Ltd., 1953), p. 72.

Shall the son of Man be born again in the litter of scorn?

The image 'son of man' suggests the redemption which is in turn to be made possible through his martyrdom. But they know that the present is perilous and a change for the better hardly possible 'ill the wind, ill the time, uncertain the profit, certain the danger'. From the first touch of sharpness ('our brains unskinned like the layers of an onion') the intensity of their foreboding increases. The image of croaking ('like frogs in the treetops'), used by the second Priest to reprove them, suggests their role as sinners.

The Fourth Tempter also signifies Becket's role as a sinner rather than a martyr. Who are you, tempting one with my own desires? With the Tempter's retort ('you have often dreamt them') and Thomas' appeals to be freed from the damning weight of his pride, we reach the point where the Tempter quotes to Thomas his own words concerning action and suffering. This is a classical device to show how inextricably mixed Thomas' motives still remain. Now, however, tempter and tempted, Satan and Adam begin to merge. Thomas is no longer the vigilant custodian over his own mind but is involved in a tangle of motives which he himself can only partially analyse. Some external prompting (from Divine Power) is needed to help him to his final decision.

This comes, as it must from the Chorus, his spiritual dependents, with image after image in their speech suggesting an acute sense of horror and panic: 'The Forms take shape . . . / The Lords of Hell are here.'

It is with their last cry, identifying their own balance between hope and despair with his decision, that resolution breaks across his hesitancy. 'Now is my way clear . . .' Another 'Christ' is ready for atonement of the sins of others for salvation.

Part II again opens with a chorus. First there is the sea-bird 'driven inland', convenient image for the Chorus — 'Innocent Adam', driven from their wonted security. Then there is a mention of a spring which is more like death than birth, an image for death-in-life. There is insistence on the unnaturalness of the season.

Just as Tennyson adopted the myth of a violent storm after the murder in his *Becket*, Eliot also gives the mythical storm a symbolic treatment through the Chorus' frantic cry beginning 'Clean the air' and containing the words 'A rain of blood has blinded my eye.' Along with the symbol of rain Eliot introduces the image of bleeding boughs, taken from II *ESDRAS* 5:5 'And blood shall drop out of wood, and the stone shall give his voice, and the people shall be troubled.' Afterwards, in the last speech of the Third Priest, he avails himself of the myth of the murderers' ultimate doom to exile, shipwreck, and death among the infidels. Thus the mythical images throw a new light on the motif of action and suffering, death and rebirth and provide a new perspective to the meaning of the play.

In *The Family Reunion*, the affinities with the *Oresteia* of Aeschylus seem to have suggested the purpose of the use of the Eumenides — the central mythical images in the play. The play has a modern story, which translates the myth of Orestes pursued by the Furies into terms of everyday life. The chain of guilt and retribution which began with the sacrifice of Iphigenia and ended with the absolution of Orestes is manifested anew in the chain of guilt which connects Harry's impulse to murder with his father's. Here too, as in the *Eumenides*, the suffering of the hero is not caused by personal guilt. Harry is expiating a family curse which started with the lack of love in his mother Amy who is presented as a modern and respectable Clytemnestra. Amy's coldness kills Harry's father, and shuts the prison on his son, who is deprived of his father's love and is made merely the instrument of his mother's steely determination to keep the family in being. Harry, by escaping the bondage of his mother, kills her. The mythical pattern is complete. The gaps are filled with the central images related to Euminides— the Furies.

Eliot, like O'Neill, in his trilogy *Mourning Becomes Electra* (1932), has used the myth in his own way and for his own purposes. Following Aeschylus and O'Neill, Eliot took a family curse with a double murder as his central image, and expiation at the end. Nevill Coghill remarks in his introduction commentary on the play:

> The myth was not resuscitated by Eliot for its historical interest, but to find a classic parallel to suit his own ideas of sin and expiation.

So the images related to the myth throw light on the symbolism of the Eumenides that makes sense not only with the *Oresteia* but also *The Family Reunion*. At the core of the significance of the Eumenides in ancient times lay the idea of a supernatural pursuit of vengeance for the sin of blood guilt, especially for matricide, foulest of all the crimes against blood and nature. The pursuers are thought of as female spirits, dwelling beneath the ground; though in Aeschylus they are a numberless Chorus, they are elsewhere generally identified with the Three Furies: Tisiphone, Megaera and Alecto, and even with a fourth figure Nemesis; there is a fifth called Adrasta, named by Plutarch as the daughter of Zeus and Necessity. The others have had various origins assigned to them. But all agree that they are the divine ministers or images of divine justice, inexorably stern and cruel in the pursuit of guilt and in its punishment. They are as horrifying in their nature and appearance. They punish foulness, but are foul themselves. Eliot has presented Eumenides as black and midnight hags, avengeresses of blood-guilt (the murder of a woman), that seem (to the fugitive Harry) to be foul themselves. This is the first element that Eliot has taken over from the classics for his own Eumenides.

The second element, that he has taken directly from Aeschylus, is their change of heart. In Aeschylus their hearts are changed, Orestes remains the same. In Eliot, they seem to change, at least in Harry's eyes who changes himself. They are images of Harry's psychic working and gradual conversion. As Helen Gardner remarks:

> They are purely symbols and have no dramatic life. They neither act nor speak, but simply appear or do not appear.[167]

In Aeschylus, the change in Eumenides is due to their being won over (by the promise of being honoured with altars and sacrifices in Athens), to being favourable to their worshippers there; no winds shall blow to wreck the olive groves, no civil wars shall rend the city. Grace shall be rendered for grace and love shall be the common will. These were the figures Eliot chose to be the images or the 'objective correlatives' of the spiritual forces set in motion by the curse of lovelessness transmitted from Amy and her husband, to Harry and his wife, with their attendant 'murders'.

From the very first moment of his entrance, Harry feels haunted and watched by his pursuers. He feels the reflection of his own contamination staring back at him through the eyes of the Eumenides. The imagery of the eye, therefore, is integrally related to the myth of the Eumenides and is in continual use in the course of the play:

> The eyes stared at me, and corrupted that song (I. i. 236)
> *   *   *   *
> I always see their claws distended (I. ii. 300)
> *   *   *   *
> The eye is on this house (I. iii. 108-9)
> The eye covers it (I. Iii. 108-9)
> *   *   *   *

---

167. Gardner, Helen, *The Art of T. S. Eliot*, p. 140.

> The degradation of being parted from myself,
> From the self which persisted only as an eye, seeing (II.
> Ii. 27)

*   *   *   *

Under the single eye above the desert (II. Ii. 200)

When Mary consoles him, Harry remarks:

> They are much too clever.
> To admit you into our world. Yours is no better.
> They have seen to that: it is part of the torment. (I. ii.
> 215-217)

He means that the spectres are too cunning and too evil to allow him the consolation of Mary's entering and sharing with him the nightmare world he shares with them. Apart from the 'eye' image, the trance-like ritual of mystifying mythical imagery seems to produce a chill feeling or spinal tremor in the audience at the presence of evil, supernatural manifestations.

There are three together. May the three be separated (I. iii. 109-110)

The 'three together' are the Eumenides (Alecto the Unresisting, Megaera the Jealous and Tisiphone the Avenger) taken directly from Aeschylus. Next images 'the knot that was tied' (line III) and 'the crossed bones' (113) are symbols for the family curse; 'the weasel and the otter' (116) seem to be symbols for the natural order disturbed by the supernatural. But soon the realisation follows:

> The things I thought were real are shadows, and the real
> Are what I thought were private shadows.
> O that awful
> Privacy of the insane mind ! Now I can live in public
> Liberty is a different kind of pain from prison.[168]

The conventions (like the pretence of family affection, the duty to maintain Wishwood, etc.) which Harry thought real, he now perceives to be shadows, things of no real

---
168. *The Family Reunion, pp. 149-150.*

importance, whereas the things he had thought to be his private fantasy (the Eumenides) he now sees to be a manifestation of reality itself. They are the embodiments of a spiritual world absolutely real, and not (as he had feared) symptoms of his personal insanity. Private phantoms (the sense of sin conveyed through the Eumenides) are the reality that can guide his life. This, though painful, is sanity and freedom. In the appearance of the Eumenides he has seen his purpose in life. They are there no longer to hound him, but to lead him; they are no longer foul, but bright. Harry has found in himself the strength to follow them.

In fact, right from the beginning there is a strong indication that terrible as they may appear, the Eumenides are there for Harry's good. Because only those who love Harry are privileged to see them: Mary, Agatha and Downing. Downing sees them even before Harry does (II. Iii. 244–246). On the Aeschylean plane of reference, Downing takes on the character of Pylades, the inseparable travelling companion of Orestes in the Oresteia. So the Eumenides are only images of Harry's mental transitions. They change when Harry changes. F. O. Mathiessen observes quoting Eliot's letter to Martin Browne:

> ... the furies are divine instruments, not simple hell-hounds ... and this gives the cue for the second appearance of the Furies, most patently in their role of divine messengers, to let him know clearly that the only way out is in purgation and holiness. They become exactly 'hounds of heaven'. And Agatha understands this
> clearly, though Harry only understands it yet in flashes...[169]

The Eumenides are driving Harry throughout on to the realisation that sin calls for expiation, so that at their second appearance, Harry greets them quietly.

And this time

---

169. Matthiessen, F. O., *The Achievement of T. S. Eliot: An Essay on the Nature of Poetry* (London: Oxford University Press, 1958), pp. 167–168.

> You cannot think that I am surprised to see you.
> And you shall not think that I am afraid to see you.
> This time, you are real, this time you are outside me,
> And just endurable. I know that you are ready,
> Ready to leave Wishwood, and I am going with you.[170]

He perceives them now as 'divine messengers': 'But lo, thou requires truth in the inward parts and shalt make me understand wisdom secretly'. Thus, the true meaning of the play, the conversion of Harry, is conveyed through the mythical images centring around the Eumenides. The myth makes the play an effort 'to reinterpret a theme of Greek tragedy in terms of a modern consciousness'.[171] As the chorus declares:

> And whether in Argos or in England
> There are certain inflexible laws
> Unalterable, in the nature of music.[172]

III. Ritualistic Images

The structural components of a Greek tragedy includes myths and rituals. Rituals are part of myths. Each Greek tragedy abounds in the ritualistic pattern of struggle, death, lament and rebirth of the 'year spirit', 'a pattern of fertility ritual which Gilbert Murray extended to Greek tragedy'.[173] Rituals are part of Eliot's imagistic design that he creates to express his meaning. In fact, Eliot was the first to reintroduce ritual element into modern theatre, and it plays a prominent part in his plays, especially in *The Rock, Murder in the Cathedral, The Family Reunion* and *The Cocktail Party*. The subtitle of his first attempt at a play called *Sweeney Agonistes* calls it, 'an Aristophanic Melodrama', and this points not only to its farcical elements but also to

---

170. *The Family Reunion*, p. 152.
171. Clarke, Graham, ed., *T. S. Eliot: Critical Assessments* (London: Christopher Helm, 1990), p. 549.
172. *The Family Reunion*, p. 142.
173. Segel, Graham, ed., *Oxford Readings in Greek Tragedy*, p. 3.

its ritual character. The ritual, in Aristophanes, aimed at a kind of magic to bring back the Spring. For just as a rooster believes he brings up the dawn by crowing, so humans have believed that their rituals could help to bring back their necessary sun, ejecting their darkness and guilt at the end of the year, and renewing their life with the return of Spring. Purgation and renewal are at the heart of Eliot's use of ritual. This makes 'ritual' a technical device in the formation and synthesis of structural elements, both of tragic and comic forms. For guilt in tragedy is transformed into a positive awareness of the universe and creation, only through the use of ritual. The ritual implications of Eliot's works can be comprehended in the light of F. M. Cornford's *Origins of Attic Comedy* in scholarly detail; Eliot is acquainted with Cornford's work:

> Few books are more fascinating than those of miss Harrison, Mr. Cornford, or Mr. Cook, when they burrow in the origins of
> Greek myths and rites.[174]

His method of dealing with rituals and his reasons for so doing can be traced to the influence of Sir James Frazer, whose work made such an impact on his poetry:

> Frazer's facts suggest that archaic and contemporary behavior are already juxtaposed in contemporary consciousness, and that a poet can further refine the juxtapositions . . . to disclose a ground of identity and to reveal the presence of a third entity, a metaphysical community of all men.[175]

Frazer admitted, what Jessie L. Weston firmly stated, that the inner purpose of the rites and rituals was to initiate the soul, through a process of trial and purgation, into a higher state of existence. As much as the cult of Christ, the cults of the hanged, buried or drowned gods contained, within an overt wish for fulfilment in this life, a deeper

---
174. *The Sacred Wood*, p. 76.
175. 'London Letter', *The Dial*, LXXI (October, 1921), p. 453.

desire to pass beyond it. Since each of Eliot's works is built around the motif of rebirth and transcendence, the ritualistic images are integral part of his artistic design.

Linda Leavell defines Eliot's 'Ritual method' relating it to the mythical method and the nonsense method:

> The mythical method is the past, vast and indefinite but potentially knowable; the nonsense method is like the present, immediate and non dimensional; and the ritual method, the method of *Ash Wednesday*, is like the future, a projection from immediate meaninglessness towards the infinite unknowable, the ineffable name. The ritual method, the greatest achievement of Eliot's Poetry, grows out of the mythical and nonsense methods.[176]

The Waste Land is the first poem where Eliot has used classical and Indian rituals to convey the reply to modern dilemmas. The poem begins with the classical ritual of fertility gods and ends in the Indian ritual, in the repetition of 'Datta, Dayadhvam, Damyata/Shantih Shantih Shantih'. Here the ritual is part of the myth, Upanishads and Buddhism both having grown out of the waste land myth. But more significantly, the entire myth of the waste land is, according to Miss Weston, derived from the fertility rituals of Nature cults.

The title of the first movement *The Burial of the Dead* glances at the ritual performed in the Church of England while a dead body is being committed to the earth. But more significantly, it is intended to recall the burial of the fertility gods as described by Frazer. In both cases the burial of the dead was followed by the rebirth of the dead and buried. Thus the basic motif of the poem—death and rebirth—is announced at its very opening. But this motif is contrasted with the death and burial or even living death in the modern waste land where there is little hope for rebirth. The opening images point to the irony of the

---
176. Basu, Tapan Kumar, ed., *T. S. Eliot: An Anthology of Recent Criticism* (Delhi: Pencraft International, 1993), p. 110.

Classical Images

ritual, hence ritualistic images. 'April is the cruelest month, breeding/Lilacs out of the dead land . . .' April or the Spring season in nature is the period of the rebirth or the return of life in nature after the death of the winter season. The dead earth is fertilised by the spring rains. But in the waste land life is like death itself, so death can't bring life or rebirth. This condition is a state of spiritual death. The pain of rebirth in Spring makes it the 'cruellest' month, as the images recalling the ritual suggest.

The Burial of the Dead winds up with the central ritualistic image of 'that corpse you planted last year' referred to in the conversation between the protagonist and Stetson, centring round the planting of the corpse and its dubious chances of sprouting. The planting of the corpse refers at once to the burial and re-birth of the old fertility god and to the burial and resurrection of crucified Christ. The sprouting of this god, the quickening of the slaughtered Osiris, would be tantamount to a spiritual revival. The image also alludes to a famous remark of St. Paul in the Romans: 'know ye not that so many of us were baptized as Jesus Christ was baptized into his death? We are buried with him . . . into death . . . if we have been planted together in the likeness of his death, we shall also be in the likeness of his resurrection.' With the faith in God intact, the hope in the resurrection after death, in the sprouting of new life out of the corpse of the old, is firm and unshakable. With the loss of this faith, however, death remains a certainty, but re-birth becomes dubious. The chances are that the germination of the corpse may be blasted by frost or dug up again by a dog, 'Dog that is friend to man'. By capitalising dog, Eliot obviously intended to remind us of the various associations of the animal with redemptive and resurrective processes or rituals in the fertility cult. In ancient Egypt, there was a fertility ritual in which the image of Osiris, god of fertility and vegetation, was first dismembered and its limbs scattered as an enactment of the process of death. But later on Isis, the consort of the god, collected the limbs together with the help of 'a Dog' to bring about the re-birth of the dead deity. Again, the Dog may refer to the Dog star, Sirius, rising in the hottest part of dry season to herald the rise of the Nile water and return of fertility to the parched and barren soil. So 'Dog' is also a ritualistic image.

In *The Fire Sermon*, the Smyrna merchant, the 'one eyed Merchant' is a ritualistic image whose eye of religion is now blinded, and the eye of commerce alone has survived. The 'invisible' something on his back is the fertility cult which traders of Smyrna anciently brought to Europe, when religion and commerce were united in them as their two eyes. The 'hanged god' is at once the fertility god of Frazer and the crucified Christ who has disappeared from the sordid world of Madame Sosostris.

Death by Water is woven around the most significant ritualistic image of spiritual purification and rebirth. The title of this movement refers to a ritual in ancient Egypt in which, according to Miss Weston, an effigy of the head of the fertility god was cast into the sea at Alexandria, to signify his death. The head was pursued as it was caught by the current and carried towards Byblos, where it was redeemed from water and worshipped as the god reborn. The ritual is represented in the baptismal ceremony of the Christian church where the sprinkling of holy water on the body of an initiate becomes the symbol of his redemption from sin and death. The image of rising and falling in 'as he rose and fell entering the whirlpool' is a hint at the process of renewal and rebirth of the drowned effigy of the fertility God, moving back from the point of death through all the stages of age, youth and childhood to the moment of birth. The image stresses the contrast between the fruitful drowning of the god's effigy and the destructive drowning of the Phoenician sailor, who stands for all those who 'turn the wheel and look windward'. This section shows as to how the element of water which, ritualistically, should have brought regeneration only completes the process of destruction.

Thus, such ritualistic images, which abound in *The Waste Land*, present the theme of resurrection in terms of fertility rites.

The *Murder in the Cathedral* is a 'ritual drama of sin and redemption, where all the components of strain and antithesis are externalized, discrete.'[177] Herbert Howarth remarks, 'The story of *Murder in the Cathedral* itself was a rite; the cathedral setting prepared the audience to follow a ritual and to participate in it.'[178] The basic plot structure appears to be derived from the ritual form of ancient tragedy. Part I corresponds to the *Agon*. The chief characters are the Chorus of the Women of Canterbury, Three Priests, Four Tempters and Thomas. Part II is the overt result, the epiphany of his agony with the Tempters. 'The internal conflicts of Becket and the Chorus are, as it were, microcosmical.'[179] The ritual motif aligning *Murder in the Cathedral* with *The Rock* through verbal effects reminiscent of liturgy and with *The Waste Land* through the theme of death and rebirth, endows the play with a kind of secondary pattern of images.

The Women of Canterbury are seen as rooted in rituals of toil— rituals of the seasons as sharing the dignity of their domestic and agricultural labour, as having their place within a hierarchy whose temporal head is the king. So images related to the Women of Canterbury (already discussed) are ritualistic images as well which present them as suffering the pain of rebirth along with Becket. Even the end of this drama of rebirth is presented through the ritualistic image of slaughter, murder of an

---

177. Smith, Grover, *T. S. Eliot's Poetry and Plays: A Study in Sources and Meaning*, p. 185.
178. Howarth, Herbert, *Notes on Some Figures Behind T. S. Eliot* (London: Chatto and Windus, 1965), p. 319.
179. Smith, Grover, *T. S. Eliot's Poetry and Plays: A Study in Sources and Meaning*, p. 185.

unresisting victim, a necessary act to achieve transcendence, timelessness, and rebirth. When Becket stands on the steps to meet his murder, the four swords of the murderers, in their ritual slaying, are the four spokes of a wheel of which Becket is the centre—they at the circumference, acting, as he at the still centre, patient, suffering, witnessing. As a martyr, Becket faces a similar situation as Christ, who also suffered temptation before entering upon the drama of action through suffering.

The pain of re-birth in spring is described in *The Family Reunion*, as follows:

> The cold spring now is the time
> For the ache in the moving root,
> The agony in the dark
> The slow throbbing in the trunk
> The pain of the breaking bud:[180]

It corresponds to 'April is the cruelest month' of *The Waste Land* and 'Now I fear the disturbance' of *Murder in the Cathedral*. Harry has been presented, on an allegorical level, as a ritual scapegoat. In classical Greece, prisoners could be put to torture and sacrificed as scapegoats for the community. But in Christianity it must be a willing and conscious sacrifice, knowledge of which must precede expiation. Harry is to symbolise redemption of the family from the paternal course by being 'its bird sent flying through the purgatorial flame'. Several details imply an analogy between Harry and the ritual hero of myth, such as the eight-year variant of the ritual term of wandering, the 'birth- mystery' in Harry's question: 'Tell me now, who were my parents' and, indeed, the whole identification with Orestes. Eliot also uses the ancient Greek folk-ritual of spring with its cyclic death and rebirth and also the Christian ritual that celebrates the crucifixion and resurrection of Easter. 'Spring is an issue of blood, a season of sacrifice' (II. 2589). According to Northrop Frye, 'Harry's

---
180. *The Family Reunion*, p. 108.

Classical Images

action makes his Wishwood another Chapel Perilous in which one must die to be reborn.'[181] In the original Chapel Perilous the lights of the Chapel are gradually extinguished during the Knight's vigil. This rite is performed on the candles of his mother's birthday cake, while Amy, all her hopes for Wishwood annihilated by Harry's refusal to stay there, is dying off stage. As Harry's awakening starts, Mary moves into a kind of trance or vision of what is happening to Harry - the joyful pain of his rebirth:

> Pain is the opposite of joy
> But joy is a kind of pain
> I believe the moment of birth
> Is when we have knowledge of death
> I believe the season of birth
> Is the season of sacrifice . . .
> And what of the terrified spirit
> Compelled to be reborn
> To rise toward the violent sun
> Wet wings into the rain cloud
> Harefoot over the moon?[182]

Harry's earthbound nature (symbolised by the images of wet wings of a mayfly and the deformity of a harefoot) has to rise to painful heights. For this ritual cleansing of the soul (symbolised by the image of 'hot bath' in line 380, Part I derived from ancient Greek drama) is a primary condition. The cleansing starts when Harry 'sees his part in the 'sin'. Thus, various images related to Harry's conversion can be categorised as ritualistic images as well presenting the ritual of rebirth through death.

The ritualistic use of the Furies, more patently in their role as Divine messengers, lets Harry know clearly that the only way out of the family curse and guilt is purgation and holiness. As his vision of the Eumenides undergoes

---
181. Frye, Northrop, *T. S. Eliot* (Edinburgh and London: Oliver and Boyd, 1963), pp. 92–93.
182. *The Family Reunion*, p. 109.

a change, he is being liberated through the understanding of his part in the story of the curse; he comes out into the light under the eyes of God or Conscience that gives final judgement; he feels himself cleansed by vomiting or excretion. This ritual of cleansing suggests that the expiation of sin is an ancient and wide-spread religious view, by no means confined to Christianity. Thus, Harry's sense of belonging to a contaminated world also reflects the Christian doctrine of the Fall of Man which, in the present century is popularly regarded as a fable connected with the story of Adam and Eve and with which the hereditary depravity (called original sin) and transgression is supposed to have handed on forever to the whole human race. For the atonement of this guilt the ritual / purgatorial fire of spiritual suffering is the only way out suggested to Harry by Agatha. He feels himself sent out into the wilderness; following the 'bright angels'. At the end of the play, he is taking the first step along the road of detachment and renunciation.

Similarly, in *The Cocktail Party*, Eliot has followed the ritual pattern of the Alcestis of Euripides with 'satyric' variations: Agon, Death and Resurrection, Marriage, and Komos. Eliot borrows all the elements of the ritual: the 'death' motif; 'resurrection' by the Herculean figure, Sir Henry, the wedding of Edward and Lavinia 'in spirit and in truth'. The reunion of the Chamberlains involves a 'rebirth' and a new order in society.

The ritualistic images and mythical images are significant in the sense that as the world of regeneration grows, the world of his poems and plays comes into a sharper focus. To create a vital model, both the world of reality and the world of myth must remain in focus. In short, the archetype cannot destroy the particular which dramatises it. So it is significant that the realistic surface doesn't give way before the ritual under-pattern. Traditionally, this ritual of rebirth and regeneration involved 'epiphany' in Greek dramas. In the tragic pattern the individual is purged of his guilt and readmitted into society; in the comic pattern harmony is restored to the society and the cosmos. When the epiphany is regenerative in accordance with cultural beliefs, the ritual expectation of the audience is satisfied. This kind of resolution is the measure of Eliot's meld of classical and modern structures meeting into images.

7

Manichaean Images

Eliot's interest in mythology and anthropology led him to study ancient myths of various cultures and religions in detail. A deeper study of Eliot's works reveals the traces of Manichaean mythology which aims at the expulsion of evil with the help of the Primal Man, using him as a warrior or *Knight* of the forces of light. Just as classical myths have provided structural images to Eliot's poems and plays, so do the Manichaean myths which are related integrally to the modern dilemma of duality. This is Eliot's major concern. Explaining the myth of Manichaeism, Terry Gifford and Neil Roberts point out:

> The religion of Mani, which originated in Mesopotamia in the third century A.D., posited a state of war between spirit and matter, light and darkness, good and evil. Its mythology explains the present mixed state of things as the result of a partially successful assault by the darkness on the light, and the whole duty of man is to restore the separation, largely by ascetic practices. A major figure in its mythology is Primeval Man, a warrior of the forces of light, who clad himself in his armour and set forth to do battle with the cohorts of matter, of darkness, of evil. The armour consisted of his five light elements and in sum they constituted not merely his armour but his own being, his proper 'self', his soul.[183]

---

183. Gifford, Terry and Neil Roberts, *Ted Hughes: A Critical Study* (London: Faber and Faber, 1981), p. 14.

Eliot's Prufrock, Tiresias, Becket, Harry etc. are the modern equivalents of the Manichaean hero, embarked on the quest of restoring reason, light and truth by attacking the dark forces. Duality is at the heart of Manichaean mythology as well as Eliot's works, as established by Eliot's response to Yeats' philosophy that 'only beautiful things should be painted':

> The essential advantage of a poet is not to have a beautiful world with which to deal, but to be able to see beneath both beauty and ugliness; to see the boredom, the horror and the glory.[184]

Eliot, thus, deals with duality like Ted Hughes who is a typical *Manichaean* poet. Peter Porter sees Ted Hughes' works 'as *Manichaean* due to the presence of horror and protest and the opposed elements of darkness and light'.[185] We find the presence of *Manichaean* philosophy, 'the boredom, the horror, the glory, the beauty and the ugliness' in *The Waste Land, Four Quartets, Murder in the Cathedral, The Family Reunion, The Cocktail Party* and most of the other works of Eliot. The imaginative world of Eliot's works with its stark opposition of death and rebirth, sterility and fertility, guilt and purgation might seem to support such a view. All the images springing from this duality are *Manichaean* images which illuminate the 'creative-destructive' elements of modern consciousness.

The sensuous world of 'facts' in Eliot's poetry is assimilated, from the very beginning, into a world of struggle between opposing forces. The first 'facts' — the poetic 'first principles' — which set in motion a creative response in Eliot, seem to be associated both symbolically and literally with the paradoxical qualities, 'perceiving' eye notices. As in *Prufrock*, when the protagonist speaks

---

184. Arnold, Mathew, *The Use of Poetry and the Use of Eroticism: Studies In the Relation of Criticism to Poetry in England*, 2nd ed., (London: Faber and Faber, 1964), p. 106.
185. Gifford, Terry and Neil Roberts, *Ted Hughes: A Critical Study*, p. 14.

of the 'evening . . . like a patient etherized upon a table' one feels mesmerised by the *Manichaeistic* way in which evening (symbol of beauty in Nature) is opposed to the ugly realistic picture of the 'etherized patient'. It is a variation of Mani's doctrine of dual reality with the etherized patient implying all that is undesirable (more so because consciousness caught in a flux is symbolic of matter and darkness) and the 'evening' pointing towards beauty and light. All such images in the opening lines of *Prufrock*—'half-deserted streets', 'the yellow fog' and 'the yellow smoke' rubbing its muzzle on the window-panes, 'a soft October night' curled about the house like a cat—are felt as negative elements of modern psyche, questioning the sanity of the protagonist. What is distinctive about the images is the pressure of division which weighs upon the human psyche.

Eliot has also used the *Manichaean* figure of the *Knight* in his poems, who is a warrior bringing back the forces of light. The Knight is the Primeval Man. Eliot's protagonists, with a split consciousness, bear a close resemblance to Primeval Man. As Marc Manganaro observes in his article *Dissociation in Dead Land: The Primitive Mind in the Early Poetry of T.S. Eliot*:

> What Eliot seems to have found especially engaging was the relationship between the nature of the primitive mind and modern mentality and, even more particularly, the question of what modern man has lost in the process of becoming civilized.[186]

In Eliot's works we find a rejection of the self-sufficient ego, in the guise of spirit, or of intellect, or of heroic endeavour, and of the embattled suppressive attitude to matter and darkness that is figured in the myths of Primeval Man. Eliot, in fact, was greatly influenced by the famous anthropologist Lucien Levy-Bruhl, whose first

---

186. Basu, Tapan Kumar, ed., *T. S. Eliot: An Anthology of Recent Criticism* (Delhi: Pencraft International, 1993), p. 27.

book on primitive mentality, *Les Fonctions Mentales dans les Societies Inferieures* (How Natives Think), published in 1910, Eliot had read in the original French in 1913.[187] The *Manichaean* myth can be better understood when studied in relation to the associations brought forth by this book. In this volume Levy-Bruhl asserts that the mentality of primitive man which he calls 'pre-logical' or 'mystical', differs essentially from that of modern man in that it does not operate by rules of Aristotelian logic. Rather, the primitive perception has a mystical and emotional base, which produces a completely different kind of thinking.

According to Levy-Bruhl, what we see as faulty perception on the part of the primitive is just another way of looking at reality. This perception, in the light of Mani's philosophy, may be termed as 'Manichaeistic perception', for it corresponds to Bruhl's concept of doubt and split.

Levy-Bruhl's philosophy revolves basically around two concepts. The first that of 'collective representations', refers to those mystical perceptions of reality that the individual inherits from the society in which he is reared. One sees in the descriptions of these 'representations' features that Eliot came more and more to believe in. In his early poetry we see products of the breakdown of such a system in characters like Prufrock and Gerontion who represent modern man divorced from unquestioned belief and left to flounder in his self-doubt. In the later poetry, Eliot gives descriptions of the strength of collective religious belief in the face of individual scepticism, descriptions which bear strong resemblance to Bruhl's accounts of the Primitive Man's unflinching faith in collective representations:

---

[187]. Eliot's first-known reference to Levy-Bruhl's *Les Fonctions Mentales dans les Societies Inferieures* is in Royce's seminar in the fall of 1913. Quotations from Levy-Bruhl's work, unless otherwise noted, have be taken from authorised English Translation *How Natives Think*, trans. Lillian A. Clare (Washington Square Press, 1966). This edition will be cited hereafter as *HNT*.

> You are not here to verify,
> Instruct yourself, or inform curiosity
> Or carry report. You are here to kneel
> Where prayer has been valid.[188]

The Primal Man of Mani is also an embodiment of faith in divinity, light, power and wisdom.

The second concept, the 'law of participation', Levy Bruhl defines as that fundamental belief of primitives that:

> Objects, beings, phenomena can be, though in a way incomprehensible to us, both themselves and other than themselves. In a fashion which is no less incomprehensible, they give forth and receive mystic powers . . . which make themselves felt outside, without ceasing to remain what they are.[189]

Eliot himself was fascinated by this idea of 'participation' and wrote of it in a review of a book by Clement C. J. Webb. In this review, published in 1916 in the *International Journal of Ethics*, Eliot makes a good defence for Levy-Bruhl:

> The mystical mentality, though at a low level, plays a much greater part in the daily life of the savage than in that of civilized man.

Eliot agrees with Levy-Bruhl that:

> Every object contains for the primitive mind mystic properties that are inseparable from it, and with these mystical properties comes a host of mystical connections that unite that object to other objects, to the tribe, and to the individual. The result is a 'complex network of spiritual links and the realization that, according to the primitive mind, there is no phenomenon which is, strictly speaking, a physical one.[190]

---

188. 'Little Gidding', *Collected Poems, 1909–1962* (London: Faber & Faber, 1963), p. 201.
189. *HNT*, p. 61.
190. *HNT*, p. 31.

This version of reality is wholly accepted by the primitive. It is modern man who has difficulty with such a concept precisely because he has, while becoming civilised, made divisions between the physical and the spiritual and in the process has excluded even the possibilities of perceiving the spiritual in the material world. Mani terms it as the victory of 'Darkness' over 'Light'. Levy-Bruhl refers to this process of division as 'dissociation' and claims that as long as it does not occur, 'perception remains an undifferentiated whole'.[191] Eliot's 'dissociation of sensibility', in a way corresponds to the philosophy of Mani and Levy-Bruhl. This famous phrase 'dissociation of sensibility', appeared first in Eliot's essay *The Metaphysical Poets*.[192] In his essay, Eliot distinguishes between two types of poetry in much the same way that Levy-Bruhl makes his distinction between two kinds of thinking. In the first type, which is characterised by Donne and poets previous to him, all the varieties of human experience are part of a whole and expressed as such in the poetry; in the second type, characterised by the post-metaphysical poets such as Tennyson and Browning, the varying experiences of the poet have no seeming relation to each other—here the disparate images of the poet's life do not cohere. Here, according to Eliot, 'dissociation of sensibility' has set in.

In the Manichaean poetry of Eliot (as in Ted Hughes) a society of dissociation is portrayed through images separating the physical from the spiritual to the extent that the nonphysical is no longer considered 'real'. This poetry of dissociation, which culminates in *The Hollow Men* often, presents personae who realise the spiritual impotence of their environment but are powerless to act upon their longings. Prufrock, as mentioned earlier in this chapter, is just such a character, one who knowingly lives in a world divested of mystical connections between

---
191. Ibid.
192. Eliot, T. S., *Selected Prose* (Harmondsworth: Penguin Books, 1953), pp. 105–114.

the seen and the unseen. Prufrock does have realisations of the spiritual, but these links are private rather than collective. However, the spiritual can be entered into only temporarily. The voice of the Primal Man, the spiritual voice acts, 'Till human voices wake us, and we drown'. This Manichaean disparity between ideal private vision and reality as seen by a fragmented society is virtually nonexistent in primitive culture—in Prufrock's world it acts ultimately as a destructive force. Still the temporary awakening of spiritual voice gives some hope which is substantiated through various images in the proceeding poems.

In fact, the positive message or hope springs from the dualistic theory itself by which Mani explains the existence of evil:

> Light is synonymous with God. Satan arose from darkness.
>
> It is man's duty in life to fight the forces of Darkness and bring about the final triumph of Light over Darkness. . . . Mani holds matter to be the root of evil. Mortification of body, therefore, becomes a virtue in his system. All bodily desires are evil. They should be stifled and killed. Mani advocates quietistic, ascetic, passive virtues.[193]

This dualistic philosophy is the foundation not only of Manichaean myths but also of Hindu religion as described in Indian scriptures, the Vedas and the Puranas, the crux highlighted in 'Aham Brahmasmi', the union of matter and spirit. Like Indian scriptures, Manichaeism was a type of Gnosticism—a dualistic religion that offered salvation through special knowledge of spiritual truth. Like all forms of Gnosticism, Manichaeans thought that life in this world was unbearably painful and radically evil. Inner illumination or *gnosis* reveals that the soul which shares in the nature of God has fallen into the evil world of matter and must be saved by means of the spirit of intelligence. This knowledge is the only way to salvation.

---
193. Radhakrishnan, S., ed., *History of Philosophy: Eastern and Western*, Vol. 2 (London: George Allen and Unwin, 1953), p. 18.

Eliot, being well-versed in various mythologies, religions and scriptures, makes the Manichaean dualism the woof and warp of his imagistic network. For the sake of clarity in interpretation the Manichaean images can be studied at two levels:
1. Eliot's poetic ingenuity: Manichaean synthesis of polarities
2. Manichaean myth of Primal Man or Knight: a Warrior of the Forces of Light

Eliot has 'an image-forming power', and his [Manichaean] 'philosophy' or body of 'ideas' is arrived at by 'studying the conceptual implications of the structure of his images'.[194] Eliot, like Ted Hughes, tends to identify, by metaphor and images, the opposed aspects of cyclical movement in nature. Winter, death or old age, night, ruins and the sea have ready-made associations with each other, and so have spring, birth or youth, dawn, the city, and rain or fountains. But these images gain intensity when presented in a shocking opposition to each other, as in 'April is the cruelest month', since it does not signify birth or spring, but death and numbness.

The December setting of *Murder in the Cathedral*, the cold March of *The Family Reunion*, the 'midwinter spring' of *Little Gidding* are deeply wrought into the Manichaean philosophy since these images suggest something beyond 'what the eyes perceive'. In Eliot's works death necessarily suggests rebirth through death of temporal existence. Physical death is a means to attain spirituality. So Eliot's poems from *Prufrock* to *The Waste Land* 'give expression to a basic existential anxiety within the self which appears in various forms'.[195] In *Prufrock*, it is a nightmare of being

---
194. Frye, Northrop, *T.S. Eliot* (London: Oliver and Boyd, 1963), p. 48.
195. Amur, G. S., 'The Poetry Does Not Matter—Progress of the Self in T. S. Eliot's Poetry' in *Asian Response to American Literature*, ed., C. D. Narasimhaiah (Delhi: Vikas Publications, 1972), p. 64.

trapped in an unreal world; in *Portrait of a Lady*, it is the fear of being deprived of self-possession; in *Gerontion*, it is a despair born of too much knowledge; in *The Waste Land*, it is the erosion of spirit by loveless sex and greed. All the protagonists, by implication, have split personalities. That is why all the images reflect this Manichaean division and make up an opposition.

The Love Song of J. Alfred Prufrock deals with the Manichaean drama of two selves. Prufrock, the protagonist, is a victim of what Martian Buber calls 'self-contradiction', 'the failure to work out and realize the inborn Thou or what meets it'.[196] Prufrock is aware of the deep split in his personality which inevitably leads to passivity and inaction, suggested by the cat-yellow fog imagery of the poem. The Manichaean split is caused by Prufrock's intense awareness of the difference between the claustrophobic world he lives in, where communication is impossible and the visionary world into which he has had an occasional entry. He oscillates between: 'There will be time . . . time to turn back . . .Do I dare disturb the universe? . . . And how should I begin? Shall I say . .?' and 'I'm no prophet', 'I am Lazarus', 'I'm not Prince Hamlet'. He is torn between two contradictory desires, the desire to lead a purely instinctive life (because he has felt the unnerving effects of knowledge) and the desire to play the role of a prophet. The integration of the divided self is sought and glimpsed on a visionary plane but it is thwarted by the disillusioning human voices. *Prufrock*, thus, illustrates the frustration of the self in its attempt to reach out to the other and heal the inner split. This Manichaean attempt to attain a perfect vision in *Prufrock* takes the form of the mythical Knight 'attacking darkness' in the positive voice

196. Buber, Martin, *I and Thou*, tr., R. S. Smith (Charles Scribner's Sons, 1958), p. 71.

of spiritualism in later poems. It is, therefore, worthwhile to note that the disgust with vulgarity and meaninglessness of city life marks *Prufrock, Portrait of a Lady, Gerontion, Preludes* and *The Waste Land*, for Eliot himself wrote that 'the contemplation of the horrid or sordid or disgusting by an artist, is the necessary and negative aspect of the impulse toward the pursuit of beauty' and the 'negative is more importunate'.[197] The images of fog, dusk, evening and of 'saw-dust restaurants with oyster-shells' which form the varied horrible aspects of Prufrock's consciousness are juxtaposed to his view of glorious and heroic aspects of the life of a martyr, prophet and hero, though negatively felt. So Eliot's way of seeking the absolute is not by escaping from experience into anything else, but by so intensifying it that it yields its universal meaning.

Stephen Spender suggests that Prufrock has 'after all a positive aspect because he knows what he lacks'.[198] Modern man's loss of identity and his pitiful efforts to find a socially acceptable substitute for it is an idea that occurs in Prufrock's cry: 'There will be time/ To prepare a face to meet the faces that you meet.' It is true that Prufrock is 'a (Manichaean) searcher, and his quest, like that of other individuals in Eliot's poems, is for a grail'.[199]

Prufrock's dilemma, apparently born of a conflict between longing and the lack of fulfilment, is essentially grounded in a complex alienation which is partly social and sexual and partly religious. This can be termed as Manichaean alienation as well. Eliot presents Prufrock, Gerontion and the lovers in *Portrait of a Lady* as miserable beings alienated from some enlivening truth which could revitalise the harmony of their souls:

---

197. Eliot, T. S., 'Dante', *The Sacred Wood: Essays on Poetry and Criticism* (London: Methuen and Co. Ltd., 1950), p. 18.
198. Srivastav, Narsingh, *The Poetry of T.S. Eliot: A Study in Religious Sensibility* (New Delhi: Sterling Publishers, 1991), p. 32.
199. Ibid.

> But though I have wept and fasted, wept and prayed,
> Though I have seen my head (grown slightly bald)
> brought in upon a platter,
> I am no prophet—and here's no great matter.

Prufrock cannot identify himself with the martyr and Lazarus; he can only visualise them. These imagined ideals of self-denial and spiritual rebirth make the cardinal points in Eliot's Manichaean quest for meaning and purpose in life. In the early poems the absolutism of a character's consciousness is reduced to a relativity of digressions into past and future— dreams and desires, reality and fantasy. The failure of will and the resultant confusion and uncertainty are the starting points of Eliot's interest in human consciousness, even as the purification of motive through action without desire for reward is the end of it. From the will lost (*Prufrock* and *Gerontion*) to the will restored in its purified form (*Four Quartets* and *Murder in the Cathedral*) is the whole story of Eliot's Manichaean progression, and it is in the course of this pilgrim's progress that belief is negated, discovered, accepted, strengthened and established as the final truth.

This is what Manichaean religion establishes in the concept of the 'Present Time' while throwing light on the 'Three moments'. In the present time, Darkness invades Light and Light, in turn, enters Darkness. The struggle ends when one wears out the physical passions (that is 'the oppressive and aggressive limits of nature') and the luminous nature is saved by liberating the soul from the shadow. The separation of shadows is what marks the Former Time in its natural state, and this distinction will prevail in Future Time as well in its enforced state as a result of human or psychic efforts. Hence the liberation is attributed to the human mind which overcomes all evil and temporal impulses. This psychic equilibrium is what Manichaean and Shamanistic practices aim at.

Eliot's poems are attempts at mediation or reconciliation. *Portrait of a Lady* presents the emptiness of a life of negative love seen from outside by the observing eye of the poet; and this forms a counter-picture of the life of spiritual harmony which the poet-prophet was in quest of. Feeling and desire are revealed, only to be rejected. Dichotomy between one's changing, undetermined feeling and the meaningless cycle of time is conveyed through Manichaean images of temporal cycle. Moving from December to April to October, the yearly cycle also ironically suggests the constant set pattern of the lady's life, without purpose or goal. The sadness of 'what might have been', which recurs in many poems of Eliot, resonates in the eager and then wistful desires of the lady within a world not capable of fulfilling them.

'The smoke and fog of a December afternoon' marks the time of her hopeful beginnings, the image suggesting death reinforced by 'Juliet's tomb'. Opposition between the lady's speech and the narrator's mental commentary emphasises their mutual isolation in self. For her their relationship is like musical harmony; for him it is first faintly tiresome and then positively confining, the winding of violins becoming a tom-tom, grating and absurd. Like Prufrock, the lady realises the separation between her intense feelings and the disparate pieces of her external life, a 'life composed so much, so much of odds and ends'. Unlike Prufrock, she presumes, pressing her need for intimacy on the embarrassed visitor: 'I have saved this afternoon for you', 'To find a friend who has these qualities, / who has, and gives / Those qualities upon which friendship lives'. Revealing her desires, she acts as Prufrock could not, and her only discovery is that no shared feeling does exist.

The second section conveys, through the intense Manichaean images of 'cracked cornets' and 'a dull tom-tom', the young man's need to escape. Her Chopin melody is for him a 'Capricious monotone', a 'definite false note'.

Like other characters of Eliot's early poems, he finds any action or expression of life troubling and alien. There is a dichotomy between their worlds: the lady raising an intense and intimate inner life, the man finding relief only in a public world without suffocating intimacy and embarrassing demands:

> Let us take the air, in a tobacco trance,
> Admire the monuments,
> Discuss the late events,
> Correct our watches by the public clocks.
> Then sit for half an hour and drink our bocks.

The Manichaean image of 'tobacco trance' emphasises the irony of his escape, his wish to 'take the air'. Suggesting a deliberate loss of awareness, a refusal to acknowledge desire, 'trance' is associated specifically with public events, clock time and freedom from human involvement beyond social conversation. As in *Prufrock*, the inner worlds are opposed, and neither offers any meaning. The young man's external world is painless but valueless, only an escape from emotion and commitment.

The movement of the second section parallels that of the first from the lady's self-exposure to the narrator's clashing emotions and dubious escape. It is now April, the month Eliot later called cruel for reawakening hope without promising fulfilment, and lilacs are in the room. Twisting lilacs in her hands, symbols of sexual tension, the lady's speech alternates between hope and resignation while his thoughts consistently focus on escape. The images of music maintain the sense of utter separation, and the refrain, 'I shall sit here, serving tea to friends', defines split between her inner experience and the temporal pattern of days and hours.

The relationship which seemed hopeful in December but already strained in April comes to a close in October. As she speaks of his impending departure, his 'smile falls heavily among the bric-a-brac'. A fitting image as it associates itself with the fragmented bits and pieces of the external world and not with the flow of feeling. Refusing to enter her inner world, he is but another impersonal object on which, for a time, she imposed her own feelings. Finding no answer she returns, resigned, to serving tea.

The Manichaean images present two alternatives, maintained throughout the poem: shared intimacy associated with musical harmony and depersonalised behaviour determined by 'public clock'. In choosing to live by the latter, the young man rejects and denies the possibility of communication, love or sympathy. The poem ends on an oddly unresolved question: 'Would she not have the advantage, after all?' He is left uncertain in the end. Neither *Prufrock* nor *Portrait of a Lady* offers any resolution to the separation between subjective and objective life. The latter is subject to the control of time and consists of conventional actions without purpose. The former seems repressed or incapable of communication. Yet the escape is conceived in human relations, which fail them. Each goes beyond simply being aware. Prufrock thinks about his dilemma and imagines other lives; the lady actually speaks. Awareness, thus, is symbolic of slight gestures towards life, though made with difficulty and ending in frustration but rousing hope.

In *Rhapsody on a Windy Night*, Eliot portrays a protagonist who wanders in the streets one night, recollecting various images from his past in a pattern which has no apparent logical connections. The world presented to the reader is typically 'modern' — lonely, desolate, sterile — yet the mode of recollection as described by Eliot in the opening stanza is a breakdown of civilised memory:

> Twelve o' clock
> Along the reaches of the street
> Held in a lunar synthesis,
> Whispering lunar incantations
> Dissolve the floors of memory
> And all its clear relations,
> Its divisions and precisions

If Eliot had read James Frazer's *Adonis, Attis, Osiris* by 1911, which is probable, he would have learned of what Frazer termed 'the doctrine of lunar sympathy', whereby the moon, with its waxing, 'renew(s) sympathetically the life of man.'[200] Frazer took pains to point out that 'lunar sympathy' was not moon worship, but rather a sympathetic rejection of an object invested with spiritual qualities or, as Levy-Bruhl would put it, an act dependent upon the primitive law of participation. And what is being 'dissolved' in the poem is the 'logical process' of the civilised mind, a process which, 'disposes our memory preferably to retain the relations which have preponderating importance from the objective and logical stand point' (*HNT*, 91). What is being restored in the poem is the primitive order of memory, which is the Manichaean order as well, calling together diverse images from the past based not upon their logical or sequential relations to each other, but upon the emotional intensity of those images to the speaker:

> The memory throws up high and dry
> A crowd of twisted things;
> A twisted branch upon the beach Eaten smooth, and polished
> As if the world gave up
> The secret of its skeleton,
> Stiff and white
> A broken spring in a factory yard,
> Rust that clings to the form that the strength has left.
> Hard and curled and ready to snap.

Levy-Bruhl characterises primitive memory as 'both very accurate and very emotional' (*HNT*, 93); we can readily see that the protagonist's recollections and images fit that description. The Manichaean images vis-a-vis dissolving of 'divisions and precisions', the madman shaking the geranium, the lapping tongue of the cat, the automatic

---

200. *Adonis, Attis, Osiris*, Part IV, Volume II of *The Golden Bough: A Study of Magic and Religion*, 3rd ed., (London: Macmillan, 1913), p. 140.

gesture of the child, the vacancy behind the child's eye, the instinctive reflex of the crab, the moon's loss of memory, the dead geranium, the pin, the twisted driftwood and the rusty spring, the mechanical toy, the paper rose, the reek of airless places, the bed waiting for its occupant etc. besiege the speaker's consciousness, for he cannot evade them: what is more dismaying, they constitute his soul. However, what the protagonist lacks of the primitive experience is exactly what was wanting in *Prufrock* the 'collective representations' shared by society which reach a permanent faith in mystical connections between the visible and the invisible. That implies the speaker's entry into the Manichaean world of darkness and ignorance. The last stanza of the poem leads the speaker back to his own door, back to the routine order of living, devoid of mystical links signified by the Primal Man of Mani:

> The bed is open; the toothbrush hangs on the wall,
> Put your shoes at the door, sleep, prepare for life.

It is noteworthy that in *Prufrock*, *Portrait of a Lady*, *Rhapsody on a Windy Night* and the other early poems, the positive, spiritual vision of the Primal Man surfaces only temporarily, to be inevitably absorbed by the cohorts of darkness implied by the material world.

According to Northrop Frye, 'Human consciousness cannot identify permanently with light or with darkness, with innocence or with experience'.[201] These worlds of the subway and the rose-garden may be called respectively, using terms from *The Hollow Men*, 'death's dream kingdom and 'death's other kingdom'. They are the 'objective correlatives' of the two levels of personality exampled by Prufrock. Death's dream kingdom is the world of experience of *Prufrock* and *Gerontion*, the 'cracked and known' waste land, the stubble field of the hollow men. Being a world without identity, it is a world of 'deliberate disguises', usually symbolised in Eliot as animals. The narrator in *Portrait of a Lady* says:

---

201. Frye, Northrop, *T. S. Eliot*, p. 57.

> And I must borrow every changing shape
> To find expression . . . dance, dance
> Like a dancing bear,
> Cry like a parrot, chatter like an ape.

Those who accept experience voluntarily can only do so through detachment, not through identification, still less through the dead-alive indifference which, in the third section of *Little Gidding*, is carefully distinguished from detachment. The Chorus in *Murder in the Cathedral* achieves a momentary identification with experience in the 'death-bringers' Chorus, which thereby becomes an epiphany of Hell; hence its imagery is full of animals, leading to 'the horror of the ape'. In the rose-garden episode of *Burnt Norton*, innocence becomes, for an instant, an epiphany of Paradise. We notice that Becket's comment on the Chorus and the thrush's comment on the rose-garden vision are the same. 'Humankind cannot bear very much reality'.

Death's other kingdom is, besides the vision of lost innocence, the heaven of religion, appearing in this form in *The Hollow Men* as the 'multifoliate rose' of Dante's *Paradise*. Many do not believe in a future or eternal life, but another aspect of death's other kingdom is irrefutable – the past. The great cultural achievements of the past remain in the present to represent another world which is both here and out of reach. Thus a sense of innocence is practically inseparable from consciousness.

The two kingdoms, contrasted in the minds of Prufrock and Gerontion, exemplify a theme, running through all of Eliot's works, of assuming a double role, a Manichaean role. In addressing 'you' who is also themselves, they follow a dialectic which separates the world they are in, and have committed themselves to, from a paradisal world set over against it, which they contemplate until they feel finally separated from it.

The Waste Land is a perfect Manichaean world with its polarities and the attempt to restore order and light. This world is physically above ground but spiritually subterranean, the world of shadows, corpses and buried seeds. The inhabitants live the 'buried life' (a phrase from *Portrait of a Lady*) of seeds in winter: they await the spring rains resentfully, for real life would be their death. Human beings who live like seeds, egocentrically, cannot form a community but only an aggregate, where 'Each man fixed his eyes before his feet', imprisoned in a spiritual solitude. To impart a three-dimensional solidity to the life he presents, Eliot works out a continuous Manichaean parallel between antiquity and modernity.

The basic function and effect of the operation of the continuous parallel is to underline the perennial predicament of man and to suggest a way out in the same fashion as suggested by Mani—the way of spiritual values and discipline taught by Sri Krishna to Arjuna in *The Gita*. The very title of *The Waste Land*, and the Manichaean sense in which it has been used, seems to be inspired by the *Upanishads* and *The Gita*. The full title of *The Gita* is *Sri Bhagvad Gita Upanishad*. The *Upanishads*, a remarkable group of scriptures, are, in fact, the main source of *The Gita*, hence, the need to relate the latter with the former. The words 'Waste Land' brings to our mind the image of dry land with 'no water', just the mirage of water, suggested by such sounds as 'drip drop drip drop'. It creates in the mind of the traveller only a fantasy of water. This picture gets further impetus from the repeated references Eliot makes to physical waste land: for instance 'the land' (1.2), 'stony rubbish' (1.20), 'the rock and no water and the sandy road' (1.332), 'the cracked earth' (1.369), 'the arid plain' (1.424), and so on. By inversion, the fertility symbol of water is implied in the title *The Waste Land*, and this relates Eliot's poem to *The Gita* (e.g., 3.14 and 11.28) and the *Upanishads*. By implication and transposition, the title of Eliot's *The Waste Land* seems to be a variant of the *Brihadaranyaka Upanishad*, for Eliot, like many other literary artists, was highly inspired by the Hindu Scriptures. Ayyappa Paniker asserts in *The Gita In World Literature*: 'Eliot's protagonist, who may bear different names in different poems, is his Arjuna, as he explicitly states in "The Dry Salvages" '. Section 111 begins as follows: 'I sometimes wonder if that is what Krishna meant / Among other things . . .'

The above mentioned *Upanishad*, which contains six chapters, is called 'Aranyaka' as being spoken of in a desert, and Brihad (great) from its extent.[202]

Like Mani's teachings, Eliot's poem, too, is a kind of *Paramam Guhyam* (*The Gita:* 11.1), a secret message delivered in a desert to its inhabitants to liberate themselves from the Mayajal, the net of Maya, the illusory golden hind.

To suggest the metaphysical and spiritual sterility, Eliot presents antithetical images of water, a symbol of regeneration and fertility, thus reiterating the associations driven forth by the title. Here 'the river's tent is broken' (1.73), 'Ganga was sunken' (1.395), 'the deep sea swell. . . . /A current under sea / picked his bones in whispers' (II.312–15). In *The Waste Land*, the river carries the weight of sin, original and new, of history and metaphysical thought;, the sea is a menace. It is the scene of human tragedy.

So water in *The Waste Land* is a Manichaean image of the devil, of evil, mischief and death—the suggestions highlighted by the two myths on which the Manichaean philosophy is partly based. According to Terry Gifford and Neil Roberts,[203] Joseph Campbell, in *The Masks of God: Primitive Mythology*, related a pre-Christian and Christianised version of the same basic myth. In the pre-Christian version, the Great Spirit tells a waterfowl to dive into the water and bring up earth and clay. The bird does so; the Great Spirit uses it to create the land and blesses the bird. In the Christianised version it is Satan, challenged by God, who dives into the water. Christ blesses the morsel of mud that he comes up with and creates a flat, smooth

---

202. Shankaracharya, Introduction: *Brihadaranyaka Upanishad*, Adyar, 1931, p. 4.
203. Hughes, Ted, *A Critical Study*, pp. 18–19.

earth out of it. But Satan has concealed some of the mud, and out of this the mountains are made. Campbell points out the obvious contrast between the innocence of the one version and ethical dualism of the other, which assigns the rugged parts of nature to an evil creator. *The Waste Land*, with all its attendant images, occupies an interesting place between the two 'genuine' myths. Eliot's protagonist, Tiresias, is equally capable of good and of evil, as the images and allusions of antiquity and modernity seem to indicate.

Polarities appear from the very first section as a psychic reality. 'The Burial of the Dead', introduces water as a cause of a state of death-in-life. Here, when the lack of water is felt, it assumes a positive character. For, as Cleanth Brooks comments:

> *The Waste Land* is built on a major contrast—a device which is a favourite of Eliot and to be found in many of his poems, particularly his later poems. The contrast is between two kinds of life and two kinds of death. Life devoid of meaning is death: sacrifice, even the sacrifice death may be life-giving, an awakening to life. The poem occupies itself to a great extent with this paradox, and with a number of variations on it.[204]

That explains the first line 'April is the cruelest month'. Death is preferable to life. The protagonist's feeling towards both winter and April, towards suspension of life in which he is living, and towards a rebirth, is ambivalent, 'mixing memory and desire'. One impulse of both memory and desire is towards apathy and oblivion of winter. The possibility of renewal, the thought of being stirred into potency and growth, the compulsion towards it felt in the images of 'April', 'rain', 'dull roots' stirred by rain, amalgamated and mingled with a fear and reluctance which drive him back to safe forgetfulness.

---

204. Rajan, B., ed. *T. S. Eliot: A Study of His Writings by Several Hands* (London: Dennis Dosson Ltd., 1947), p. 8.

The entire passage records death in the midst of renewal; it documents the inhabitants' failures: their inability to love, their rootlessness in the present—without a past, desperately searching the horoscope for a glimpse of the future. The blighted loves of Rudolph and Maria of Mayerling. Tristan and Isolde, the Hyacinth garden lovers are reflected in the spiritual aridity of the damned. The speaker, like the others, is neither living nor dead, knowing nothing as he looks into 'the heart of light, the silence'. A sterile planting, evoking images of Ennui closes the first part. Yet Adonis' sacrificial burial has been hinted at. Contrasting the revelation of modern man's heart of darkness is the admonishing voice of Ezekiel, the vestigial rituals, the echoing promise of transfiguration in 'Those are pearls that were his eyes'. All the Manichaean images reflect the split between the living death of the waste land and the surrender to the symbolic death which may bring rebirth.

The second part, 'A Game of Chess', deals directly with the artificiality and sterility in the central 'fertility' situation, the marriage relation of men and women. The satiated, synthetic richness of the upper-class is contrasted with the unclean, vacuous smugness of the pub women. Violation is universal in the image of Philomel, in Lil's abortions, in the madness of Ophelia that closes the passage. Symptoms of the disease of the society are laid bare in the neuroses of the speakers, in their lack of communication, in their distraction. The solution hinted at the close of 'The Burial of the Dead' is thwarted by the lethargy pervading an entire society. They do nothing. Eliot's comment in his essay on Baudelaire is especially significant here: 'So far as we are human, what we do must be either evil or good; so far as we do evil or good, we are human; and it is better in a paradoxical way, to do evil than to do nothing; at least we exist.'

'The Fire Sermon' juxtaposes the fire of lust with the fire of rebirth. The fragmentary answers of the past—

Spenser's *Prothalamion*, Marvell's lovers, the tragedy at Thebes, the love of Elizabeth and Leicester— become vulgarised in the modern world as the lifeless coupling of the typist and her boyfriend. The image of tarred and drifting Thames suggests modern London, the infernal city of fragmented lives where the speaker can connect nothing with nothing. For the second time in the poem, however, the passage ends with the suggestion of a ritual purgation by fire through the voices of Augustine and Buddha. Bernard Bergonzi rightly observes:

> All these cultural references, so bewildering in their diversity and range, and juxtapositions, point beyond themselves to the true underlying themes of the poem. And these can be stated simply: sexual disorders, the lack and need, of religious belief.[205]

'Death by Water' holds tentatively the promise of a 'sea change into something rich and strange'. Denied to Phlebas and others caught up in the profit and loss, the mode of salvation, death and rebirth, echoes in the whispers of the sea.

All the images in the first four sections seem to be mocking at the positive associations suggested by them. Spring, season of regeneration and fruition, is 'the cruelest month'. Violet time, suggesting a time of vision in Dante's *Earthly Paradise* when the tree of man was grafted to the tree of Christ, is the hour for bats. Dawn, the time of Christ's appearance on the journey to Emmaus, is the brown dawn in the unreal city. Garden, image of fertility, sensuous efficiency (Hyacinth garden) and source of rebirth (buried corpse of Adonis) is juxtaposed with the failures in the garden. Sacred Garden of Gethsemane is witnessing the betrayal of Christ. Chapel perilous is empty. Churches (St. Mary Woolnoth, Magnus Martyr) are opposed to Mrs. Porter's brothel house. Water is presented as a source of life

---

205. Srivastava, Narsingh, *The Poetry of T. S. Eliot: A Study in Religious Sensibility* (New Delhi: Sterling Publishers, 1991), p. 37.

in the shower of rain heralding summer, ritual washing of Christ's feet; as a source of transformation in 'full fathom five' and the thunder announcing rain and conveying Divine message. The regenerative faculty of water is juxtaposed to the reality of the waste land: the absence of water, empty cisterns, desiccated land, no rain; empty social rituals 'water at ten'; Phlebas' death by Water, Mrs. Porter's perversion of water ritual and the pollution of the Thames.

The Earth, image of life and regeneration, is a desert here. Fire, image of cleansing (in Augustine's sermon, Buddhist burning, Arhant Daniel's leap into purgatorial fires in Dante's *Commedia*) is the fire of madness (Game of Chess), destruction (falling cities) and lust (Carthage). Air, source of wisdom (the spoken words from the *Upanishads* in 'what the thunder said'), symbolises the only spiritual way to the dilemma of sterility but then it is wisdom suggested in an alien tongue and the wind is doing 'nothing'. Spiritual love of Rudolph and Maria, Tristan and Isolde, Hyacinth girl and the quester, Antony and Cleopatra, Elizabeth and Leicester, Marvell's lovers, is contrasted with love turned to lust through the passionless coupling of the typist and the young man, loss of love in the garden, Lil's abortions, Eugenides' deviations, violation of Thames' daughters and Rhine maidens, violation of Philomel and La Pia (Dante's *Purgatorio*).

Thus, the 'yoking together' of juxtaposed associations of Manichaean images brings into sharp focus the need of the wastelanders for a 'Knight' who can restore fertility and life to the sterile desert.

The Manichaean 'Knight' appears in the form of King Fisher, the hanged god in the perspectives of the fertility cults and Christianity and lastly, the Upanishadic myth of the renewal of self. These myths have been synthesised to bring home to us the 'necessity' and possibility of purgation of our debased earthly existence. They symbolise the potential to restore life to the dead land. The hooded figure in 'What the Thunder Said' gives an idea of Eliot's belief in the incarnation which finds its fullest expression in the Facsimile edition of *The Waste Land* preserving a discarded fragment as a short poem, 'I am the Resurrection and the life'. The unknowability of the Knight or the Warrior of the forces of light or god presented here in Emerson's style in *Brahma* reveals Eliot's own religious emotion:

> I am the Resurrection and the life
> I am the things that stay, and those that flow
> I am the husband and the wife
> And the victim and the sacrificial knife
> I am the fire, and the butter also.[206]

Tiresias, the overseeing imagination of the poet, mediates between us and the protagonist; he enables us to see God struggling to be born in Man. Eliot connects the entire context of the moral degradation and spiritual death with the supernatural by making us listen to the divine sound of the 'Thunder' coming above the normal temporal existence.

This reference to an oriental idea of redemption from the life of lust and narrow selfishness is related to the implicit central motif of right action which is introduced as an antithesis to the panorama of inaction and wrong action of which the wastelanders are incurable victims. The tale of Prajapati has similarity with the Manichaean myth with its divine messenger. Eliot's originality lies in drawing the image of the thunder from the epithet 'thundering' used for qualifying the voice of Prajapati in *Brihadarnakya Upanishad* where he appears in his divine form as a person, nay as a veritable father addressing his own sons in response to their prayers offered in a moment of crisis. Eliot makes out of this archetypal sound a poetic image of universal truth. The triple derivatives of 'Da' (*Datta, Dayadhvam, Damyata*)

---

206. Eliot, Valerie, ed., *T. S. Eliot, The Waste Land, A Facsimile and Transcript of the Original Drafts*, (New York, 1971), p. 111. Also included in *The Collected Poetry and Plays*, p. 606.

are used for suggesting an antidote of moral and spiritual degradation of the inmates of the waste land as well as way out of it. Through the sound of the thunder we are led to witness within the 'heap of broken images' or the 'rats alley' a Manichaean light that reveals the redeeming truth and affirms the possibility of resurrection 'in a handful of dust'.

Significantly, the thunder speaks when the disgusting panorama of carnality and nerve-wrecking alienation have been fully visualised and the antithetical theme of ascetic purgation advocated by Mani has been introduced through Buddha and Augustine:

> Burning burning burning burning
> O Lord Thou pluckest me out

It evidences Eliot's understanding of the fact that morality as an ethical concept that governs our ways of life, essentially emanates from the basic foundations of a religious ideal. Eliot's elaboration of the three derivatives of 'Da' constitute the replies or the interpretations of the implied commands of the divine father. The subtle irony implied in the replies reveals the double aspects of human conduct—the intensely shared experience of love (*Datta*) and the inadequacy of mere sexual relations; the unbounded sense of unity with one's fellow beings (*Dayadhvam*) and the solitary imprisonment of the egoistical self; the harmonious order of a perfectly restrained existence (*Damyata*) and a disordered and negative life of sexual gratification.

> What have we given?
> My friend, blood shaking my heart
> The awful daring of a moment's surrender

It is left for us to see whether the image of giving which is symbolic of the perpetuation of human race is to be an act of an all-embracing love or a mere tyranny of blood, a physical involvement. The heart-searching, leading to an acceptance of the command, forms the basis of right understanding.

The second response, *Dayadhvam*, hints at Eliot's purpose to arrive at a poetic affirmation through negation. Through a concrete image of a prison tower he sets into sharp focus the pitiable state of our negative isolation bred by our egoistical self. It is a Manichaean image suggesting ironically that real sympathy is an act of giving oneself to someone or something outside one and the lack of which causes both individual debasement and national curse. Devoid of true sympathy everyone breeds a Coriolanus within oneself eventually to suffer a self-imposed banishment and final doom. The image implies that the prison wall has to be shattered for a true liberation of the self.

The last of the triple path of liberation forms the third response to the divine sound, given by the gods in the Upanishad. The vivid image of a boat, directed by controlled hands and floating with a rhythm of joy on the calm surface of the sea, evokes the state of a self-poised being. Obviously, the image seems to be based on that of a barge used by Lord Krishna in *The Bhagvad Gita* (11, 67–68) for admonishing Arjuna on the necessity of self-control as a pre-condition of spiritual liberation. Lord Krishna tells Arjuna that as the wind carries away a barge upon the waters, even so of the wandering senses, the one to which the mind is joined takes away his discrimination. Eliot's originality lies in employing the basic image to picture a joyful voyage of a poised mind on the calm waters of the sea. It is no wonder, then, that Eliot, who read *Patanjali* and *The Bhagvad Gita* thoroughly at Harvard, employs this image as an effective antidote to lust (Kama) which is the root cause of all our debasement and hollowness. The life of lust, depicted in all its variants in *The Waste Land* on the one hand, and the admonition of self-control on the other, relate the loss of the sacred aspect of sexuality, which makes it fertile and life-giving. Hence, the lust for flesh or money must need be suppressed through a purging practice of inner restraint (*Damyata*) and transcended through self-effacing acts of giving and all-embracing sympathy. Hands 'expert with sail and oar' are not, as Hugh Kenner suggests; 'the imagined instruments of comparably sensitive human relationship',[207] but in a Manichaean juxtaposition to the 'heart responding gaily when invited, beating obedient / To controlling hands', they connote more accurately the idea of an integrated personality, hands embodying the controlling mind. The response of the heart would have been 'gaily' only if it could obey the controlling hands, and the joy of a poised life (*Shantih*) can be attained only in such a state of the integrated self, realised through an inner control. The relief suggested by the final words of the poem 'Shantih, Shantih, Shantih', is experienced as the consequence of an inner discipline of liberation from the sensual bondages. What is needed for the attainment of 'shantih' is obviously the complete concord between hand and the heart— an integrated personality which lends wholeness to our life. This psychic equilibrium is what Manichaean and Shamanistic practices aim at. Manichaeism also attributes liberation to the human mind which overcomes all evil and temporal impulses.

The movement from *Gerontion* to *The Waste Land* is a movement from the loss of God as Love to a communion with God as Law. The haunting image of the lost father suggested repeatedly by the allusion to *The Tempest* melts finally in the restored image of the cosmic father who out of his fatherly benevolence, offers us his commands of right action that bring order in a disordered world and restore light to dark souls.

In *Murder in the Cathedral*, Becket has 'assumed a double part', separating his inner immortal self from the impurified part of himself. This latter part appears in front of the audience as Four Temptations which, in a sense,

---
207. *The Invisible Poets* (London, 1960), p. 152.

reiterate the one dominant theme of which all the plays of Eliot are variations—the quest for self-fulfilment. The nature of this quest is indicated in a highly significant analysis of the two selves in Man made by Edward in *The Cocktail Party*: 'The self that can say, "I want this or want that"/ The self that wills—he is a feeble creature;/ He has to come to terms in the end / with the obstinate, the tougher self; who does not speak / who never talks, who cannot argue / And who is some men may be the guardian / But in men like me, the dull, the implacable, / The indomitable spirit of mediocrity / The willing self can contrive disaster / Of this unwilling partnership— but can only flourish / In submission to the rule of the stronger partner.'[208] The Manichaean quest in which all Eliot's major characters are engaged is the attempt to make the feeble, self-centred, desire-ridden self come to terms with the 'tougher' self, which if properly developed can play a role similar to that of Plato's 'guardians', who were noble-minded and altruistic public servants or to that of Mani's 'Knight' who is the spirit which prevails over matter. Given scope, it leads a person to self-knowledge and self-fulfilment, thus making for salvation. Denied scope, it leaves the feeble, self-centred self to dominate the personality, which therefore, lacks vision and remains blind to spiritual values.

In the protagonist of Eliot, the better self has a high potential which is developed during the course of the play and is usually flanked by the 'tougher' or 'weak' selves. Becket, in *Murder in the Cathedral*, also combines the roles of the helper and the seeker. The Tempters represent the element of the 'blind' in Becket, which he overcomes with the help of his 'tougher' self. A moment comes when the path of his spiritual journey is 'clear' and the meaning of his quest 'plain': he will not yield to the temptation of willing to become a martyr because it will be doing 'the right deed for the wrong reason', falling a prey to self-will rather than patiently waiting for the behest of God and

---
208. *Collected Plays* (London, 1962), pp. 153–154.

obeying it. He now understands the paradox of 'action and suffering'. The last temptation, ironically, is a gift of grace.

Of the four worlds, there is no place for the rose-garden: we begin in experience, represented by the Chorus. The Chorus becomes increasingly aware that experience is the doorway to hell. The ambivalent attitude of the common Women of Canterbury is suggested through the paradoxical Manichaean image.

> Are we drawn by danger?
> Is it the knowledge of safety, that draws our feet
> Towards the cathedral?
> *   *   *   *
> The New Year waits
> Winter shall come bringing death from the sea . . .
> *   *   *   *
> Sweet and cloying through the dark air Falls the stifling sense of despair
> *   *   *   *
> What signs of a bitter spring?

Becket discloses to these anxiety-ridden Women of Canterbury the meaning of agony and ecstasy in moments of adversity:

> This is your share of the eternal burden,
> The perpetual glory. This is one moment,
> But know that another
> Shall pierce you with a sudden painful joy
> When the figure of God's purpose is made complete.[209]

They are, he means to say, passing through the despairing darkness of soul but their soul will certainly experience the dawn of the 'Invisible Light'. The Priests, being afraid of danger to his life, request him to run away to the altar to save himself but he only affirms his belief in the meaning of life and death:

---

209. *Collected Plays*, (London 1962), p. 43.

> All my life they have been coming, these feet.
> All my life I have waited.
> Death will come only when I am worthy,
> And if I am worthy, there is no danger.
> I have therefore only to make perfect my will.[210]

Being 'near to death' does not amount to 'being in danger', he says. He has a premonition of his death which exhilarates his soul; he is feeling the bliss of death:

> I have had a tremor of bliss, a wink of heaven, a whisper,
> And I would no longer be denied; all things
> Proceed to a joyful consummation.[211]

It is Christian humility that Becket is affirming here. He has triumphed over his beastly passions, now he will conquer the foes by suffering, as did Christ. The moment of his death is 'out of life', 'out of time'. The Manichaean image of wheel, thus, is central to the play. True martyr is one who has, in the midst of this turning world of flux, found his still centre in God and is truly unchanging in this ever-changing cycle of nature and life. Hence the persistence of the wheel in the play.

The Third Priest, who is perfectly enlightened spiritually, underscores the meaning of the Archbishop's martyrdom:

> ... the church is stronger for this action,
> Triumphant in adversity. It is fortified
> By persecution: supreme, so long as men will die for it.[212]

On the other hand, he condemns through paradoxical images, the death- in-life state of 'the lost erring souls, homeless in earth or heaven' living a life of insignificant toil; of meaningless thought, of make-believe but not of belief:

---

210. Ibid., p. 43.
211. Ibid., p. 44.
212. *Collected Plays*, p. 52.

> In the small circle of pain within the skull
> You still shall tramp and tread one endless round
> Of thought, to justify your action to yourselves,
> Weaving a fiction which unravels as you weave,
> Packing forever in the hell of make-believe
> Which never is belief; this is your fate on earth.[213]

Becket, in a sense, becomes the Manichaean figure of the Knight. His conquest and his surrender are against the material world, he conquers by surrendering to his re-absorption into it. The play echoes the philosophy of *The Gita*. Surrender implies 'cinder' — combustion (extinction) of ego. One who surrenders his ego, he surrenders to a greater consciousness and, thus, conquers his self and becomes a 'self-aware' person. But this surrender must be self-giving and spontaneous. Such a man becomes all-pervading.

The Gita advocates renunciation not of action, but renunciation in action; renunciation of the self sense and re-absorption into the universal good: *Loksamgraha*. Arjuna, the pupil of Lord Krishna, a variation on the Primal Man, typifies the representative human soul seeking to reach perfection and peace. He fights with the forces of darkness, falsehood and immorality, which bar the way to the higher world. The whole teaching of Krishna and Mani requires man to choose the good and realise it by conscious effort. Man, the subject, should get mastery over man, the object. 'Being' should overcome non-being on way to 'becoming'. In *Murder in the Cathedral* the overwhelming sense of non-being communicated by the Chorus is balanced by the rhetorical twist that death is also rebirth. 'It feels like the world/Before your eyes ever opened' — an idea conveyed by Eliot in *The Waste Land*. Thus all the images in Eliot's works typify the dualism of death and rebirth. Physical death is the pre-condition of rebirth.

The same Manichaean dualism is at the heart of *The Family Reunion* conveyed through paradoxical images. According to M. K. Naik:

---
213. Ibid.

> *The Family Reunion*, richest in imagery of all Eliot's plays, has not one dominant image but a linked set of symbols, which expresses its prevailing spirit. Images of cold and dark, ghosts and shadows, light and warmth, journey and frontier, and disease and curative magic form a persistent under-song in the play which Agatha describes as '. . . a story of sin and expiation' .[214]

Harry's sufferings are conveyed through such Manichaean images as 'solitude in a crowded desert', 'voice in the silence', 'cold spring' etc. His searing with suffering finds expression in such images: 'you all look so withered and young,'[215] 'In a thick smoke, many creatures moving. . . . In flickering intervals of light and darkness;/ The partial anesthesia of suffering without feeling'.[216] When Harry sees his own sin as part of the family curse, he feels released from the past and proclaims that liberty is 'a different kind of pain from prison'. In her reply, it is almost as though Agatha were taking up the image of the open prison door, providing a glimpse of the 'rose-garden'. This image as opposed to that of 'desert' (when both Harry and Agatha speak of their experiences of dragging themselves through deserts) symbolises love and innocence, its memory leading to purgation.

We can take the first rose-garden as the garden of (Agatha's) erotic love (for Harry's father), whereas the rose, in the second instance, has been transformed into the symbol of trans-erotic love (as in Dante's *Paradiso* 23). As in *Murder in the Cathedral*, it would again be a case of literally the same, rose-garden yet, spiritually, worlds apart: for Thomas, damnation or salvation, for Harry, being haunted or following his own road. On the whole, the rose-garden is a Manichaean image, denoting anti-thetical suggestions for different characters. One can also accept the rose-garden, in *The Family Reunion*, as the same, in kind, as the one in

---
214. Naik, M. K, *Mighty Voices: Studies in T. S. Eliot*, p. 97.
215. *The Family Reunion* (Delhi: Oxford University Press, 1963), p. 79.
216. Ibid., p. 82.

the opening movement of 'Burnt Norton': as an image of the plentitude of an unaccountable moment's experience which provides clarity and meaning. He expresses this moment of enlightenment again in Manichaean images of reality and shadows:

> The things I thought were real are shadows, and the real
> Are what I thought were private shadows.[217]

He, along with Agatha, looks back from the new stand point upon the hollow past, finding in the present moment its fulfilment and an end which is also a beginning.

Agatha, in fact, is the Manichaean Knight bringing light to the dark soul of Harry. She has known moments of fulfilment when 'there seems to be no past or future,/ only a present moment of pointed light / when you want to burn'.[218] Hence, she is able to make Harry realise the true nature of his malady and can also suggest the solution which is 'the pilgrimage of expiation'. Harry's spiritual struggle makes him a seeker who is brought out of his doubts by Agatha:

> This is like an end
> And a beginning.[219]
>
> * * * *
>
> O my child, my curse
> You shall be fulfilled
> The knot shall be unknotted
> And the crooked made straight.[220]

Thus, Eliot's knowledge of the ancient myths, his study of anthropology, his concern with the world with all its dualities (matter and spirit, death and rebirth, sin and expiation, temporality and spirituality, sterility and

---
217. *The Family Reunion*, p. 150.
218. *Collected Plays*, p. 104.
219. *The Family Reunion*, p. 149.
220. Ibid., p. 153.

fertility), his suggestive logic to control the temporal energy and channelise it to universal good, his Manichaean preoccupation with articulating being and becoming and the myth of the Primal Man or the Warrior of the forces of light are the basis of his imagistic pattern. Images, indeed, are the vehicles for the expression of modern dilemma with all its complexity. Eliot shares with Manichaeans the knowledge of the relationship of human mind with the forces within and without. His Manichaean images, dominating in his works, expose the psycho-neurotic state when this relationship is disturbed and suggest the ways to restore balance. Mani's importance in the making of Eliot's mind lies in the fact that Manichaeism provided an answer to Eliot's problem of redemption which lay in the attainment of the 'still centre' — the state of the '*Istithaprajna*' of *The Gita* or '*kayvalya*' of *Patanjali*. Eliot described it later as the point 'where past and future are gathered' and which, at its practical level of flowing consciousness, involves the inner freedom from the practical desire: 'The release from action and suffering, release from the inner and outer compulsion' (*Four Quartets*). It is interesting to note that this idea is common to the Manichaean myth, *The Gita*, *Patanjali*, Buddhism and Christian asceticism, particularly the mysticism of St. John of the Cross. They all assert the same philosophy: the soul cannot be possessed by the divine union, until it has divested itself of the love of created beings. Thus, salvation within this world is suggested through the reflection of the universe as a system of contradictions, a mere appearance of reality.

8

Conclusion

In the present age the poet's main concern seems to use new and striking images as a technical device to dramatise the theme. Coleridge remarked: 'Images, however beautiful, do not of themselves characterize the poet. They become proof of original genius only so far as they are modified by a predominant passion; or by associated thoughts or images awakened by that passion.' What Coleridge implies is that a poem should have a unifying theme passionately conceived and passionately developed. In order to be functional, images should be inter-linked by a running theme. In Eliot's works images are functional. Therefore, they are not conventional but given with the ideas to which they correspond. They become modes of thought rather than ornaments of speech. Since each of Eliot's images participates in the reality symbolised by it his images are 'accurate, precise and definite'.

The principle that organises Eliot's images is a concord between image and theme, the images lighting the way for the theme and helping to reveal to the poet the theme as it gradually develops. But Eliot's ingenuity lies in the way he combines images with incongruous ideas, which at first seems to be mind-boggling. But a deeper study reveals a remarkable relation between the image and the corresponding association on the psychic level. For Eliot's major concern is the inner life and psychic processes of modern mind which do require special complex images to interpret their realities. Hence same images recurring through Eliot's works denote diverse associations in the context of different personae and situations. The same object evokes different ideas and concepts from different perceivers. What is significant is not the object of perception, but the concept that is given birth through the perception in a particular psychic condition. So all the images used by Eliot have been studied at the conceptual level which is definitely related to perceptual level.

The poetic mode of Eliot works by fusion of elements. For him, the poem is a particular medium 'in which impressions and experiences combine in peculiar and unexpected ways'. Poetic apprehension means for him the emotion 'wholly evoked by the object of contemplation to which it is adequate'. The theme or philosophy of a poem, thus, appears not as a narrative structure but as a pattern of images.

The primary theme which stirs Eliot's poetry into quaint-looking images, (temporal, spatial and psychological) is the barrenness of man's contemporary spiritual state. It assumes many imagistic forms—sand and dry rock, gashouse ugliness, sandwich-paper litter, parvenu vulgarity, prostitution, hysteria, death and half-death; underlying all of which are the two main tokens of spiritual failure—neutrality and separation. The crowd that flows over London Bridge each morning to the drab necessities of urban employment is likened to the ruined souls whom Dante's Hell rejects—moral isolationists who could not make a choice, damned followers of a wavering banner. Dante describes them through the image of sand—its dryness, barrenness and non-resistance to the wind. Eliot thickens the imagery by evoking in the next line another scene from the Inferno—the second circle, where lust, once so alive, has withered into a stereotype, an attitude, dull gnawing restlessness without hope of comfort, fulfilment, or release and where the only light — as in Blake's engraving of the scene — is an ever-dimming memory of lost joy. The larger theme of the individual's isolation, his estrangement from other people and from the world is also related to the ultimate subject throughout Eliot's work: the estrangement between man and woman. Hence, the images highlighting these two themes are psychological images. In *Portrait of a Lady* the young man's 'self possession' means not only his poise but, in the context of Eliot's major theme, his isolation, his inability to give himself to or to possess others. In *Prufrock* the theme of isolation is pervasive and represented in various images, from the 'patient etherized upon a table' at the beginning, to 'the mermaids', at the end who will not 'sing to me' — but especially in the images of 'claws' and 'sea'. *The Waste Land* presents a procession of characters locked within themselves: 'We think of the key, each in his prison/Thinking of the key, each confirms a prison . . .'

When we turn to the plays, we find characters either accepting isolation or struggling to escape from it. Thomas is, by definition, set apart from ordinary humanity. Hence images suggesting this isolation are religious images. Harry, towards the end of *The Family Reunion*, says, 'where does one go from a world of insanity?' — and his sharpened sense of spiritual awakening leads him towards the way of the saint and the martyr. The theme of isolation is conveyed through the circle image in one of the choruses in the play:

> But the circle of our understanding
> Is a very restricted area.
> Except for a limited number
> Of strictly practical purposes
> We do not know what we are doing;
> And even, when you think of it,
> We do not know much about thinking.
> What is happening outside of the circle?
> And what is the meaning of happening?

Eliot has defined Harry's isolation by vividly portraying the world from which he is alienated. A person's identity is defined by his world, and to escape one is as difficult as to escape the other.

Characteristically, the moments and images of beauty in Eliot's works are meagre and brief and are obviously calculated to serve as a contrasting emphasis on the opposite, as in *The Waste Land*:

> ... the nightingale
> Filled all the desert with inviolable voice
> And still she cried, and still the world pursues,
> 'dirty' to Jug Jug ears.

Up through *The Waste Land*, Eliot's poetry is richly furnished with the images of the sordid, the disgusting, and the depressing. In the poems of the 'Prufrock' group, there are one-night cheap hotels and sawdust restaurants, the vacant lots, faint stale smells of beer, a thousand furnished rooms and the yellow soles of feet, the dead geraniums, the broken spring in a factory yard, all the old nocturnal smells, the basement kitchens, and the damp souls of housemaids. In the poems of the 'Gerontion' group (1920), there are 'rocks, moss, stonecrop, iron, merds'. *The Waste Land* and *The Hollow Men* (1925) are also full of obnoxious images as the titles are indicating clearly enough the grounds of alienation.

This idea of isolation, of the impossibility of communication and understanding has a direct bearing on Eliot's imagistic patterns and the structure of his poems, for the thematic problem is not only that of communication between one person and another but finally, that of articulation itself. Prufrock declares:

> It is impossible to say just what I mean!
> But as if a magic lantern threw the nerves in patterns on a screen

This statement is relevant to Eliot's entire early poetry. A familiar complaint about Eliot's early poetry, including *Prufrock*, was that it was difficult and obscure, that it did not clearly and directly say what it means. But once one has understood the pattern of images evolved in the study, the interpretation of Eliot's poems and plays becomes easily comprehensible and the works of Eliot greatly enjoyable. Every poem and play of Eliot is like a series of slides impinging on the mental and social screen. Each slide is an isolated, fragmentary image, producing its own effect, including suggestions of some larger action or situation of which it is but an arrested moment. For example, *Prufrock* proceeds from the half deserted streets at evening, to the women coming and going, to the yellow fog, to Prufrock descending the stairs, and so on, to the mermaids at the end of the poem. Each part of the poem, each image, each fragment, remains fragmentary even within its given context. A series of larger wholes is suggested , and yet the series of suggestions or images is itself a kind of whole. It is the poem. It is Prufrock. He has gone nowhere and done nothing. He has conducted an 'interior monologue', as the critics have said, and he is the monologue. All the scenery of the poem, indoor and outdoor, is finally the psychological landscape of Prufrock himself and all the images — the streets, evening, restaurants, rooms, people, and fancies of the poem are psychological images since they all register on Prufrock's consciousness. This is the general imagistic pattern of a characteristic poem of Eliot: ending on the note of the fragmentary, which is a part of the unity of the poem.

The various images in the poems following *Prufrock* like *Gerontion* and *The Waste Land* deepen, expand and complicate features of the preceding poems. Same is true of Eliot's plays, since all the recurring images are inter-related. As the in-depth study of the various poems and plays of Eliot has revealed that all the broken images are assembled into the heap which is the work itself, the perfect amalgam of Manichaean images of past and present, memory and desire, death and rebirth, sterility and fertility, darkness and light. The series of fragments work through various images to compress and intensify the technique, the mode of expression, which has operated throughout the work.

This fragmentariness is part of Eliot's technique as he reveals in his response to the question whether *Ash-Wednesday* had begun as separate poems: 'Yes, like *The Hollow Men*, it originated out of separate poems. Then gradually I came to see it as a sequence. That's one way in which my mind does seem to have worked throughout the years poetically—doing things separately and then seeing the possibility of fusing them together, altering them and making a kind of whole of them.' A 'kind' of whole—that is an apt and significant description of Eliot's imagistic patterns.

Each image, like the individual parts of *Four Quartets* allows itself the separate unity in relation to its context, and at the same time becomes a part of the larger pattern. For each work of Eliot, whether a poem or a play, has an affinity with other works in terms of themes of time, alienation, isolation, articulation, spiritual barrenness. This affinity obviously contributes to the continuity. And so does a steadily developing pattern of interrelated images and symbols.

There are, for example, the images of desert and garden, water and underwater, rain and river and sea, flowers and animals, music, stairs, human parts, time of the day, months, seasons, streets etc. All these images remain enigmatic unless related to the similar images in Eliot's other works. This is simply because all these images yield no simple or consistent meaning and undergo radical changes. An attempt has been made in this study not only to evolve a pattern of images but also to correlate them with various works of Eliot. For instance, the 'sea' image shows the most revealing change: a 'splitting' effect in which the image keeps some of its early meanings, but sheds others which then re-emerge in a different imagistic form. *Prufrock* ends with a complex image (mermaid, sea, song, his wished-for journey) representing an intricate emotional blend, desire for a freer life, for beauty and love, fear of risk, despair and unheroic resignation. *Marina* also uses the sea as part of a complex image, but shifts its attractive qualities elsewhere. The sea is merely the condition of the sea-voyage whose goal is represented in the islands, the birdsong and the pine trees. Even its latent dangerousness has been diluted since what may wreck the boat is not 'water lapping the bow', but the 'granite islands'. And further, though Prufrock's mermaids have disappeared, some of their qualities remain. The haunting birdsong through the fog embodies their seductive aspect; the relation between Pericles and his daughter fulfils and transforms the mermaids' promise of love, and where Prufrock, resigning the heroic role, does not expect the mermaids to sing to him, Pericles hears the birdsong and speaks himself to his daughter.

Similarly one persistent element in Eliot's works, which takes imagistic form but also exists as an idea in the consciousness of the personae, is the element of journey. Eliot's poems and plays are full of taken and untaken journeys, along streets, down rivers, over mountains, across seas. The lover in the *Portrait of a Lady* reports visits to his mistress, one an unwilling climbing of stairs, and ends with thoughts of going abroad. Prufrock invites to a journey through streets, imagines his return from the dead, and ends standing on a beach looking over water which he would like to but will not cross. Gerontion's mind is full of vain journeys, real and metaphorical, and he thinks of death as a journey into nothingness. *The Waste Land* is a long legendary quest which finds expression in various spatial images centring around land and desert. Its protagonist is constantly on the move in the desert over the mountains, to the ruined chapel, in the water and the journey ends in spiritual awakening through air, 'thunder'. *Journey of the Magi* concentrates on the journey taken (instead of the traditional moment of the arrival), and *Marina* pre-supposes a nearly concluded sea-voyage. *Ash-Wednesday* III recounts a journey upstairs, and VI exhorts to a final move away from the sea into the desert. *Four Quartets* adopts the endless journey as the appropriate metaphor for human life, whether on the sea, up a river, or along 'the edge of a grimpen'.

In Christian thought, the journey is, of course, a venerable image, and Auden has given a cogent explanation for this which throws light on the difference between Eliot's later and earlier use of journey image:

The Christian concept of time as a divine creation, to be accepted, and not, as in platonic philosophy and stoic philosophy, to be ignored, made the journey or pilgrimage a natural symbol for the spiritual life.

Upto and including *The Waste Land*, journeys are merely dreamt of, or vainly aspired towards, or if taken, disappointing, of uncertain value. But in *Marina* the journey is fruitful, though dangerous, and the speaker has to build his own boat to make it. (In contrast are the dreams of Prufrock and the hypothetical boating-trip at the end of *The Waste Land*). Again, in *Ash-Wednesday* III, the speaker struggles purposefully upstairs past a vision of renounced, innocent sexuality (innocent because renounced), instead of like Prufrock—hesitantly towards a corrupt sexuality which bores and frightens him. In *Four Quartets*, *Murder in the Cathedral*, and *The Family Reunion*, journeys are actually taken, instead of being dreamed about or proving illusory and therefore, are valued. The vague promise imagined by Prufrock becomes the unknowable certainty pursued by the traveller in *Four Quartets* and *The Family Reunion*. Marina is the earliest poem to show what this involves: the necessary access of purpose (the boat), and the taking of the risk (the granite that will wreck the boat), which Prufrock both lacks and fears.

Thus, the change in the 'sea' image or 'journey' image or any other image is associated with the continuity as well as the development of an exquisite imagistic pattern. The 'splitting' effect which makes the sea merely a medium, and which projects its original promise of freedom and romance onto the island images, takes place when the journey across the sea is undertaken. Similarly, the valuable journey, with what it suggests of choice and will-power, of 'resolution and independence', is intimately related to the general development of imagery, to the process of simplification, clarification of emotional texture, growing generality, the polarisation of experience and the withdrawal from the reader of its most significant level.

This last process, in fact, can be seen indirectly at work in the way the journey image itself develops, if we examine not its structural aspect, but the texture, the actual scenery of the journey. The new decisiveness that takes the traveller onto the sea, towards islands, deep into the ocean, also takes him away from streets, houses, cities and people. The transition begins in *The Waste Land*, where the observer-protagonist starts in the city (Madame Sosostris, the crowd on London Bridge, the church clock, the boudoir, the pub) moves to the river bank, then down-river ('o city city') towards the sea that drowns Phlebas, and on whose shore the Fisher King finally sits meditating. (Meanwhile various centres of Western civilisation have been declared unreal, and London Bridge is falling down). The germ of the movement lies in the early poems' use of the sea as a means of imagined escape from the stifling triviality of metropolitan culture, and in *Coriolon* we see its full flowering. Finally, in *Four Quartets*, city scrapes have become phantasmal, mere occasions for something more real to declare itself. The authentic scenery is found in gardens, the country, the villages of the titles of each poem, the journeys on marsh, cliff and sea; and the traveller is always on his own, 'a spirit unappeased and peregrine'.

Thus, the images from one poem or play to another change so radically that interpreting their recurrence is a complex matter, and may even lead one to question whether 'recurrence' is a particularly fruitful way of discussing them. Secondly, these changes in imagery provide an approach to the poetry and plays which respects its integrity and does not involve a reduction of the works to mere 'expressions of the thought'.

In relating themes and images of a work to earlier poems or plays, Eliot re-interprets and re-evaluates them. This is not to say that the earlier apparent meanings or suggestions carried out by the images are cancelled out by the later poems any more than one quartet cancels out another or the later plays cancel out the earlier plays and poems. While each image remains itself, it takes on an additional aspect, a qualification of meaning, in the larger context. The same theme, recurring in many works may be highlighted through different images or one image recurring in many works may be related to different themes. The image of hyacinth girl, or 'rose-garden', suggesting failure of communication in *The Waste Land*, changes its implications in relation to other emerging themes, especially religious ones, as it does in *Ash-Wednesday, Four Quartets, The Family Reunion* and *The Confidential Clerk*.

Considering the recurrent themes, intricate implications of constantly changing images, accumulation of meaning, merging or overlapping of one image with another, a retroactive effect of later images upon earlier ones, a pattern of images which is all-inclusive is an absolute necessity. For without this, the linguistic structure of Eliot's art would remain an enigma. The pattern traced in the study—temporal, spatial, psychological, classical and Manichaean—highlights the development of Eliot's talent while it also lends a comprehensive meaning to the structure of his images. The present study shows that every image, irrespective of its various connotations, will fall under one or all of these five categories. While temporal, spatial and psychological images deal with the modern themes and create atmosphere, the classical and Manichaean images provide a solid structure, a network for the atmospheric images and hold tight the weaving of these images. This pattern is significantly indicative of the packed character of Eliot's imagery and of the interlocking network of thematic correspondences.

Eliot's preoccupation with images is also a sign of the modern poet's efforts to elucidate and control the modern scene and the modern situation by juxtaposing it against the glorious past of classical times and mythical world. This juxtapositioning brings out a way to the dilemma of split consciousness of modern man. That is why while the early poetry is richly furnished with images of the sordid, the disgusting, and the depressing the later poems and plays are replete with the religious images, bringing out the beauty of the spirit and attainment of timelessness. His images, thus, are associated not only with the perceptions of the contemporary life, but also with his conceptions.

There is no gain saying the fact that the best approach to interpret and understand the works of Eliot is through the images used by him. Efforts have been made by critics and scholars on Eliot to appreciate various images in isolation. But no exclusive attempt has been made to codify images of Eliot into a pattern with a view to enhancing the understanding of Eliot's poems and plays, since none could perceive the unity inherent in the inter-related images. That unity has now been codified into a comprehensive pattern which harmonises and binds all the images used by Eliot. The pattern of images vis-a-vis the plethora of images falling within the categories of temporal, spatial, psychological, classical and Manichaean, gives a new meaning to the overall understanding of the otherwise difficult and obscure works of Eliot.

Bibliography

Primary Sources

Eliot, T. S., *After Strange Gods: A Primer of Modern Heresy*, London: Faber and Faber, 1934.
― ― ―, *Collected Poems*, London: Faber and Faber, 1963.
― ― ―, *For Lancelot Andrewes: Essay on Style and Order*, London: Faber and Faber, 1928.
― ― ―, *Knowledge and Experience in the Philosophy of F. H. Bradley*, London: Faber and Faber, 1964.
― ― ―, *Murder in the Cathedral*, Delhi: Oxford University Press, 1963.
― ― ―, *Notes Towards the Definition of Culture*, London: Faber and Faber, 1948.
― ― ―, *On Poetry and Poets*, London: Faber and Faber, 1957.
― ― ―, *Selected Essays*, London: Faber and Faber, 1951–1961.
― ― ―, *Selected Prose*, Edited by John Hayward, London: Penguin Books, 1958.
― ― ―, *The Complete Poems and Plays*, London: Faber and Faber, 1969.
― ― ―, *The Family Reunion*, Delhi: Oxford University Press, 1963.
― ― ―, *The Idea of a Christian Society*, London: Faber and Faber, 1939.
― ― ―, *The Music of Poetry*. Glasgow University Publication—No. L-VII, Glasgow: Jackson, 1942.
― ― ―, *The Sacred Wood: Essays on Poetry and Criticism*, London: Methuen and Co., 1950.

― ― ―, *The Three Voices of Poetry*, London: Cambridge University Press, 1953.

― ― ―, *The Use of Poetry and the Use of Criticism: Studies in the Relation of Criticism to Poetry in England*, 2nd ed., London: Faber and Faber, 1964.

― ― ―, *To Criticize the Critic*, London: Faber and Faber, 1965,

Other Primary Sources Used

Bergson, Henri Louis, *An Introduction to Metaphysics*, Translated by T. E. Hulme, New York: G. P. Putnam's Sons, 1912.

― ― ―, *Creative Evolution*, Authorised translation by Arthur Mitchell, New York: Henry Holt and Co., 1963.

― ― ―, *Matter and Memory*, Authorised translation by Nancy Margaret Paul and W. Scott Palmer, London: Allen and Unwin, 1950.

― ― ―, *Time and Free Will: An Essay on the Immediate Data of Consciousness*, Authorised translation by F. L. Posson, London: Allen & Unwin, 1950.

Bradley, F. H, *Appearance and Reality*, London: G. Allen and Unwin, Ltd., 1897.

Brandon, S. G. F., *History, Time and Deit: A Historical and Comparative Study of the Conception of Time in Religious Thought and Practice*, New York: Barnes and Noble, Inc., 1965.

Chiari, Joseph, *Symbolism from Poe to Mallarme*, London: Rockliff, 1957.

Conrad, Joseph, *Heart of Darkness*, London: Penguin Books, 1973.

Dante, *The Inferno*, Translated by John Ciardi, New York: New American Library, 1954.

― ― ―, *The Paradiso*, Translated by John Ciardi, New York: New American Library, 1970.

― ― ―, *The Purgatorio*, Translated by John Ciardi, New York: New American Library, 1961.

Frazer, Sir James, *The Golden Bough: A Study in Magic and Religion*, New York: The Macmillan Company, 1935.

Heidegger, M., *Being and Nothing*, tr., John Maquarrie and Edward Robinson, London: SCM Press Ltd., 1962.

Jaspers, Karl, *Man in the Modern Age*, tr., Eden and Cedar Paul, London: Routledge & Kegan Paul Ltd., 1951.

Sartre, Jean-Paul, *Being and Nothingness*, tr., Hazel Barnes, London: Methuen & Co., 1957.

— — —, *The Psychology of Imagination*, New York: Philosophical Library, 1948.

Symons, Arthur, *The Symbolist Movement in Literature*, London: Constable, 1899.

The Bhagvad Gita, Translated by Eliot Deutsch, New York: Holt, Rinehart and Winston, 1968.

Secondary Sources

Ackroyd, Peter, *T. S. Eliot: A Life*, New York: Simon Schuster, 1984.

Benjamin, Walter, *Charles Baudelaire: A Lyric Poet in the Era of High Capitalism*, tr., Suhrkamp Verlog, 1969.

Bergsten, Staffan, *Time and Eternity: A Study in the Structure and Symbolism of T. S. Eliot's Four Quartets*, Stockholm: Svenska bokforlaget, 1960.

Blamires, Harry, *Word Unheard: A Guide Through Eliot's Four Quartets*, London: Methuen & Co., 1969.

Bowra, C. M., *The Heritage of Symbolism*, London: Macmillan and Co. Ltd., 1954.

Bradbrook, M. C., *T. S. Eliot*, London: Longmans Green, 1950.

Braybook, Neville, ed., *T. S. Eliot: A Symposium for His Seventieth Birthday*, New York: Farrar, Strans and Cudahy, 1958.

Brooks, Cleanth, *Modern Poetry and the Tradition*, London: University of North Caroline Press, 1967.

Chiari, Joseph, *T. S. Eliot: Poet and Dramatist*, London: Vision, 1972.

Davidson, Harriet, *T. S. Eliot and Hermeneutics: Absence and Interpretation in The Waste Land*, Baton Rouge: Louisiana State University Press, 1985.

Drew, Elizabeth, *T. S. Eliot: The Design of His Poetry*, New York: Scribne, 1949.

Everett, Barbara, 'In Search of Prufrock', *Critical Quarterly*, XVI, No.2., Summer, 1974.

Gallup, Donald, *T. S. Eliot: A Bibliography*, New York: Harcourt, Brace and World, Inc., 1969.

Gardner, Helen, *The Art of T. S. Eliot*, London: Cresset Press, 1949.

George, A. G, *T. S. Eliot: His Mind and Art*, Bombay: Asia Publishing House, 1962.

Gish, Nancy K., *Time in the Poetry of T. S. Eliot: A Study in Structure and Theme*, London: Macmillan Press Ltd., 1981.

Gordon, Lyndall, *Eliot's Early Years*, New York: Oxford University Press, 1977.

Gray, Piers, *T. S. Eliot's Intellectual and Poetic Development, 1902–22*, Sussex: The Harvester Press, 1982.

Gross, Harvey Seymour, *The Contrived Corridor: A Study in Modern Poetry and the Meaning of History*, Michigan: University Microfilms, 1955.

Howarth, H., *Notes on Some Figures Behind T. S. Eliot*, London: Chatto and Windus, 1965.

Ishak, Fayed M., *The Mystical Philosophy of T. S. Eliot*, New Haven, Connecticut: College and University Press, 1970.

Kenner, Hugh, *The Invisible Poet: T.S. Eliot*, New York: McDowell Obolensky, 1959.

— — —, ed., *T. S. Eliot: A Collection of Critical Essays*, New Jersey: Prentice-Hall, 1962.

Knight, Wilson G., *The Crown of Life*, London: Methuen & Co. Ltd., 1948.

———, *The Imperial Theme*, London: Methuen & Co. Ltd., 1951.

———, *The Shakespearean Tempest*, London: Methuen & Co. Ltd., 1953.

———, *The Sovereign Flower*, London: Methuen & Co. Ltd., 1958.

Leavis, F. R., *New Bearings in English Poetry: A Study of the Contemporary Situation*, Michigan: The University of Michigan Press, 1960.

Lee, Brian, *Theory and Personality: The Significance of T. S. Eliot's Criticism*, London: The Athlone Press, 1979.

Levy, William Turner and Victor Scherle, *Affectionately T. S. Eliot*, New York: J. B. Lippincott, 1968.

Lewis, C. Day, *The Poetic Image*, London: Jonathan Cape, 1949.

Litz, A. Walton, ed., *Eliot in His Time*, Princeton: Princeton University Press, 1973.

Lynen, John F., *The Design of the Present: Essays on Time and Form in American Literature*, New Haven: Yale University Press, 1969.

March, Richard, and Tambimuttue, eds., *T. S. Eliot: A Symposium*, Chicago: Henry Regnery, 1949.

Martin, Graham and P. N. Furbank, eds., *Twentieth Century Poetry: Critical Essays and Documents*, London: Open University Press, 1979.

Matthiessen, F. O., *The Achievement of T. S. Eliot: An Essay on the Nature of Poetry*, London: Oxford University Press, 1958.

Miller, James E., *T. S. Eliot's Personal Waste Land*, University Park: The Pennsylvania State University Press, 1977.

Miller, J. Hills, *Poets of Reality*, New York: Athenaeum, 1969.

Minor, Robert N., *The Bhagvad Gita: An Exegetical Commentary*, New Delhi: Heritage Publishers, 1982.

Montgomery, Marion, *T. S. Eliot: An Essay on the American Magus*, Athens: University of Georgia Press, 1969.

Moody, A. D., *Thomas Stearns Eliot: Poet*. London: Cambridge University Press, 1979.

Poulet, Georges, *Studies in Human Time*, tr., Elliott Coleman, New York: Harper & Brothers, 1956.

Rajan, Balachandra, ed., *T. S. Eliot: A Study of His Writings by Several Hands*, New York, Haskel House, 1964.

Sanjuan Jr., E., *A Casebook on 'Gerontion'*, Columbus, Ohio: C. E. Merrill Publishing Co., 1970.

Schneider, Elizabeth, *T. S. Eliot: The Pattern in the Carpet*, Berkeley: University of California Press, 1975.

Sen, Sunil Kanti, *Metaphysical Tradition and T. S. Eliot*, Calcutta: Firma K. L. Mukhopadhyay, 1965.

Smidt, Kristian, *The Importance of Recognition: Six Chapters on T. S. Eliot*, London: Routledge and Kegan Paul, 1973.

Smith, Grover, *T. S. Eliot's Poetry and Plays: A Study in Sources and Meaning*, Chicago: The University of Chicago Press, 1956.

Southam, B. C., *A Guide to the Selected Poems of T. S. Eliot*, New York: Harcourt, Brace and World, Inc., 1969.

Spurgeon, Caroline, *Shakespeare's Imagery and What It Tells Us*, London: Cambridge University Press, 1965.

Tate, Allen, ed., *T. S. Eliot: The Metaphysical Perspective*, Carbondale: Southern Illinois University Press, 1963.

Tobin, David Ned, *The Presence of the Past: T. S. Eliot's Victorian Inheritance*, Michigan: the University Research Press, 1983.

Traversi, Derek, *T. S. Eliot: The Longer Poems*, New York: Harcourt, Brace, Jovanovich, 1976.

Unger, Leonard, *T. S. Eliot: Moments and Patterns*, Minneapolis: University of Minnesota Press, 1966.

Williams, Helen, *T. S. Eliot: The Waste Land*, London: Edward Arnold, 1970.

Williamson, George, *A Reader's Guide to T. S. Eliot: A Poem-by-Poem Analysis*, New York: Noonday Press, 1964.

Witrow, G. J., *The Natural Philosophy of Time*, London: Thomas Nelson & Sons, 1961.